Railroads of
New Jersey

Railroads of New Jersey

FRAGMENTS OF THE PAST IN THE GARDEN STATE LANDSCAPE

Lorett Treese

STACKPOLE BOOKS

For Mat

Copyright © 2006 by Stackpole Books

Published by
STACKPOLE BOOKS
5067 Ritter Road
Mechanicsburg, PA 17055
www.stackpolebooks.com

Printed in the United States of America

10 9 8 7 6 5 4 3 2 1

First Edition

Cover design by Caroline Stover

Photos by the author and illustrations from the author's collection unless otherwise noted

Front cover: *CNJ Jersey Central Baby-Face with Seashore Train* **by Andy Romano, 2001.**
ANDY ROMANO, TRAINUTZ.COM

Back cover: John Stevens 1825 steam locomotive at Hoboken, New Jersey, by Fulvio Giudici. STEVENS INSTITUTE OF TECHNOLOGY LIBRARY, SPECIAL COLLECTIONS

Library of Congress Cataloging-in-Publication Data

Treese, Lorett, 1952–
    Railroads of New Jersey : fragments of the past in the Garden State landscape / by Lorett Treese.–1st ed.
      p.   cm.
    Includes bibliographical references and index.
    ISBN-13: 978-0-8117-3260-4 (pbk.)
    ISBN-10: 0-8117-3260-6 (pbk.)
    1. Railroads–New Jersey–History.   I. Title.
HE2771.N5T67   2006
385'.09749–dc22

                    2005024739

CONTENTS

SECTION TWO: Skylands Region

Great Railways of the Region

Rail Stories of the Region

The Region's Railroad Giants

Sampling the Region's Railroad History

The Region's Rail Trails   90

SECTION THREE: Gateway Region

Great Railways of the Region

Rail Stories of the Region

SECTION FOUR: Shore Region

SECTION FIVE: Greater Atlantic City Region

SECTION SIX: Southern Shore Region

PREFACE

While researching my book on the railroads of Pennsylvania, I realized that I was telling only half of a fascinating story on railroad transportation in the Mid-Atlantic states. Most entrepreneurs constructing railroads in Pennsylvania in the nineteenth century wanted their freight and passengers to reach New York City as well as Philadelphia, because New York was growing faster and had a fine port through which merchandise could be shipped elsewhere. Conversely, farmers and businesspeople in New Jersey with products to sell or a resort to promote wanted to make residents of Pennsylvania their customers. So I decided to follow up my book *Railroads of Pennsylvania: Fragments of the Past in the Keystone Landscape* with a volume on the development and fate of rail transportation in New Jersey.

New Jersey holds a special place in American railroad history: It was the home of John Stevens, sometimes called the "Father of American Railroads." Stevens earned his reputation by publishing a groundbreaking pamphlet titled *Documents Tending to Prove the Superior Advantages of Rail-Ways and Steam-Carriages over Canal Navigation.* This concept became abundantly evident during the nineteenth century, but Stevens expressed it in 1812, a time when America had few canals and no long-distance railroads with which to compare them. Stevens wrote that he expected to be "stigmatized as a visionary projector," so, near his estate in Hoboken, New Jersey, he constructed America's first operating steam demonstration railroad, just to show the world it could be done.

By the 1820s and 1830s, railroads were springing up all over the eastern United States, where they transported agricultural products and natural resources to urban consumers, as well as manufactured goods and machinery to rural areas. Railroads opened markets and encouraged the development of unsettled areas. They linked Americans residing in distant regions, helping to truly unite our new nation. They also provided opportunities for many another American visionary, giving ambitious men a way to make a living—or a fortune.

Like America's other railroads, those operating in New Jersey saw a decline in freight and passenger business through much of the twentieth century, but today that is changing. Freight is moving smartly over rails in New Jersey, and new passenger lines are being opened, perhaps more rapidly in this state than any other.

I've lived all my life in the Keystone State, but like many other Pennsylvanians, I've spent a lot of time across the Delaware River. An aunt and two uncles lived in Elizabeth before they retired to Lakewood, and on holidays, we'd meet them halfway to dine in restaurants in Princeton or Stockton. My dad built a vacation home in Stone Harbor, across the street from its famous bird sanctuary, where we retreated just about every weekend except during the summer, when we rented the house to other Pennsylvanians. I still like the Jersey coast and its shore towns best in the dead of winter.

This volume is not intended to be a comprehensive history of transportation in New Jersey, nor does it provide complete information on every railroad that ever operated in this state. *Railroads of New Jersey: Fragments of the Past in the Garden State Landscape* is part history and part travel guide, intended to place the state's railroads and railroad artifacts in historical context. The word "fragments" in its subtitle is from the science fiction time-travel classic *Time and Again* by Jack Finney, who describes New York's vintage buildings and neighborhoods as "fragments still remaining . . . of days which once lay out there as real as the day lying out there now: still-surviving fragments of a clear April morning of 1871, a gray winter afternoon of 1840, a rainy dawn of 1793."

The text consists of short essays organized into six sections, roughly corresponding to the regions of the Garden State as defined by the New Jersey Commerce, Economic Growth and Tourism Commission (the official travel guide published by this agency lists accommodations and other attractions in the same regions). For the convenience of travelers, I wrote the text so that they could open the book anywhere and start reading.

In each section, "Great Railways of the Region" includes brief histories of the major railroads associated with the region—how they were organized, how they grew, and what happened to them—as well as the names of museums and historical societies that interpret their history. "Rail Stories of the Region" presents various tidbits and footnotes of railroad history, plus information on local chapters of the National Railway Historical Society, whose members often are actively involved in rail heritage preservation. "The Region's Railroad Giants" gives brief biographies of those who made their names or fortunes from the region's railroads and related enterprises. "Sampling the Region's Railroad History" offers information on operating railroads, museums, tourist railroads, and other places readers can go to find railroad artifacts. "The Region's Rail Trails" provides information on the state of rail trail construction in the area. Full citations for published histories of railroads from which material is quoted appear in the Bibliography.

I am grateful to all those who helped me research and write this book. My husband, Mat Treese, accompanied me on all my rail heritage treks and enriched my research with his own observations and the perspective of a businessman who is also a scholar. The staff and collections of the Mariam Coffin Canaday Library at Bryn Mawr College were tremendously helpful, particularly the patient members of the interlibrary loan department. I also thank the staff at the Hagley Museum and Library. Finally, I thank Stackpole Books, my editor, Kyle Weaver, and associate editor, Amy Cooper, for the opportunity to continue studying and sharing America's rich railroad history.

Delaware River Region

Great Railways of the Region

The Pennsylvania Railroad Company

In the early nineteenth century, New Jersey shared with every other state in the new union the problem of creating transportation systems that would support the growth of America's population and its expansion to the frontier. Some citizens looked to the federal government for help in building canals and turnpikes as well as the latest innovation in transportation: railroads. Presidents Jefferson, Madison, and Monroe shared the opinion that only a constitutional amendment would properly give the federal government such sweeping powers, but Congress failed to deliver, and transportation became the business of the states and private entities yet to be born.

In 1825, neighboring Pennsylvania passed legislation appointing canal commissioners to explore linking Philadelphia, Pittsburgh, and Lake Erie with canals so that Philadelphia could remain competitive with its rival Atlantic seaports, New York and Baltimore. New Jersey's John Stevens had obtained a charter to build a railroad between Philadelphia and the Susquehanna River in 1823, but too few potential investors shared his enthusiasm for railroads, and the project languished for lack of capital. By 1834, Pennsylvania finally had a statewide system that combined both means of transportation: It incorporated a railroad similar to what Stevens had envisioned between Philadelphia and Columbia, followed by 172 miles of canals to the base of the Allegheny Mountains, 36 miles of inclined planes to get cargo over the mountains, and 104 more miles of canals to Pittsburgh.

But Pennsylvania's Main Line of Public Works, also called the State Works, cost a great deal to maintain, and by the mid-1840s, Pennsylvanians were ready to entertain an even more ambitious idea than the one that had originated in the creative mind of John Stevens: one long, continuous railroad between Philadelphia and Pittsburgh. On April 13, 1846, Pennsylvania's governor signed legislation creating a private entity called the Pennsylvania Railroad Company, originally empowered to build between Harrisburg and Pittsburgh, superseding the least efficient portion of the Main Line of Public Works.

The future Standard Railroad of the World was able to triumph over the Alleghenies with the Allegheny Tunnel and the engineering marvel called the Horseshoe Curve. In 1855, its Harrisburg-to-Pittsburgh line was complete and open, and in 1857, the Pennsylvania Railroad was sufficiently successful to purchase the old State Works for $7.5 million. By the end of the 1860s, it had linked Philadelphia to the Midwest and Great

Lakes by acquiring the Pittsburgh, Fort Wayne & Chicago Railway as well as the Pittsburgh, Cincinnati, Chicago & St. Louis Railroad, popularly called the Pennsy's Panhandle Lines.

Yet in the same time period, New York had surpassed Philadelphia and grown into America's premier seaboard city. The Erie Canal had been providing cheap transportation to the West since it opened in 1825. In 1853, a number of New York State railroads merged into what would become the Pennsy's leading rival, the New York Central Railroad. By 1867, a single line linked Buffalo and New York. Meanwhile, Philadelphia had lagged in the development of adequate waterfront terminals and auxiliary business services, such as banks and brokerage houses, and ocean transport from Europe to Philadelphia cost more than to New York.

In the 1949 *Centennial History of the Pennsylvania Railroad Company, 1846–1946*, George H. Burgess and Miles C. Kennedy wrote that during the mid-nineteenth century, the competitive situation among America's railroads "made it highly desirable that the Pennsylvania should reach New York over its own rails, or a controlled route." In other words, in order to thrive as a railroad, the Pennsy needed to run trains through New Jersey.

In 1862, the Pennsylvania Railroad Company began negotiations with a New Jersey business group commonly called the Joint Companies (including the Philadelphia and Trenton Railroad Company, Camden and Amboy Railroad and Transportation Company, and Delaware and Raritan Canal Company, later called the United Companies) to construct a connecting line that would join the Pennsy's tracks to the Joint Companies' route across Jersey to New York City. By 1863, the Pennsy had a deal empowering it to build a 6.4-mile line from West Philadelphia across the Schuylkill to a junction point in North Philadelphia. The connecting line was completed by the middle of 1867 and leased to the Philadelphia and Trenton Railroad Company for 999 years.

The arrangement was anticipated to send a great deal of traffic over the Joint Companies' rails, so the Pennsy accordingly expected them to enlarge their northern terminal facilities. In 1867 and 1868, they made improvements at their Jersey City terminal and purchased land for new terminals in Jersey City and Harsimus Cove. The Joint Companies were not inclined to invest much more once their experience demonstrated that they had agreed to a rate system that kept their profits on the new traffic low.

The Pennsy could have purchased land and built its own terminals in northern New Jersey, or even embarked on the expensive alternative of building a competitive railroad through the neighboring state. Instead, it leased all the liquid and fixed assets of the United Companies for a period of 999 years at a rate favorable to the companies effective December 1, 1871.

A stock audit conducted that year showed that the Pennsy had acquired not only four major canal and railroad companies (the Camden and Amboy, Delaware and Raritan, Philadelphia and Trenton, and New Jersey Railroad), but also holdings in thirteen smaller railroads, as well as ferry companies, steamboats, turnpikes, and bridges. In terms of rolling stock, the United Companies had owned 160 locomotives, 221 passenger cars, and more than 2,000 freight cars. The Pennsy reorganized its new holdings as its New York Division, headquartered in Jersey City, with an Amboy Division headquartered in Trenton (later Camden) controlling what had been the Camden and Amboy's original line between Camden and South Amboy.

The Pennsylvania Railroad Company embarked on a major engineering and improvement program that would extend into the twentieth century, intended to upgrade its line between Philadelphia and New York City, and enabling it to handle far more freight and passengers quickly and safely. In 1872, the Pennsy began gradually standardizing the track gauge of all its New Jersey lines. Over the years, it straightened out curves and eliminated grade crossings by elevating its rails in urban areas. It also constructed a third and then a fourth track along this main line. Millions were spent over time on improvements on Pennsylvania Railroad Company facilities in New Brunswick, Newark, and Jersey City, and eventually tunnels that took its trains under the Hudson River to the Pennsy's own magnificent terminal in the heart of New York. For the passengers who merely traveled between Camden and Trenton, the railroad upgraded its stations in Riverton, Palmyra, Delanco, Riverside, and Burlington.

In Camden itself, the Pennsy made its most extensive improvements at the turn of the twentieth century, while the railroad was also renovating the main line it had acquired to Atlantic City. Between the summers of 1900 and 1901, the Pennsy replaced Camden's separate train and ferry facilities with New Jersey's largest railroad station at that time. Its ferry terminal had four slips and was constructed directly in front of a train shed with eleven tracks. Beginning in 1902, the railroad started a building program to elevate its main lines through Camden to both Atlantic City and Cape May in order to eliminate many dangerous grade crossings.

The Pennsy continued to operate in New Jersey until its demise in the twentieth century. Its merger with its longtime rival, the New York Central Railroad, failed to save it from bankruptcy, and on April 1, 1976, known as Conveyance Day, its operations were turned over to Conrail and Amtrak. Amtrak established its Northeast Corridor over the Pennsy's quadruple-tracked route from Philadelphia through Trenton, New Brunswick, and Newark, and today Amtrak, SEPTA, and NJ TRANSIT trains continue to operate over it. In 1997, Norfolk Southern and CSX

The RiverLINE runs through Bordentown above the Delaware River at the spot where ferries once landed.

purchased all shares of Conrail and split the company between them, but since June 1999, Conrail has continued to operate in this region of New Jersey as a switching and terminal railroad for its parent corporations, Norfolk Southern and CSX, as well as local industry. Conrail sold the old Camden and Amboy trackage between Camden and Trenton to NJ TRANSIT in 1999 for its Southern New Jersey Light Rail Transportation System. Conrail still operates the tracks that commuters and tourists see running parallel to those of the RiverLINE trains.

Since 1974, the Pennsylvania Railroad Technical and Historical Society has been collecting and preserving information about the Pennsylvania Railroad Company and its subsidiaries. Also preserving railroad history is the Camden and Amboy Railroad Historical Society, located in South Amboy.

Rail Stories of the Region

The Camden and Amboy

In 1751, Joseph Borden announced that a boat would arrive at a certain Philadelphia dock every Tuesday and leave for Bordentown the following day. From Bordentown, goods and passengers could proceed by stage wagon on Thursday to a house opposite Perth Amboy, from which another boat would ferry them to New York City on Friday. Altogether, it would take thirty to forty hours and two overnight stays to travel between Philadelphia and New York.

This marked a huge improvement. Earlier in the century, the same trip had taken up to six days and was possible only during times of the year when the roads were not completely impassable because of ice or mud.

By the early 1800s, the Stevens family of Hoboken had developed an intermodal transportation system of steamboats and coaches called the Union Line, which had reduced the trip between Manhattan and Philadelphia to ten or eleven hours. But John Stevens had bigger plans. In 1811, he petitioned New Jersey's legislature for a charter to build a railroad from Trenton to New Brunswick, linking the Delaware and Raritan rivers. In 1815, the legislature finally granted him America's first railroad charter, but the use of railroads for long-distance transportation was still such a novel concept that Stevens was unable to raise sufficient funds.

By the late 1820s, railroads were no longer considered so revolutionary. On January 14, 1828, citizens gathered at the courthouse in Mount Holly to promote the idea of a trans-Jersey railroad. Among other things, they resolved "that, situated as New Jersey is, between two great emporiums of the Union, and with great resources of her own to sustain the undertaking, it is a reproach to the enterprise of her citizens that a line of internal intercourse has not been extended across her territory." Their minutes and resolutions were published in the *New Jersey Mirror* two days later. Similar meetings in Burlington, Bordentown, Princeton, and Trenton produced similar memorials in 1828 and 1829.

Other New Jersey citizens who favored improved transportation had their doubts about a steam railway and simultaneously promoted a trans-state canal. Canals had been in use much longer than railroads, and a canal promised to keep up the demand for horses, mules, and fodder that existing stage lines provided for local farmers. In 1829 and 1830, the legislators found themselves confronted by what amounted to two competing lobbies: railroad promoters headed by the Stevens family, who ran the Union Line, and canal supporters who operated its rival, the People's Line.

The legislature compromised by issuing charters to both the Camden and Amboy Railroad and Transportation Company and the Delaware and Raritan Canal Company on the same day, February 4, 1830. Unlike Pennsylvania, which undertook large-scale internal improvements at public expense, both the railroad and canal would be privately financed, with the state receiving a specified fee for every passenger and ton of freight they carried.

Within a very short time of the moment when stock in both companies was offered for sale, it became clear that railroads were the transportation of the future. In mere minutes, $1 million of railroad stock was sold, whereas it took a few days to sell $100,000 of stock in the canal. The canal might have failed completely if its key promoter, Robert Field Stockton, had not borrowed enough cash to buy the stock to get it going.

The less popular canal company approached the railroad company and proposed a merger in order to avoid competition. The legislature accepted the proposition and in 1831 passed legislation popularly called the Marriage Act, or the Act of Union, merging the two companies' policies and profits but retaining their individual corporate identities. The Camden and Amboy Railroad and Transportation Company and the Delaware and Raritan Canal Company came to be known as the Joint Companies (later the United Companies), and Robert Field Stockton and the two sons of John Stevens became a wealthy and politically powerful transportation triumvirate.

Preliminary surveys had begun in 1827 and continued in earnest after the two companies had been chartered. John Wilson, a West Point graduate and major in the U.S. Army, directed the railroad surveys. Assisting him was a young man named John Edgar Thomson, who later designed the Horseshoe Curve and served as president of the Pennsylvania Railroad Company.

Those traveling between New York and Philadelphia on the Camden and Amboy Railroad got off the train and made their way across the Delaware via steam ferry, like this one depicted in the 1845 edition of *Historical Collections of the State of New Jersey* by John W. Barber and Henry Howe.

During 1832, the Camden and Amboy Railroad concentrated on building tracks between South Amboy and Bordentown, a Delaware River port from which steamboats would take freight and passengers to Philadelphia and Camden. Workers used the standard procedure of fastening iron rails to stone blocks called sleepers. When the laborers at Sing Sing Prison failed to cut blocks quickly enough for the line to reach Amboy that winter, Robert Livingston Stevens came up with the idea of replacing the blocks with logs secured in a bed of broken rock, an improvement that made for both faster construction and a smoother ride.

By the fall of 1832, horses drew passenger cars as far as Hightstown. The next year, the railroad added its first freight cars. The first train ran from South Amboy to Camden in 1834.

Robert Livingston Stevens became the railroad's first president and chief engineer, and his brother, Edwin Augustus Stevens, was elected treasurer. By 1840, they controlled a $3 million company with scores of passenger and freight cars.

Although John Stevens had proposed a railroad between New Brunswick, at the head of navigation on the Raritan River, and Trenton, the state's capital, his sons had changed its terminals to South Amboy and Bordentown (closely corresponding to the old stagecoach route) and added a branch to Camden that could be used when ice clogged the Delaware farther north. Railroad operators quickly realized that passengers reached Philadelphia faster via Camden and improved this branch line, eventually creating a line that was double-tracked most of the way, which railroad agents began calling the railroad's "main line." Camden gained an efficient connection with New York and points north that spurred its growth in succeeding years.

Back in 1832, the Camden and Amboy had agreed to construct a branch to New Brunswick when that city was served by a connecting line to Jersey City. The citizens of Trenton demanded that this line run through their town, and in 1838, the Camden and Amboy began building a Trenton branch to connect with the Philadelphia and Trenton Railroad. By the beginning of 1839, the railroad was offering service between Trenton and New Brunswick.

That same year, the railroad strengthened the bridge across the Delaware at Trenton, enabling through service between Philadelphia and Jersey City. This allowed passengers and freight to travel between the cities an hour and a half faster, and it became the favorite route to travel and eventually the New York main line for the Pennsylvania Railroad Company.

It was also in 1832 that Pennsylvania's legislature incorporated the Philadelphia and Trenton Railroad Company to build a railroad between

The tracks of the Camden and Amboy running beneath a street in Bordentown, as depicted in *Historical Collections of the State of New Jersey* (1845).

Philadelphia and Morrisville, which was across the Delaware from Trenton. Before beginning operations, this railroad acquired a controlling interest in the bridge already constructed across the Delaware at that point, as well as a company authorized to build a turnpike between Trenton and New Brunswick. Just in case the Philadelphia and Trenton contemplated laying railroad tracks on its turnpike's right-of-way, Robert Field Stockton began buying the company's stock, and by 1836, the Philadelphia and Trenton essentially belonged to the Joint Companies, though it continued to have a separate corporate status. By the time the Camden and Amboy opened its line between Trenton and New Brunswick, its trains continuing on to Philadelphia ran over its own rails.

In the 1860s, the New Jersey Railroad and Transportation Company, which had constructed the line between New Brunswick and Jersey City over which Camden and Amboy trains proceeded, threatened to build a parallel line to Trenton. In 1867, the New Jersey Railroad was persuaded to join the Joint Companies, thereafter known as the United Canal and Railroad Companies of New Jersey or simply the United Companies. During the same time period, the corporation also leased a number of smaller railroads in this region, including the Pemberton and Hightstown Railroad; Columbus, Kinkora and Springfield Railroad Company; and Camden and Burlington County Railroad Company.

Besides canals and railroads, the corporation ran steamboats. It started with a fleet of steamboats purchased from the Union Line to ferry passengers between Bordentown and Philadelphia. In 1837, the Camden and Amboy had purchased a majority interest in the Camden and Philadelphia Steamboat Ferry Company and developed a ferry terminal and slips in Camden.

The Camden and Amboy moved both passengers and freight, but prior to the Civil War, it made more money moving passengers. During 1833, it carried 110,000 passengers, and business increased in 1839, when passengers could ride through to New Brunswick. In 1838, the railroad started running a train it called the Pea Line to serve local farmers. By 1840, the daily Pea Line could be up to sixteen cars long, stopping wherever a farmer waved it down and transporting his perishable fresh produce quickly to urban markets. The Camden and Amboy also was among the first American railroads to strike a deal with the nation's post office to transport mail.

For such a busy and profitable railroad, its owners invested in very little double tracking prior to the Civil War. Its trains were supposed to keep to a schedule and move to a siding to allow a scheduled train heading in the opposite direction to pass. If trains encountered each other along the line, one had to back up. This resulted in more accidents for the Camden and Amboy than for any other Jersey railroad. In 1836, the Camden and Amboy suffered the nation's first head-on collision between steam locomotives when a freight train loaded with lumber hit a passenger train in a thick fog. Three years earlier, when a train was speeding to make up lost time, one of its cars' axles broke, causing another car to overturn and killing two passengers. John Quincy Adams and Cornelius Vanderbilt were both aboard and both survived, though Vanderbilt suffered serious injury.

Twenty-four passengers died and more than a hundred were injured in the Camden and Amboy's worst accident, which occurred in 1855. North of Burlington,

In 1891, the Pennsylvania Railroad Company honored the Camden and Amboy Railroad with this monument still standing in Bordentown.

the engineer on a northbound train spotted an oncoming southbound train and started backing up to the nearest siding. His rear car, which he could not see, collided with a team of horses pulling a carriage over a crossing. The rear car derailed, pulling others with it. New Jersey residents cried out for an investigation and long-overdue improvements.

Both the Reading Railroad and the Pennsy sought to absorb the Camden and Amboy, but the Pennsy had more money. By the time the Camden and Amboy joined the Pennsy family, it had served New Jersey not only as its first railroad, but also as the inspiration for the creation of a great many independent feeder lines that linked their rails to those of the Camden and Amboy. It continued being a vitally important part of the Pennsylvania Railroad Company as that company's own critical link to New York.

The Delaware and Raritan Canal

In the 1790s, if not earlier, Jersey residents began talking about a canal across the state's narrow waist in the fairly level ground between Trenton and New Brunswick. In 1804, William Patterson and other members of the New Jersey Navigation Company were granted a charter by the state legislature to excavate existing streambeds and construct the dams and locks for such a canal, but these entrepreneurs failed to attract sufficient capital.

A second canal company was incorporated in 1824, but its authorization was contingent on permission from the Keystone State to draw water out of the Delaware River. Pennsylvania came up with a number of conditions onerous enough to doom this effort, including the right to renege if it could be determined that the canal had reduced the water level in the Delaware.

After Pennsylvanians had constructed a canal on the Delaware's western shore and were no longer in a position to object about someone else taking water out of the river, Jersey residents again agitated for a trans-state canal in mass meetings, and two conventions mounted in Princeton in 1827 and 1828.

The Delaware and Raritan Canal was chartered in 1830, on the same day as the Camden and Amboy Railroad. It became part of the conglomerate known as the Joint Companies (later the United Companies) by legislation passed the next year.

Ground was broken in Kingston in 1830, and construction began on a Y-shaped system that would run from Lambertville through Trenton to Bordentown, with a second branch from Trenton through Princeton to the beds of the Millstone and Raritan rivers and thence to New Brunswick. A feeder canal that was also navigable was constructed from Bull's Island to a point near Bordentown to keep the Delaware and Raritan supplied with water.

Construction on the Delaware and Raritan Canal began in Kingston, perhaps near these artifacts, a lock and locktender's house.

The Delaware and Raritan Canal was extremely well built. Its 43-mile main line between Bordentown and New Brunswick was 75 feet wide, with a water level maintained at 7 or 8 feet, making it navigable for that period's oceangoing vessels. It included aqueducts that allowed vessels to cross smaller streams, and the bridges that crossed over the canal could be turned to allow masted vessels to pass.

The Delaware and Raritan Canal opened in the spring of 1834, with a victory regatta of barges carrying the governor and other dignitaries traveling its length while residents gathered at its bridges to cheer them on.

Business was slow at first, but the canal's strategic location between Pennsylvania's eastern coalfields and the coal consumers of New York and New England guaranteed steadily increasing eastbound tonnage from the 1840s. Its feeders included Pennsylvania's Schuylkill Canal and the Reading Railroad, and its competition consisted mainly of coastal carriers. By the end of the Civil War, the canal was considered to be about as profitable as the Camden and Amboy Railroad.

The peak business year for the Delaware and Raritan Canal was 1871, the same year that the Pennsylvania Railroad Company leased the United Companies. The Pennsy regarded the canals it owned as far less important than its railroads, and its rates and policies encouraged its shippers to prefer rail transportation. In 1932, the Pennsy filed certificates with New Jersey's secretary of state to abandon the Delaware and Raritan Canal.

New Jersey established a commission to figure out what to do with the canal. In 1942, the commission's *Report on the Final Disposition of the Delaware and Raritan Canal* concluded that although continued maintenance of the entire operation would be uneconomical, so would its total dismantlement. The commissioners argued that the Delaware and Raritan could continue to serve the state by transporting water to the industrial communities that had grown up along its route. They also said that New Jersey needed more recreational areas and proposed that portions of the canal be adapted for bathing, fishing, boating, and barge parties.

The canal and its structures were granted a place on the National Register of Historic Places in 1973. Delaware and Raritan Canal State Park was created in 1974 by a new canal commission, which designated more than 60 miles of the old canal as state park land. A portion of the corridor of the Belvidere Delaware Railroad was added to the park in the 1980s.

The 1942 report had acknowledged the historic value of the Delaware and Raritan Canal. Together with the Chesapeake and Delaware Canal and the Dismal Swamp Canal, the Delaware and Raritan had been part of a system making tidewater navigation possible in early America all the way between New York and Georgia.

The Camden and Amboy's Monopoly

Monopolies got a bad name in the late nineteenth and early twentieth centuries, but back at the beginning of the 1800s, certain commodities were regarded as natural monopolies, transportation systems among them. It cost a lot of money to construct a turnpike or railroad, and potential investors liked to be assured that they could enjoy profits for considerable time without having to worry that a charter might be issued to some competitor that wanted to build another railroad or turnpike right alongside theirs.

The fledgling Camden and Amboy Railroad and Transportation Company offered the state of New Jersey a thousand shares of stock for the assurance that no other railroad would be chartered between Philadelphia and New York. After the Camden and Amboy had been united with the Delaware and Raritan Canal to form the Joint Companies, they gave the state another thousand shares and guaranteed that the state would receive $30,000 in annual dividends and transit duties. This ensured revenue plus the promise to construct a branch to New Brunswick earned the Joint Companies legislation passed in 1832 that included this phrase: "That it shall not be lawful . . . to construct any other rail road or rail roads in this state, without the consent of the said companies, which shall be intended or used for the transportation of passengers or merchandise between the cities of New York and Philadelphia."

By the mid-nineteenth century, the Joint Companies contributed a significant portion of the state's revenue and dominated its politics. Their managers advanced from lobbying the legislature for favorable measures to getting friendly representatives elected to its seats. They controlled the development of other New Jersey railroads as well as interstate commerce. Detractors came up with a new slogan for New Jersey: "The State of the Camden and Amboy."

The Joint Companies' opposition included the merchants of Philadelphia, New York, and Delaware, who petitioned Congress in the 1840s to break the monopoly. The noted economist Henry Charles Carey was another critic, who pointed out that the monopoly was gouging the public and suppressing the state's economy. Letters written by Carey appeared in the *Burlington Gazette* starting in January 1848, addressed to New Jersey's legislature and signed simply by "A Citizen of Burlington."

In rousing language, Carey cried out for revolt against the tyrannical monopoly. In a letter dated January 28, 1848, which was reprinted in a collection of letters published the same year, Carey wrote, "Among the causes that should lead to a Revolution in this State is the belief, universally entertained, that no bill can become a law, however necessary to the convenience and advantage of its people until it has received the Royal Assent, signified by viceroys acting on the part of the Railroad Kings of New Jersey." In another letter, reprinted in a booklet satirically titled *Beauties of the Monopoly System of New Jersey,* Carey compared the Joint Companies to the ancient Colossus of Rhodes: "Resting one foot upon the Camden ferry monopoly, the other is securely placed among the associates and lottery-dealers of Jersey City. With its right hand it grasps Amboy, and with its left, Trenton Bridge and thus it holds almost every avenue by which any Jerseyman can pass out of the state, or any stranger pass into it, while its deputies pick the pockets of all for the purpose of swelling their already enormous revenues."

The publishers of other newspapers weighed in, including Horace Greeley of the *New York Tribune,* and the state established a commission to investigate. The commissioners' generally favorable report quieted the opposition only temporarily. By the early 1850s, proposals were being made that the federal government build a national railroad from New York to Washington.

Despite these outcries, the Joint Companies triumphed over potential rivals for almost two more decades. When their managers relinquished their power and privileges to the Pennsylvania Railroad Company in 1871, they did so on favorable terms. On May 21 of that year, the *New York Herald* cynically editorialized: "The halo of New Jersey's glory has left her. Her Ichabod hath departed. The Camden and Amboy road, the pride of the State and ruler of Legislatures, has been ceded to Pennsylvania; and Tom Scott [then president of the Pennsy], like Commodore Stockton of old, carries the little borough in his breeches pocket."

John Bull

Soon after the Camden and Amboy Railroad was chartered, John Stevens's son Robert Livingston Stevens traveled to England, where he purchased a locomotive from a company that had built others for a British railroad. The manufacturer shipped the locomotive, which had been named the John Bull, to Philadelphia, where it was hauled by sloop to Bordentown in August 1831.

Its separate pieces arrived in several packing crates, with some assembly required but no written instructions. A young man named Isaac Dripps, who had been employed to repair steamboats, was summoned to construct a technologically advanced machine that he had never seen. But Dripps was equal to the task, and he later became a master mechanic for the Camden and Amboy and, later still, an executive for the Pennsylvania Railroad Company.

By November 12, 1831, the John Bull was ready for an exhibition run along roughly 1,000 feet of track that had been laid outside Bordentown in a place locally known as Mile Hollow. Members of New Jersey's legislature were invited to occupy two passenger coaches, but several accounts written about the event recorded an initial reluctance to participate on the part of some elected representatives.

Robert Stevens then offered a ride to anyone who wanted one and found a taker in one of the residents of Point Breeze, which was the nearby estate of Joseph Bonaparte, the older brother of the emperor Napoleon and an ex-king of Naples and Spain. Princess Caroline Murat, Napoleon Bonaparte's niece by marriage, became the first woman to ride a train in New Jersey.

The John Bull needed a few modifications. It had not come equipped with a tender, a car designed to carry wood and water for the steam engine. Camden and Amboy Railroad workers mounted a whiskey barrel on a flatcar, and a Bordentown shoemaker reportedly made a leather hose to carry water to the locomotive's boiler. When the John Bull later displayed an alarming tendency to derail on sharp curves, Robert Livingston Stevens invented a feature to stabilize it, first called a pilot truck, but later commonly known as a cowcatcher.

The John Bull ran on the Camden and Amboy Railroad from 1833 until 1866. It then was retired to the company's shops until 1876, when it began its second career as a revered railroad artifact. Following an appearance at the Centennial Exposition in Philadelphia that year, it traveled to the Columbian Exposition in Chicago in 1893, to Baltimore in 1927, and the World's Fair in New York in 1939.

The Pennsylvania Railroad Company eventually donated it to the Smithsonian Institution. In 1981, the museum's magazine carried an account and photographs of the John Bull's 150th birthday run on tracks beside the Potomac. Today the John Bull is housed in the National Museum of American History, where it is honored as one of the first successful locomotives in the United States and the world's oldest operable locomotive.

The Philadelphia and Trenton

In February 1832, Pennsylvania's legislature incorporated the Philadelphia and Trenton Railroad Company, a system linking those cities that was also empowered to purchase stock in other transportation companies, including railroads and turnpikes. Its Pennsylvania promoters actually envisioned a system between Philadelphia and New York that would cross the Delaware farther north than the Camden and Amboy and traverse New Jersey, to connect with the line being advocated from Jersey City to New Brunswick. To this end, the Philadelphia and Trenton bought control of the Trenton and New Brunswick Straight Turnpike Company in 1833.

Construction began that year, and by the spring of 1834, passengers could travel by rail from Bristol to Morrisville, a town just across the river from Trenton. The Philadelphia and Trenton was later extended south to Kensington, while a connecting railway eventually enabled passengers to travel directly to the Pennsylvania Railroad Company's expanding facilities in West Philadelphia. The Philadelphia and Trenton officially opened for business in 1834, offering two round-trips per day, one train hauled by horses, the other by a Baldwin locomotive.

While construction was in progress, one of Philadelphia's leading lawyers appeared before the New Jersey legislators to argue that they had the power to revoke the Camden and Amboy's monopoly and should do so. A New York lawyer joined Daniel Webster in his opinion that the Trenton and New Brunswick Straight Turnpike Company did not need additional legislation to empower it to construct a railroad (instead of a turnpike) over its own right-of-way. Robert Field Stockton defended the Joint Companies and later joined the Stevens brothers in buying up Philadelphia and Trenton Railroad stock with the object of acquiring the system.

By 1836, the Joint Companies were well represented on the Philadelphia and Trenton's board. That April, the Camden and Amboy Railroad,

Delaware and Raritan Canal, and Philadelphia and Trenton Railroad reached a final agreement to share profits, thus putting an end to this early threat to the Joint Companies' monopoly.

The Delaware and Bound Brook

The Delaware and Bound Brook Railroad Company was incorporated in 1874, not long after the Pennsylvania Railroad Company leased the United Companies of New Jersey, and just a year after New Jersey passed a general railroad law enabling the Pennsy's competitors to build other railroads between Philadelphia and New York. The Delaware and Bound Brook was intended to connect Jenkintown in Pennsylvania with Bound Brook in New Jersey, which was in turn connected by the New Jersey Central to Jersey City.

Lying in the path of this right-of-way was a Pennsy branch called the Mercer & Somerset. The Delaware and Bound Brook planned to build a crossover connection called a frog near Hopewell, New Jersey, but Pennsy track crews placed a locomotive in the way. Delaware and Bound Brook workers waited until the Pennsy men moved their locomotive onto a siding to make way for a Mercer & Somerset express train, then chained the Pennsy locomotive to the siding. The Pennsylvania Railroad Company sent down another locomotive, which burst through a barrier erected by the opposition, but the militia arrived in time to prevent any further violence and make the Delaware and Bound Brook victorious in what was called the Hopewell Frog War.

A judge upheld the right of the Delaware and Bound Brook to build a railroad across New Jersey, truly putting an end to the era of railroad monopoly in New Jersey. By the time the Centennial Exposition opened in Philadelphia in 1876, the Delaware and Bound Brook had a printed brochure advertising a new route that New Yorkers could take to the fair: the New Jersey Central ferry and rail line from Liberty Street in New York City to Bound Brook in New Jersey, then the Delaware and Bound Brook to a connection with the North Pennsylvania Railroad, which ran to Philadelphia.

In 1879, the Philadelphia and Reading Railroad (known to most today simply as the Reading Railroad) leased the Delaware and Bound Brook for 999 years, making this railroad part of its own New York Division. The Reading was by then a large anthracite hauler, having been established to transport coal from the Schuylkill County coalfields to Philadelphia, where it could be shipped by water to New York and New England. The Delaware and Bound Brook enabled the Reading to run coal trains directly to New York Harbor.

The period following the Civil War was a time of attempted growth for the Reading, when its management hoped it would become a trunk line to the West. After Franklin B. Gowen became the company's president in 1870, he made the decision that the Reading needed to purchase the coal lands it served to ensure a source of freight. This did not result in sufficient profit to prevent the company from entering receivership in 1880, ending its grandiose transcontinental expansion plans.

Three Englishmen Travel through Jersey

Throughout America's history, there has been no lack of travelers who needed to get between New York and Philadelphia, and those who recorded travel accounts at different times in the nineteenth century demonstrate the progress of rail transportation.

From 1833 to 1835, when the Camden and Amboy Railroad was new, a British actor named Tyrone Power traveled to major American cities, where he performed at various theaters. In 1836, he published a two-volume account for the British reading public in which he described the American scenery in flamboyant but often condescending tones, as in the following excerpt:

> Here [at Amboy Landing] we left our boat, and were immediately transferred to the cars of the new railroad connecting the Raritan with the Delaware, and pursued our way to Bordentown, through a dreary, barren-looking country, whose only attractions were occasional orchards of a most fruitful kind, if one might judge by the plenteous gathering already in progress. In many places were piled up little mountains of apples, destined chiefly for the cider press.
>
> The loco-motives not being in condition to do duty, the horses occupied as yet their legitimate station, going at the rate of about eight miles per hour.
>
> Near the entrance to Bordentown, the present mansion of the ex-king of Spain was pointed out: it does not appear to be very happily located, but commands, I understand, an extensive view of the broad Delaware, and affords room enough to bustle in, even for one whose domain was once royal.
>
> Here we once more embarked; and hence to Philadelphia the Delaware is a broad placid stream, with low banks of alternate wood and meadow, having sprinkled among them numbers of well-built houses of all sizes, from the shingle cottage to the imposing-looking mansion with its lofty portico of painted pine.

James Silk Buckingham, a British Quaker, arrived at Amboy Landing on a February day and penned an account dedicated to the queen but also published in New York in 1841:

Here we found the commencement of the railroad to Philadelphia; and, embarking in the cars provided for that purpose, we set forward on our journey. These cars are not so comfortable in their arrangements as the carriages on our English railroads. They are very long omnibuses, sufficiently broad to admit a passage up the middle, on each side of which is a range of seats going across the breadth, each capable of accommodating two persons, who sit with their faces toward the engine, and not facing each other, as in omnibuses generally. The car in which we sat had twenty such cross-seats on each side of the central passage, and therefore contained eighty passengers. In the centre of the car was a stove, well supplied with fuel, which warmed the whole interior, and rendered the atmosphere agreeable.

The rate at which we traveled was about sixteen miles an hour; the road was good, but the scenery was very monotonous and uninteresting, being mostly uncultivated land, covered with small trees and brushwood, and the few villages through which we passed were neither picturesque nor beautiful. The dreary season of winter would account for much of this, it is true; but even in summer the route must be regarded as monotonous.

About two o'clock we reached the small town of Camden, on the Delaware, nearly opposite the city of Philadelphia; and, embarking there on a steamboat of peculiar construction, with iron stem and keel, called an ice-boat, we literally cut our way through the solid masses of ice in some places, and broken pieces in others, some of them from twelve to fifteen inches thick, and, safely reaching the other side of the river, we landed at Philadelphia before three.

In 1861, the *London Times* sent William Howard Russell, the paper's correspondent during the Crimean War, to see what sort of bloody row was about to commence in America. He produced an illustrated account titled *My Diary North and South,* in which he described a trip from New York to Washington by means of railroad through New Jersey. Here he talks about his first night on the train:

The whole of my luggage, except a large bag, was taken charge of by a man at the New York side of the ferry, who "checked it through" to the capital—giving me a slip of brass with a number corresponding with a brass ticket for each piece. When the boat arrived at the stage at the other side of the Hudson, in my innocence I called for a porter to take my bag. The passengers were moving out of the capacious ferry-boat in a steady stream, and the steam throat and bell of the engine were going whilst I was looking for my porter; but at last a gentleman passing said, "I guess y'll remain here a considerable time before y'll get any one to come for that bag of yours," and taking the hint, I just got off in time to stumble into a long box on wheels, with a double row of most uncomfortable seats, and a passage down the middle, where I found a place beside Mr. Sanford, the newly-appointed United States Minister to Belgium, who was kind enough to take me under his charge to Washington.

The night was closing in very fast as the train started, but such glimpses as I had of the continuous line of pretty-looking villages of wooden houses, two stories high, painted white, each with its Corinthian portico, gave a most favorable impression of the comfort and prosperity of the people. The rail passed through the main street of most of these hamlets and villages, and the bell of the engine was tolled to warn the inhabitants, who drew up on the sidewalks to let us go by. The passengers were crowded as close as they could pack, and as there was an immense iron stove in the centre of the car, the heat and stuffiness became most trying, although I had been undergoing the ordeal of the stove-heated New York houses for nearly a week. Once a minute, at least, the door at either end of the carriage was opened, and then closed with a sharp crashing noise, that jarred the nerves, and effectually prevented sleep. It generally was done by a man whose sole object seemed to be to walk up the centre of the carriage in order to go out of the opposite door—occasionally it was the work of the newspaper boy, with a sheaf of journals and trashy illus-trated papers under his arm. Now and then it was the conductor; but the periodical visitor was a young gentleman with a chain and rings, who bore a tray before him, and solicited orders for "gum drops," and "lemon drops," which, with tobacco, apples, and cakes, were consumed in great quantities by the passengers.

Local Chapter of the National Railway Historical Society

The National Railway Historical Society grew from the marriage of two local clubs: the Lancaster Railway & Locomotive Historical Society of Pennsylvania and the Interstate Trolley Club of Trenton. In 1935, their officers consolidated to create a larger organization with local chapters whose members could celebrate railroad heritage at a time when the Depression was taking its toll on the railroad industry.

Additional chapters were created in 1936 and throughout the course of the Second World War. By 2004, the National Railway Historical Society had become America's largest railfan organization, with nearly two hundred chapters worldwide and about eighteen thousand members. Its headquarters are in the Robert Morris building in Philadelphia, at Seventeenth and Arch Streets, where members of the research staff can be con-tacted for help in the use of its library. Local chapters may be associated with individual preservation efforts of railroad artifacts, sometimes oper-ating railroad museums or actual equipment and rolling stock. Other chapters build and maintain model railroads, collect data and documents on railroad history, and encourage rail transportation.

The West Jersey Chapter was established in this region in 1944 and meets regularly in Haddonfield, where speakers conduct programs on historic railroads in New Jersey or Pennsylvania, or their modern successors such as Amtrak and Conrail. During the winter, the chapter conducts a film festival with old movies that may include vintage railroad promotional films or Hollywood productions such as *Buster Keaton Rides Again,* featuring the silent film star in a movie set on a train. Members enjoy frequent field trips on operating transit or tourist lines and also visit railroad facilities not generally open to the public, such as the Southern New Jersey Light Rail Transportation System shops in Camden.

The chapter publishes the *West Jersey Rails Quarterly* and has produced a number of books, including its popular three-volume collection of illustrated articles on southern New Jersey railroad history, titled *West Jersey Rails I, II,* and *III.* Railfans can order copies of these publications or prints of photos from the chapter's Edward Trebino Collection through the chapter's website at www.nelliebly.com/westjersey/.

This region is also home to a club whose members operate a miniature steam railroad called the Iron Acres Railroad, in Jackson. This is not open to the general public, but those interested in becoming members can apply via e-mail at the group's website, ironacresrailroad.homestead.com/index.html.

The Region's Railroad Giants

Robert Field Stockton (1795–1866)

Robert Field Stockton was born to a very prominent Princeton family. His father was a lawyer and U.S. senator, and his grandfather had been one of the original signers of the Declaration of Independence.

Stockton is well remembered in the history of the U.S. Navy. He dropped out of Princeton to join the Navy as a midshipman in 1811, when he was just sixteen years old. He served under Commodore John Rodgers and took part in the defense of Baltimore during the War of 1812, later serving in the Mediterranean and Europe. He commanded the Pacific Squadron off the coast of California during the Mexican War in the 1840s. Together with Lt. Col. John C. Frémont, he organized a civilian government for California and managed its military operations until it was ceded to the United States. Upon his retirement, he returned to Princeton and was elected to the U.S. Senate, serving from 1851 to 1853.

During the 1830s, Stockton had been one of the key promoters of canals over railroads and the man who obtained the charter for the

Delaware and Raritan Canal Company. After he came to terms with the Stevens family, he became the most visible and commanding leader of the Joint Companies. He officially became president of the Delaware and Raritan Canal Company in 1853 and served in that position until his death in 1866.

In 1828, Stockton inherited his family's Princeton estate, called Morven. Since that time, Morven served for many years as the official residence of the governor of New Jersey. Following a multimillion-dollar renovation, Morven is now open to the public as Morven Museum and Garden.

Robert Livingston Stevens (1787–1856)

Son of the visionary John Stevens, Robert Livingston Stevens was born in Hoboken and is known for his naval as well as railroad innovations. He was privately tutored and assisted his father in his early experiments with steam engines.

After operating a steamboat ferry on the Hudson, he helped design and build the *Phoenix,* which he sailed from New York to Philadelphia in 1809, a historic journey marking the first time a steamboat survived the open sea. The *Phoenix* ferried passengers between Philadelphia and Trenton as part of the Stevens family's steam ferry transportation system, which also included service between New York and Hoboken. Stevens designed and built nearly twenty other steam vessels and took pleasure in the sport of sailing.

Many authors have repeated the story of Robert Livingston Stevens's chief innovation for the railroad industry: the T-rail. In 1830, he sailed for England to purchase a locomotive and make arrangements for acquiring iron rails for the fledgling Camden and Amboy Railroad and Transportation Company. While en route, he carved a wooden model of the Birkinshaw rail then in use in England, adding a broad base so that much less iron hardware would be needed to hold the rail in place. After he found a mill willing to manufacture his prototype and worked out the production difficulties, Stevens's design became the standard for the Camden and Amboy and later all American railroads. In his many years as a president of the Camden and Amboy and its chief engineer, he also invented the hook-headed spike and other rail fastenings that improved the strength of railroad joints.

In England, he observed the public testing of the locomotive called the Planet and ordered a similar engine for the Camden and Amboy. After Isaac Dripps assembled the locomotive, which the railroad named the John Bull, Robert Livingston Stevens personally tested it on its trial run in Bordentown in 1831.

Edwin Augustus Stevens (1795–1868)

Also the son of John Stevens and, like his brother, privately tutored, Edwin Augustus Stevens became the unofficial chief executive officer for the various Stevens family enterprises. In 1812, he began managing the family's ferry service between Philadelphia and Trenton or Camden, and he stayed involved as the family expanded its ferry and stagecoach transportation system.

In 1830, he became treasurer and manager of the Camden and Amboy Railroad and Transportation Company, assuming the presidency of this company when his brother, Robert, died in 1856. It was Edwin Augustus Stevens who initiated leasing certain operations of the United Companies to the Pennsylvania Railroad Company. He retired in 1867.

Stevens took an interest in naval warfare and together with his brother constructed an armored vessel called the Stevens Battery. He later built the *Naugatuck,* which became part of the fleet to attack the *Merrimack* in the Civil War.

Edwin Augustus Stevens's will endowed the Stevens Institute of Technology for engineering education on the old Stevens family estate in Hoboken. Opening in 1870, the Stevens Institute is currently one of America's leading technological universities, offering bachelor's and master's degrees and doctorates.

Benjamin Fish (1785–1880)

Benjamin Fish was born on his father's farm in Ewing Township. Moving to Trenton in 1808, he helped establish Hill, Fish and Abbey, a firm that transported merchandise between Philadelphia, New York, and Albany. During the War of 1812, it transported commissary stores and ordnance for the U.S. Army.

In 1825, he joined the Stevens's Union Line empire, and he became a director of the Camden and Amboy Railroad when it was organized in 1830. Fish is said to have driven the horses for the very first run of the Camden and Amboy from Bordentown to South Amboy before the railroad acquired a locomotive. He also helped organize and direct a number of other New Jersey transportation systems, including the Delaware and Raritan Canal Company, Camden and Philadelphia Steamboat Ferry Company, Freehold & Jamesburg Agricultural Railroad Company, and Delaware Bridge Company.

Isaac Dripps (1810–1892)

Born in Belfast, Dripps immigrated to Philadelphia with his parents, where he became an apprentice to a manufacturer of marine engines.

Robert Livingston Stevens discovered him repairing a steamboat and hired him for the family business.

Dripps distinguished himself by successfully assembling the locomotive John Bull, even though he had never seen a steam locomotive. He later copied and improved its design and built seven other locomotives while in charge of the Camden and Amboy's shops outside of Bordentown.

In 1853, he became superintendent of the Trenton Locomotive & Machine Works. He became superintendent of machinery for the Pittsburgh, Fort Wayne & Chicago Railway in 1859 and inspector of shops, tools, and machinery for the Pennsylvania Railroad Company, which leased this line. He designed and equipped some of the Pennsy's car shops at Altoona and conducted important tests and studies of locomotives on mountain grades.

Dripps retired to Philadelphia in 1876. The Pennsylvania Railroad Company honored him when it erected a monument commemorating the first movement of a steam locomotive in New Jersey in Bordentown in 1891.

Sampling the Region's Railroad History

The PATCO Speedline

In the Jersey suburbs of Philadelphia, there's a railroad that's relatively new yet already historic. The system now called the PATCO Speedline offers frequent rapid rail service to Philadelphia that's almost always on time. Its riders actually prefer it to their cars.

PATCO stands for Port Authority Transit Corporation, an entity officially incorporated in 1967 by the state of New Jersey and the commonwealth of Pennsylvania, a wholly owned subsidiary of the Delaware River Port Authority. It is the successor of a system once operated by the Philadelphia Rapid Transit Company and the Delaware River Joint Commission that used to be called the High Speed Line, the Bridge Speed Line, or simply the Bridge Line.

The bridge in question is the Benjamin Franklin Bridge. When it opened on July 4, 1926, it was the world's longest single-span suspension bridge, stretching from Sixth and Vine Streets in Philadelphia to Sixth and Penn Streets in Camden. It had been designed to accommodate not only six lanes of automobile traffic, but also rapid-transit trains and trolley cars.

By the time the bridge opened, trolleys were being phased out in favor of buses for city transit, so trolleys never crossed the Benjamin Franklin Bridge. The Delaware River Joint Commission did construct a Camden-to-Philly railroad, which opened in 1936, across the bridge. The Bridge Line had two stations in Camden and two in Philadelphia, one of them permitting free transfer to Philadelphia's subway system. The Bridge Line proved to be more popular than ferry service across the Delaware, which was eliminated in 1952.

The Delaware River Port Authority (DRPA) was created that same year and empowered to operate rapid transit farther out in the suburbs of Camden. During the late 1950s, its consultants studied the idea of a tunnel under the Delaware, but the DRPA opted for a far less expensive system incorporating the Bridge Line and extending via Haddonfield to the Kirkwood Station in the borough of Lindenwold on the old Pennsylvania-Reading Seashore Lines.

Designers and engineers adopted concepts from the transit systems of other American cities. Their guiding objective was to create a system that could compete successfully with the private automobile. At the request of the mayor of Lindenwold, the transit system, which had been dubbed the Kirkwood Line while it was under construction, was christened the Lindenwold High Speed Line, a name by which it was known for many years.

Trains began running between Lindenwold and Camden in January 1969, and service to Philadelphia was inaugurated on February 15. Seventy-five new cars replaced the old subway cars of the Bridge Line. The fleet was expanded by forty-six more cars in 1980. The trains ran with subway frequency during rush hour, and they ran around the clock. They still do.

In a traditionally labor-intensive industry, the system has always managed with very few employees. One person operates each train, regardless of its number of cars, because PATCO Speedline trains operate automatically. The train accelerates smoothly to maximum speed, and the brakes go on when it gets within a certain distance of a station so that it can stop precisely at the center of the platform. PATCO Speedline stations are unmanned, and passengers deposit their fares in a machine that dispenses a ticket. The PATCO Speedline currently has 325 full-time employees, including thirty-five police officers.

On its first weekday of operation, the line collected eighteen thousand fares, a number that rose to an average of thirty-six thousand in 1971. Success prompted the managers to add parking spaces at various locations and create special and express trains that did not stop at every station. PATCO estimates that about thirty-eight thousand commuters now ride the line every day.

In 1975, a regional transit improvement program for southern New Jersey proposed that the PATCO system be expanded with lines extending to several other New Jersey suburbs, but these lines were never built.

Haddonfield, a station stop on the PATCO Speedline.

In 1984 and 1985, PATCO replaced the tracks over the Benjamin Franklin Bridge. In 1988, it began renovating the viaducts originally constructed by the Pennsylvania Railroad Company during the early twentieth century, which elevated its trains over Camden. Most recently, PATCO refurbished its stations and replaced its wooden ties with concrete ones as part of a $100 million renovation program.

In 2005, the DRPA opened public hearings to consider extending the PATCO Speedline system deep into South Jersey, as far as Glassboro in Gloucester County, or even Millville in Cumberland County. In Philadelphia, the system might incorporate a light rail line on Columbus Boulevard.

The RiverLINE

When it opened in March 2004, the RiverLINE was America's longest light rail line. Twenty diesel-powered vehicles plied its thirty-four miles of riverfront corridor between Camden and Trenton, stopping at each of twenty stations every thirty minutes during regular operating hours, and more frequently during rush periods.

The RiverLINE had materialized quickly. Most accounts of its development credit the original idea to New Jersey state senator William Haines, who promoted the old Camden-to-Trenton route of the Camden and Amboy over two other routes under consideration in 1995 for mass transit in South Jersey. Once NJ TRANSIT's board voted to proceed, the project moved rapidly without the need for review by the Federal Transit Administration because no federal funds were being sought. A low bid from Bechtel Group, Inc. won the contract to build and operate the RiverLINE, and construction began in 2000.

The RiverLINE cost the taxpayers of New Jersey more than $1 billion in principal and interest. Tracks and grade crossings were rebuilt. A new steel-arch bridge replaced an aging bridge over Rancocas Creek in 2001, but while the bridge was being floated on a barge toward the new piers on which it would rest, the barge collapsed, resulting in a delay of nearly four months before the eight-hundred-ton bridge could be righted.

Considerable expense also went into making the open-air stations attractive. Railfans will recognize the Tuscan red roofs and wrought-iron lampposts, benches, and other fixtures as Pennsylvania Railroad Company nostalgia. Sculptor Marilyn Keating, ceramicist Katherine Hacki, and painter Hiroshi Murata collaborated to design the tiled panels that decorate each station, generally depicting plants and animals that dwell in the nearby Delaware River.

Heated controversy attended the RiverLINE's construction. In April 2001, South Jersey's *Courier-Post* published a three-part series of articles in which Richard Pearsall addressed whether the RiverLINE had been a "billion-dollar boondoggle." Instead of providing a mass-transit alternative through one of South Jersey's more congested traffic corridors, the River-LINE connected old factory towns that for the most part had stopped growing decades earlier. Although its southernmost terminal was the increasingly popular entertainment complex on the Camden waterfront, the RiverLINE shared tracks with Conrail, and its passenger trains had to be off the rails to make way for freight trains too early at night for the RiverLINE to be convenient for those attending concerts at the Tweeter Center or ball games at Campbell Field. At its northern terminal, passengers

New Jersey's newest railroad, the RiverLINE, at Camden's recently refurbished Broadway Station. Note the lampposts and other metalwork decorating the station, purposely reminiscent of architectural ornamentation used by the Pennsylvania Railroad Company.

Like the Old Camden and Amboy and the Pennsylvania Railroad, the RiverLINE is single tracked through Burlington.

found themselves a mile away from the government buildings where most commuters to Trenton worked. Pearsall reported that the justification for the RiverLINE's existence quoted by proponents had subtly shifted over the years from much-needed mass transit to hopes for economic development in the river towns it served. The *Courier-Post* series reported that both supporters and critics agreed that the RiverLINE could succeed only if more people moved into the riverfront corridor after it opened.

In the summer of 2004, the RiverLINE averaged forty-two hundred riders on weekdays and forty-eight hundred on Saturdays, well below the number of people who ride the PATCO Speedline. Yet it serves the greater good of populous Burlington County by making it possible for residents to reach not only Camden and Trenton, but also Philadelphia, Newark and its airport, and New York City by rail. It also gives those residing on the western shore of the Delaware an alternative to SEPTA's R7 line between Philadelphia and Trenton. The RiverLINE may take a little longer, but it's cheaper to ride, its trains operate more frequently, and it's something new.

The PJ&B, or Dinky

Its official NJ TRANSIT name may be the Princeton Branch, but Princeton students have called the one-car train that serves their campus the PJ&B (Princeton Junction and Back) for generations, and more recently, the Dinky. This train makes more than forty weekday round-trips between a modest stone station on University Place and the Princeton Junction Station, where Amtrak and NJ TRANSIT trains stop. The trip is 2.7 miles long and takes four minutes, making it possibly the shortest scheduled passenger railroad line in America.

In 1865, the route of the Camden and Amboy that would become the Pennsy's main line through Jersey was shifted east from Princeton Basin in order to straighten the tracks. Both town and gown elements protested the increased distance they had to travel to catch a train, so the railroad constructed a short spur. Initially, this little railroad provided six round-trips a day, hauling both passengers and freight.

In the early 1900s, the PJ&B made it possible for fans of college football and other sports to make an easy day excursion to Princeton University. The Pennsylvania Railroad Company cooperated by offering special game-day trains from New York, Boston, and Washington, D.C., that parked on sidings in special layover yards until the fans went home. The PJ&B was double tracked in 1905, and today NJ TRANSIT adds a second car during holiday seasons, when more students travel, assuming that it has an extra car available.

For nearly half a century, Princeton Branch passengers arrived at a small stone station built in the 1870s to replace an earlier wooden structure near the university's Blair Hall, a building that boasted an impressive stair and arch intended to be the entrance to the campus for those who arrived by

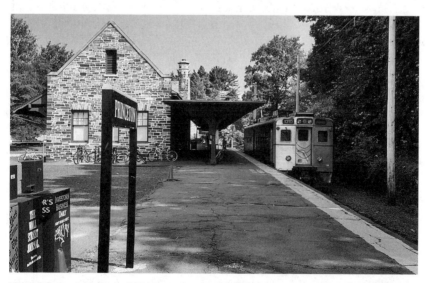

The Princeton terminal of what may be the world's shortest regularly scheduled commuter railroad, popularly known as the PJ&B (Princeton Junction and Back) or Dinky.

rail. Perhaps only those involved in the railroad industry appreciated the fact that Blair Hall had been named for John I. Blair, a descendant of Princeton faculty who made millions investing in railroads.

As Princeton University expanded, students began complaining about the noise and soot of steam locomotives too close to their dorms, prompting the Pennsylvania Railroad Company to move the terminal south to its present location in 1920 and electrify the line in 1936. Today Dinky riders purchase tickets from machines on the platform near a station that was designed to match the style of Princeton's campus architecture. The station is closed except to NJ TRANSIT employees.

Many famous Princetonians and Princeton visitors have ridden the Dinky, including Albert Einstein, while he was a faculty member at the Institute for Advanced Study, and John Nash, the real-life subject of a recent film titled *A Beautiful Mind.* In 1913, Woodrow Wilson began his trip to Washington, D.C., for inauguration as president with a ride on the Dinky. Before Princeton went coed in 1969, the Dinky station was the place where students picked up their dates, who stayed for the weekend in boardinghouses in town. Most passengers today study, teach, or work at Princeton University or live in town and commute to jobs elsewhere.

In 2004, there was some talk of replacing the Princeton Branch with a more flexible bus route, but the idea was not terribly popular on campus.

Trenton's Railroad Heritage

For nearly a century, those wishing to travel between Philadelphia and Trenton could choose to ride either the Pennsy or the Reading Railroad's Delaware and Bound Brook route. The Pennsy's main line ran across the Delaware River and under the Delaware and Raritan Canal to a station on South Clinton Avenue. The Reading deposited passengers at a Ewing Township station, from which they could take a short spur to a station on Trenton's North Warren Street near Tucker Street.

Today's commuters ride the same two routes on trains operated by a single transportation system officially called the Southeastern Pennsylvania Transportation Authority but commonly known as SEPTA. SEPTA's R7 line still arrives at a station on Clinton Avenue, where passengers can catch connecting trains to New York. The R3 terminates at West Trenton Station in Ewing, New Jersey, which is no longer connected to Trenton proper by rail and mainly serves those who live in the Trenton area and commute to Pennsylvania.

By the 1950s, both the Pennsy and the Reading were losing money on commuter operations and responded by cutting services, raising fares, and even threatening to discontinue passenger service unless they were awarded

View of Trenton from the other end of its remarkable bridge, as depicted in the 1845 edition of *Historical Collections of the State of New Jersey* by John W. Barber and Henry Howe.

government subsidies. Loss of passenger rail service would have meant increased congestion on metropolitan Philadelphia's highways and streets, not to mention a population immobilized in bad winter weather.

A transportation study conducted in the entire Philadelphia–New Jersey Delaware Valley region resulted in a federally assisted commuter railroad demonstration project called SEPACT I. One of its key objectives was to reverse the decline in commuter ridership by offering better service, newer trains, and cheaper fares. SEPACT I also pioneered regional cooperation between a city and its suburbs and led to the 1964 creation of SEPTA, the modern-day heir to both historic routes between Philadelphia and Trenton.

A different government agency, New Jersey's Department of Transportation, has promised Trenton a greatly expanded and modernized rail station with larger waiting areas and more retail space. This is planned to open in 2006 following an expenditure of about $50 million.

Trenton's transportation history has left the city a number of interesting bridges—artifacts of the enduring need to get trains and other vehicles safely and efficiently over the river from Pennsylvania. The first bridge across the Delaware at Trenton required the cooperation of both New Jersey and Pennsylvania. In 1798, both states authorized stock subscription commissioners for the construction project, and both granted charters in 1803. Construction began in 1804, and two years later, the

The first bridge across the Delaware at Trenton, which opened in 1806 and was adapted later for the use of the Philadelphia and Trenton Railroad.

Trenton Delaware Bridge Company opened its bridge with a parade and a gun salute.

The bridge had been designed by noted bridge engineer Theodore Burr. Over 1,000 feet long, it had five arches resting on four piers and abutments built of stone. It was covered with a cedar-shingled roof, and both ends of the bridge had facades with arched entrances. In the 1845 edition of *Historical Collections of the State of New Jersey,* John W. Barber and Henry Howe write, "It reflects credit upon Mr. Burr, its architect, combining as it does, the three great objects, convenience of traveling, strength, and durability."

After the Philadelphia and Trenton Railroad was built as far as Morrisville, railroad track was laid over one of the bridge's wagon lanes, making this the first bridge in the United States adapted for interstate railroad traffic. This left only a single lane for wagons, so a traffic coordinator had to be stationed at each end to ring a bell signaling oncoming traffic to halt whenever a wagon entered the bridge. To address this inconvenience, the bridge was widened in 1848 and a separate lane created just for trains. In 1860, the bridge's roof was removed after a spark from a locomotive caused a fire in a span near the Jersey shore.

In the years following the Civil War, the historic bridge was aging, and sometimes heavy wagons broke through its rotting floorboards. Many feared that a train accident would be far worse. In *A History of Trenton, 1629–1929,* Edwin Robert Walker describes the further evolution of this structure. The Pennsy contracted with the Keystone Bridge Company to replace the Burr bridge with an iron bridge. Engineers adapted the piers and abutments for the new bridge, which was constructed right beside the Burr bridge and then moved into place in 1876. In 1898, the American Bridge Company used a similar technique to replace the iron bridge with a steel one.

In 1928, after yet more adaptations to the piers and abutments, the bridge became the double-lane Lincoln Highway Bridge, now spanned by Route 1. What happened to the trains? They had been crossing the Delaware on a stone-arch bridge constructed by the Pennsylvania Railroad Company in 1908 a few hundred yards to the south; this bridge is still used by passenger trains.

In the late nineteenth century, during the period when the iron and steel successors to the Burr bridge had been handling railroad traffic only, other vehicles were crossing the Delaware on an iron "wagon bridge" built by the Keystone Bridge Company in 1876. This bridge, with its five iron spans but relatively narrow roadway, is still used by local traffic and has since been graced with enormous letters spelling the slogan "Trenton Makes The World Takes," making it a famous Trenton landmark easily visible to passengers crossing the river on trains.

Trenton's other bridge, called the Calhoun Street Bridge, opened in 1860 and was rebuilt following a fire in 1884. Early in the twentieth century, it accommodated trolleys between Trenton and Morrisville.

Pemberton

Though far smaller than Trenton, the Pine Barrens community in Burlington County called Pemberton once boasted excellent rail connections. The Pemberton Branch, an extension of the Burlington County Railroad between Camden and Mount Holly, opened in the 1860s and later became part of an alternate way to travel between Philadelphia and Long Branch, known to Pennsylvania Railroad Company employees as the "back road."

In 1864, the state of New Jersey authorized the incorporation of the Pemberton and Hightstown Railroad. The Camden and Amboy assisted with funding and later leased this line, which it intended to use as an alternate route between Camden and Hightstown. After the Pennsylvania Railroad Company merged the Pemberton and Hightstown into its system, its managers tried to shut down all traffic except daily mail service in 1888, justifying themselves by citing years of regular losses.

The Pemberton and Hightstown then became a genuine farmers' railroad, thanks to the Burlington County farmers who had come to depend on it to get their commodities, mainly milk, to consumers. Local business leaders raised the funds to begin operating the Union Transportation Company, headquartered in nearby New Egypt. Well into the twentieth century, this local line served passengers and delivered milk, cranberries, hay, and straw, not to mention a whole lot of ripe Jersey tomatoes headed for the Campbell Soup Company in Camden.

In 1872, Pemberton took its place in railroad history when the Pennsylvania Railroad Company tested George Westinghouse's triple-valve air brake system on the Pemberton and Hightstown Railroad. In 1905, its successor, the Union Transportation Company, experimented with concrete ties near New Egypt.

Pemberton became far busier in the years after 1917, when a large army base, Camp Dix (now Fort Dix), opened in the Pine Barrens just to the north. During World War II, troop trains passed through Pemberton regularly.

New state highways allowed cars and trucks to serve the Union Transportation Company's regular customers, causing the number of trains bound for Pemberton to decline in the 1950s. The last passenger train between Camden and Pemberton ran in 1969, and the Penn Central abandoned this line in the 1970s.

Today Hightstown has few traces of railroad history, save for the remains of two abutments built by the Pennsylvania Railroad Company near Rocky Brook and a row of old stone sleepers from the Camden and

Pemberton's railroad station, constructed in 1892 and now open to the public as a museum.

Old railroad viaduct abutments dominate the main intersection of Hightstown.

Amboy lined up behind the town's freight station, which has been moved and attached to a historic house maintained by the town's historical society. Pemberton, however, has a railroad station constructed by the Pennsylvania Railroad Company and the Union Transportation Company in 1892. It was painstakingly restored between 1996 and 1999 and is currently owned by the township of Pemberton. It replaced an earlier station that opened on this site in 1863 and burned down in 1891.

The Pemberton Township Historic Trust maintains a museum inside the station and conducts programs there. The small frame building is filled with maps, spikes, and other hardware excavated in the surrounding area, and railroad station artifacts such as ticket boxes and tickets from the Pemberton and Hightstown and connecting railroads. Other objects are also on display. These include local artifacts such as milk bottles, attesting to the continued importance of the milk industry in this area, as well as donated items that the historic trust simply did not turn down, such as a photograph of a steam locomotive from the East Broad Top Railroad that seems very far from its home in Orbisonia, Pennsylvania.

Some township officials would like to use state grant money to purchase the site of Pemberton's old rail yard, which they hope to transform into a railroad village suggesting Pemberton at the turn of the twentieth century. Plans were stalled in 2004 by discord over a proposal to build a large convenience store on some or all of this property. Convenience-store proponents argued that private enterprise would bring in more tax revenue than a historic site. The recently located and identified foundations and fragments

Remains of the Camden and Amboy in Hightstown include a row of stone sleepers on display behind the historical society.

of actual buildings in the Pemberton rail yard remain obscured by weeds, quietly awaiting a verdict on their final disposition. Museum visitors can sign a petition and take home a copy of a diagram of the site's proposed structures, which include a freight house, lumber shed, general store, turntable, and roundhouse.

Long-A-Coming Berlin

The 1868 edition of *Historical Collections of New Jersey,* a history of New Jersey written by John W. Barber and Henry Howe, mentioned a town called Long-A-Coming, "situated among the pines" fifteen miles from Camden. It had two hotels and about forty dwellings. There is still speculation whether the village's unusual name was an anglicized version of the Native American name for this particular spot or was bestowed by those traveling via stagecoach between Philadelphia and Absecon Island, who used it as a rest stop and wearily proclaimed that it always seemed to be extremely long-a-coming.

The name was officially changed to Berlin in 1867, some years after the town became a station stop on the Camden and Atlantic Railroad, whose service no doubt made it seem less inconveniently distant. Trains continued to stop at Berlin after this railroad became part of the Pennsylvania-Reading Seashore Lines.

A small frame railroad station called the Long-A-Coming Depot, constructed in Berlin in 1856, has since become the oldest surviving railroad station in New Jersey—or at least, it was the oldest one listed on the National Register of Historic Places when it was awarded this honor in 1997. The borough of Berlin leased the building in 1992, and members of the Long-A-Coming Historical Society began restoring it in 1994.

The station is not open to the public. It is small enough, however, for visitors to view by peering in the windows.

Constructed in the Italianate style popular in the mid-nineteenth century, the station has a freight room with some original sliding doors,

New Jersey's oldest surviving railroad station, constructed in 1856 in the town of Berlin, then called Long-A-Coming.

office, and passenger waiting room. The office was built with a bay projecting onto the platform so that railroad personnel could see trains coming down the tracks. The structure is a good example of how a whole new type of building was evolving to serve the needs of expanding railroads, and how those designing early railroad stations combined functionality with style, even in what would have been a small rural town.

Lorett Treese Travels

I had never really noticed the red directional signs leading me through the Gallery shopping mall in downtown Philadelphia to the PATCO Speedline station at Eighth and Market, but then, I had never looked for them before. They led my husband and me to the PATCO Speedline turnstiles and ticket dispensers, artifacts of the late 1960s that were the biggest headache of riding the PATCO Speedline when we made our maiden voyage in the summer of 2004.

The ticket dispensers would not accept paper currency, so purchasing a ticket was a two-step process involving the dollar bill changer installed at every station. The tickets operated by older magnetic rather than digital technology, and the typeface and condition of mine indicated that it had been recycled in the PATCO Speedline system for a very long time.

The PATCO Speedline website promised us that a new smart-card system would be piloted in 2005, but the 2004 fare-collection equipment did give us a brief glance of something I had not witnessed in years. Among the coins meted out by the dollar bill changer were a Sacajawea and a Susan B. Anthony dollar. So that's where they all went!

Stairs led to a narrow platform between two tracks that seemed dark compared with the well-lit expanses of SEPTA's Market East Station. We gazed right and left, wondering which track the Jersey-bound trains ran on, and finally asked a gentleman in a basketball jersey and bandanna who looked like a regular PATCO Speedline rider. As a train approached, the computerized sign that had been blinking the time and the name of the Delaware River Port Authority's website generated an arrow pointing to one of the tracks and identified the terminus for the oncoming train as Lindenwold. A recorded announcement repeated the information and told us that this train made all stops.

We got a seat near the front of the train, where I was able to share the operator's view as we rounded the underground curves leading to daylight. We emerged on elevated tracks level with roof gardens and the windows of apartments and offices as we climbed the grade onto the Benjamin Franklin Bridge.

The windows on PATCO Speedline cars are large and provide a fine view of either the advancing Camden waterfront or retreating Philadelphia skyline, depending on which way your seat faces. Those occupying seats on the bridge side of the train experience more evidence of the grade as the train rises to the level of the bridge deck and speeds past the cars traveling alongside it. I'd spend the cash to take this ride just for the view, especially at night when the city lights are burning and one can't see just how far beneath the car the choppy surface of the Delaware seems to be.

Camden's revitalized riverfront and new ballpark are just a short walk from the PATCO Speedline's City Hall station, formerly a station on the old Bridge Line. Riders can also reach the waterfront attractions via the RiverLINE by getting off at the transportation center recently named for Camden state senator Walter Rand, although it was still identified as Broadway on PATCO Speedline tickets and maps at the stations in 2004.

We gazed down from rails elevated a century before at Camden row homes and then the backyards of suburban neighborhoods where the homeowners seemed to be in competition over who could own the finest pool. Haddonfield, a destination we had selected for its reputation of shaded streets, colonial architecture, and historic sites, is known in Jersey transportation history for the colonial road that still bisects it, called the King's Highway. We were strolling this venerable thoroughfare, admiring its upscale shops and deciding which restaurant to patronize for lunch, when a server at one of them informed us that Haddonfield was a dry town. Fortunately, the PATCO Speedline runs every twelve minutes, even on Saturdays, and the fine wines and microbrewed beers of Philadelphia's dining establishments were just a short ride in the opposite direction.

On another trip, as the PATCO Speedline rushed us over the Delaware River, we tried but failed to spot from the air any vestige of the Pennsy's old Camden Terminal, which once included a passenger station, ferry slips, roundhouse, and repair facilities for locomotives and passenger cars. It took up so much space that it effectively isolated Camden residents from the city's waterfront. We saw instead the facilities of Camden's newest industry, tourism, including a new marina, the state aquarium, and the battleship *New Jersey* proudly berthed in the river.

After exiting the PATCO Speedline at the Walter Rand Transportation Center, we crossed the street to ride a successor to the Pennsy and earlier Camden and Amboy, NJ TRANSIT's Southern Jersey Light Rail Transportation System and its RiverLINE trains. We waited until a train was in view to validate the tickets we purchased from an automatic dispenser, so they were good for a whole two hours of rail travel no matter how many stations we visited.

At midmorning on an August weekday, enough passengers boarded to half fill the train. We found a pair of purple-and-red-upholstered seats at the front, where we could once again share the operator's view and gaze over his shoulder at the controls. We climbed an embankment and speeded up as we passed Pavonia Yard, the largest classification yard in South Jersey, where we spotted a CSX locomotive and quite a few freight cars parked between the RiverLINE and the river. As we approached the Route 73 station, we could spot two Delaware River bridges, one of them the Delair Bridge, a railroad drawbridge built by a Pennsylvania Railroad Company subsidiary in 1896. As our car passed under its approach, we could look up through the ties and rails overhead.

Now that trolleys have all but disappeared in the Delaware Valley, it's an odd sensation to proceed by rail right down a suburban street and past the borough hall, as we did in Palmyra. NJ TRANSIT buses paced us and occasionally passed us.

At Riverside, we found a restaurant advertising $1 off any item to customers who came in with validated RiverLINE tickets. The town's former Pennsylvania Railroad passenger station was open for business as a thrift shop, and the sounds of construction emanated from an elaborate and massive building being renovated as the Watchcase Office Complex. Most of its windows were still broken and boarded, but we saw plants

The Pennsylvania Railroad Company built this station in Riverside. It is now open to visitors as a shop.

and blinds in the windows of the first and second floors, and the clock in its tower told the correct time.

After catching the next train north, we crossed the Rancocas Creek on the line's new bright blue steel bridge. We did not exit at Delanco, but I noticed several square, light-colored stones lined up near the parking lot, as if someone intended to remind railfans of the stone sleepers that had been phased out while the Camden and Amboy was under construction.

Traffic approaching the Burlington-Bristol Bridge halted for our River-LINE train, and we passed another old Pennsy passenger station just before we moved to the single track that runs down Burlington's Broad Street. Rail lore has it that Burlington bigwigs never allowed the Pennsy to double track its line through this town.

When the Camden and Amboy laid tracks between Camden and Trenton, Burlington was one of only two towns of any significance along the route. Founded by Friends in the late 1600s, Burlington still has dwellings of colonial and early American vintage along its narrow streets, mainly functioning as private residences. Burlington's High Street, which once separated the town lots of Quakers who had come from London and those from Yorkshire, is now lined with shops and restaurants leading to an attractive riverfront park and promenade. A large building on a corner of Broad and High Streets, once a fine hotel called the Beldin House, occupies the site of the earlier Blue Anchor Tavern, where Camden and Amboy passengers boarded the train until the 1860s. It now belongs to the city and was awaiting an occupant in 2004.

Back on the train, we passed the Burlington Yard office of Conrail as we sped toward Florence. The remains of a mill in Roebling intrigued us and invited exploration, but it looked as if it was nowhere near ready for guided tours, so we stayed on the train.

As we drew near Bordentown, I realized we were passing White Hill, the place where the Camden and Amboy Railroad had built the maintenance shops for its locomotives and passenger cars. The RiverLINE's Bordentown station is very near the spot where the Camden and Amboy's Camden branch joined its original main line to South Amboy. Stand there long enough and you can hear unseen freight trains heading in that same direction.

When the Camden and Amboy was new, passengers arriving in Bordentown mounted steps from the platform to Farnsworth Avenue, which ran over a stone bridge across the tracks. Today's passengers find themselves on the new Park Street Bridge, overlooking what a sign identifies as Bordentown Beach, the place where ferries once landed and people now quietly picnic, fish, or put small craft in the water.

Farnsworth Avenue is now home to bookstores, restaurants, and shops offering jewelry and decor items. When the staff of the historical society is manning the old Friends Meeting House on this street, they will sell you a guide for a walking tour of Bordentown's historic buildings. The face of Bordentown's founder, Thomas Farnsworth, looks down from the wall of a restaurant that bears his name at the old Pennsylvania Railroad

The site of a tavern where passengers boarded Camden and Amboy trains until the 1860s, when this hotel was constructed in Burlington.

monument, known to the locals as the John Bull monument, occupying a prominent spot in the center of town.

The Pennsylvania Railroad Company constructed this monument in 1891, on the sixtieth anniversary of rail operations in Bordentown. It's a big granite block set on a foundation of original stone sleepers surrounded by a circle of iron formed of two rails from the old Camden and Amboy line. A bas relief depicts the locomotive John Bull, together with its improvised tender and passenger cars that resembled stagecoaches. A more recent plaque informs visitors that the monument was moved to its present location in 1970 by Penn Central as a tribute to Edward S. Shott, "whose interest in rail transit keeps a watchful eye on its preservation." The monument is protected by a gate and fence erected by the Bordentown Rotary Club.

Just beyond the Crosswicks Creek Bridge, north of the Bordentown Station, RiverLINE passengers might find it difficult to recognize the remains of the Delaware and Raritan Canal. Even after a rainy summer, it held little more than puddles and weeds.

In Trenton, the train stopped first at Cass Street, then Hamilton Avenue, where we could see the Sovereign Bank Arena. While approaching the RiverLINE's northern terminus, passengers get a reminder that its trains can negotiate pretty steep inclines. Passengers emerge at an intersection where quiet Mercer Cemetery is located diagonally across from the busy Amtrak–SEPTA–NJ TRANSIT Station, which proved to be the destination for most people riding our train. Nearby streets named Canal Street and Yard Avenue hint at the historic significance of this spot as a transportation hub.

The train was slightly more crowded on our trip back to Camden later in the afternoon approaching rush hour, but it was still nowhere near full. Whether the line will achieve ridership expectations remains to be seen. It may be that the line already has more riders than its revenue would indicate. At nearly every station, it took us at least three attempts to get any of the station's vending machines to accept a dollar bill, a situation that sorely tempted us to steal a ride out of sheer frustration.

While we were strolling High Street in Burlington, a *Courier-Post* reporter stopped us to inquire whom we would vote for in the upcoming presidential election. When we identified ourselves as Pennsylvanians exploring New Jersey's Delaware River towns simply because the RiverLINE was there to make it possible, he seemed more than a little surprised. Maybe this reporter had contributed to his newspaper's series questioning the worth of the RiverLINE. In any case, while we chatted, I had the distinct impression that he regarded us rather like the specters that materialized in a movie where a voice had advised, "Build it and they will come."

The Region's Rail Trails

Among the benefits of the 1980 Staggers Act to the railroad industry was the provision greatly streamlining the process of selling or abandoning unprofitable branches. At the turn of the twenty-first century, America's railroads included about 105,000 miles of track, down from a peak of about 270,000 miles around World War I, thanks to the Staggers Act as well as other factors.

What to do with abandoned railroads became a question hotly debated in the 1980s. Out of the Midwest came the notion of preserving railroad corridors while removing the tracks and adapting the roadbed for recreational uses. A 1983 amendment to the National Trails System Act allowed railroad corridors to be "railbanked," or preserved for possible future reclamation for rail transportation while joggers, hikers, and cyclists enjoyed them in the meantime.

The Rails to Trails Conservancy was formed in 1986 to provide assistance for local rail-trail conversions. Its website, www.traillink.com, lists up-to-date information on trail access and conditions nationwide.

The nonprofit volunteer conservation group called New Jersey Rail-Trails is working to create more rail trails from New Jersey's eight hundred miles of abandoned rail corridor. Since 1961, New Jersey's Department of Environmental Protection has run the Green Acres Program, empowered to purchase land to add to state parks, as well as provide grants and loans to townships, counties, and trusts. The program's current administrators are particularly interested in securing connector parcels to create greenways between existing and planned parks, making them the natural allies of rail-trail proponents.

The Delaware and Raritan Canal State Park is one of the most popular state parks in New Jersey, and though the bulk of it has no rail trails, the canal's history is firmly tied to the state's railroad heritage. The D&R Canal was constructed at a time when it was not yet certain that railroads would supersede canals, and it was managed jointly with the companies that formed New Jersey's railroad monopoly. In 1932, the canal was finally closed by the Pennsylvania Railroad Company, which owned it at that time.

The state of New Jersey later operated the canal as a water supply system, and by the 1970s, it was acknowledged to be one of the country's oldest and best-preserved canals. The canal and its remaining structures were entered on the National Register of Historic Places in 1973 and became a state park the following year. In the 1980s, the Delaware and Raritan Canal State Park acquired a genuine railroad corridor when the tracks and roadbed of the Belvidere Delaware Railroad (which had since become part of the Pennsy system) from Bull's Island to Frenchtown were added.

The 65 miles of park are generously furnished with transportation artifacts, such as bridges, locks, and the dwellings of those who tended and operated them. The remains or sites of mills are also located in several towns along the canal, including Stockton, Griggstown, Kingston, and Blackwells Mills.

In 1830, ground was broken for the Delaware and Raritan Canal in Kingston, which was about halfway between Bordentown and the Raritan River. In their history of New Jersey published in 1845, John W. Barber and Henry Howe identify Kingston as the place where the Delaware and Raritan Canal intersected the turnpike between New York and Philadelphia, calling it "the great thoroughfare between New York and the South," and claiming that up to four hundred travelers could be found in town at any one time.

Just off Route 27 between Kingston and Princeton, tourists can park near a preserved lock tender's house overlooking the old Kingston Lock. Inside, an exhibit of photos explains Kingston's history and mentions that there once was a railroad station just across the lock. Park literature states that the associated railroad was the Kingston Branch of the Pennsylvania Railroad Company, but a railroad map of New Jersey printed in 1894–95 identifies it as the Rocky Hill Railroad and Transportation Company, then connecting neighboring Rocky Hill with the Freehold & Jamesburg Agricultural Railroad. Rails are still visible crossing old Route 27, which leads to the mill dam on the nearby Millstone River.

Near where Route 27 intersects the canal, users will find the trailhead for the Kingston Branch Loop Trail, which is well liked by trail enthusiasts because it makes a circuit, using the Pennsy Rocky Hill rail corridor to the Georgetown-Franklin Turnpike and the canal towpath on the way back. Users will find some mile markers stating the distances to the opposite ends of the canal.

The canal's administrative headquarters were once located in Princeton, and the canal itself was just a mile from the campus down Canal Street, now Alexander Street. A separate community called Princeton Basin grew there, with wharves, a mule barn, and a basin where vessels could be unloaded and turned in the opposite direction. As traffic increased and the canal was widened, Princeton Basin acquired coal yards, warehouses, and a lumberyard.

Princeton Basin also had structures supporting the Camden and Amboy Railroad, whose tracks were constructed close to bank of the canal. They remained there until the Pennsylvania Railroad Company embarked on a project to straighten out the route. Its passenger station and freight depot then disappeared, but a Princeton guidebook published in 1931 and updated in 1945 mentioned that a railroad hotel was still standing, as was an old locomotive water reservoir at the top of a steep bank.

Today Princeton Basin has been replaced by Turning Basin Park, a spot where tourists can rent a canoe and put it in the water in the old turning basin. All that remains of Princeton Basin's old industrial structures is the pictures of the once-thriving community on the signs erected along the trails.

In 1836, the Belvidere Delaware Railroad Company was incorporated to share the right-of-way of the Delaware and Raritan Feeder Canal, or that portion of the system running parallel to the Delaware River designed to supply water to the main canal. The man who engineered and built this railroad located the Bel-Del's yards in his hometown of Lambertville, which Barber and Howe describe in the 1845 edition of their book as the most prosperous and flourishing village in Hunterdon County and a "good place for manufacturing."

On a summer Saturday afternoon, modern Lambertville is jammed with affluent shoppers and sightseers, many of whom stop for refreshment at Lambertville Station Restaurant and Bar, an excellent example of what seems to be a nationwide trend to convert spacious and often attractive passenger stations into eateries. A table in the second-floor dining room includes a great view of the Delaware River, but a seat on the enclosed passenger platform puts one practically on top of the old Bel-Del tracks with a view of the Delaware and Raritan Canal. Guests will

Delaware and Raritan Canal State Park outside of Princeton.

Genuine railroad tracks are part of the Delaware and Raritan Canal State Park in Lambertville. They have been cleared near the main shopping thoroughfare and the popular restaurant operating in the old passenger station.

notice a lot of traffic on the state park trail, but they'll wait a long time to spot any rolling stock; the tracks are not currently used, though they have been cleaned off where they are visible to diners or those strolling along Bridge Street, implying that a freight train might go by any minute.

As they continue north, those using the Delaware and Raritan Canal State Park Trail will find a lot more railroad artifacts, including mile markers, grade crossings, unidentified ruins of former railroad structures, and identifiable passenger stations in downtown Stockton and Frenchtown. Just north of Bull's Island Recreation Area, they may notice the spot where the feeder canal begins.

Delaware and Raritan Canal State Park is the most extensive segment of New Jersey's ninety-two-mile portion of the East Coast Greenway, a system conceived in 1991 to run twenty-six hundred miles from Maine to Florida and provide a traffic-free urban alternative to the Appalachian Trail.

In Burlington County, the Pemberton Rail-Trail extends for three miles, primarily along a right-of-way of the Pennsylvania Railroad Company that was originally part of the Burlington County Railroad linking the town of Pemberton (and later Fort Dix) with Camden. At the restored Pemberton railroad station where the trail begins, the staff will provide a map when the museum is open. Users proceed along a Y-shaped trail that takes them to the former resort town of Birmingham and back along a southern spur to Hanover Street in Pemberton Borough, about half a mile south of the station.

The trail owes its existence to local grassroots activism, mainly by members of the Pemberton Rotary Club, who led in its planning and development. Because it is shaded and furnished with benches, it is very popular with joggers and hikers, including the employees of a local chemical company who often trek through on their lunch hour.

Success in Pemberton led the Wrightstown Area Rotary Club to begin creating a rail trail in Springfield Township, Burlington County, on what is now known as the Kinkora Railroad Corridor. In the 1830s, construction began on a line originating in Kinkora, in Mansfield Township near the Delaware River, but the builders never got any closer to their objective of the Atlantic coast than the town of Columbus, just a few miles from the river. Abandoned in the 1850s, the line saw new life in the 1860s. A railroad map published in 1894–95 identifies it as the Columbus, Kinkora and Springfield Railroad and shows it extending from Kinkora to New Lisbon. The railroad was taken over by the Pennsy and abandoned by the Penn Central in the 1970s.

Wrightstown Rotary Club members are grooming the trail and seeking funding for surfacing, signage, and amenities. There are long-range plans to extend the Kinkora Rail-Trail northwest to the Delaware River and south to link with the Pemberton Rail-Trail in order to develop a countywide trail system.

The Monroe Township Bike Path extends four miles in the area of Williamstown in Gloucester County. Beginning at Church Street and Railroad Avenue in Williamstown, it runs along a former right-of-way of a branch of the Pennsylvania-Reading Seashore Lines, past the locations of former stations in Robanna and Downer.

Camden Greenway is a linear park system under construction that will offer users more views of riverside wildlife and vegetation than railroad heritage. In 1993, Camden Greenways began work on an extensive plan that was incorporated into the city's master plan in 1997. Ultimately the park system will skirt the Delaware River, Cooper River, and Newtown Creek. One of its trailheads will be the Camden waterfront, where the Pennsylvania Railroad's Camden terminal used to be, and it will wind north through Cooper Point, where the Camden and Atlantic Railroad once operated a picnic area. In 1999, the city of Camden opened its first section through woods along the Cooper River. Called the Parkside Trail, it links two schools and two existing parks. Nearby Cooper River Park, located on the north and south shores of Cooper River Lake, is better known for rowing, but it also offers bike paths and other recreational facilities.

The Gloucester Township Bikeway is a two-mile trail between the communities of Blackwood and Grenloch along a railroad right-of-way. It is being expanded to connect with Bellmawr. The borough of Merchantville also has a two-mile bike path.

Skylands Region

Great Railways of the Region

The Central Railroad of New Jersey

In 1831, concerned citizens of Elizabeth secured a charter to incorporate a railroad that would compete with the Morris Canal. It would extend about twenty-five miles, from nearby Elizabethport on Newark Bay halfway across New Jersey to the town of Somerville. Work proceeded slowly on the Elizabethtown & Somerville Railroad, and in 1846, the company's creditors foreclosed their liens and reorganized it with the capital and support of several New York businessmen.

John Taylor Johnston, the railroad's new president, rebuilt the line with heavy iron rails strong enough for coal transportation. The railroad's new owners obtained a second charter in 1847 for the Somerville & Easton Railroad, which would extend their line to and across the Delaware River. The two railroads were consolidated in 1849 as the Central Railroad of New Jersey, popularly known as the Jersey Central, or CNJ.

On July 2, 1852, the railroad's directors took their first locomotive, called the Pennsylvania, decorated it with flags, and hauled eight cars of invited guests plus a hired band through the countryside of Hunterdon and Warren counties. The CNJ opened an important extension to Jersey City and the Hudson River in 1864, which included a bridge almost two miles long across Newark Bay with two draw openings to ensure that navigation could continue undisrupted.

The CNJ's first Jersey City terminal was a depot at the end of a long trestle across a field of mudflats in an old Dutch fishing village called Communipaw. The railroad had purchased the American Dock and Improvement Company in 1860, however, securing its extensive waterfront south of the basin of the Morris Canal. While Americans fought the Civil War, Johnston dealt with the protests of Jersey City residents as he imported New York City's garbage to serve as landfill on which the CNJ could expand its terminal facilities. Between 1887 and 1889, CNJ's architects, Peabody and Stearns of Boston, replaced the Jersey City depot with an elegant Gothic Revival–style structure for the convenience of CNJ passengers as well as those of the Baltimore & Ohio and Reading railroads, who also used CNJ ferries from Communipaw to the foot of Manhattan's Liberty Street.

In his 1881 *History of Sussex and Warren Counties*, James P. Snell writes that from the time the CNJ opened in 1852, the "undeveloped country began to yield up its wealth. Iron-works that had lain in ruins for the

The Elizabethtown & Somerville in Bound Brook, as depicted in *Historical Collections of the State of New Jersey.*

want of fuel since the Revolution were rebuilt, and with the advent of the thundering coal-trains began the ring of tilt-hammers; while the exchange of log cabins for beautiful dwellings, and the founding of churches, schools, etc. marked the succeeding years of the history of this road." While making such an impact on northern and central Jersey, the CNJ Central Division acquired many branches through leases, mergers, and takeovers, including the South Branch Railroad, Perth Amboy and Elizabeth Railroad, Sound Shore Railroad, and New Jersey Terminal Railroad, among many others. The Jersey Central also put names on the map, such as the town called High Bridge, where the CNJ did indeed build a high bridge over a branch of the Raritan River.

From 1856, when the Lackawanna, Lehigh Valley, and Warren railroads all opened, the CNJ made a significant portion of its money hauling coal. By 1859, it was advertising excursions into Pennsylvania's coalfields, including the scenic town of Mauch Chunk. In the late 1860s and early 1870s, CNJ managers were not pleased to learn that both the Lackawanna and Lehigh Valley intended to build or acquire their own routes through New Jersey, meaning that CNJ stood to lose two very important feeders. They reacted by expanding operations in Pennsylvania in 1871, leasing the Lehigh & Susquehanna Railroad from the Lehigh Coal & Navigation Company, whose main business was operating a canal that competed with the Lehigh Valley Railroad. This move enabled the CNJ to haul coal directly from Pennsylvania coalfields to its own tidewater facilities. It also brought the CNJ an engineering feature called the Ashley planes, designed to carry coal from Pennsylvania's Wyoming Valley over Penobscot Mountain. The CNJ kept the planes in use until 1948.

The CNJ had been cooperating with the Reading Railroad in passenger operations between Philadelphia and Jersey City since 1874, and it came under the Reading's direct control a number of times while the Reading tried to monopolize the major anthracite railroads. In 1883, the Reading's president, Franklin B. Gowen, leased all the CNJ railroads, but this arrangement fell apart a short time later when the Reading entered receivership. Gowen's successor, A. A. McLoed, leased the CNJ a second time in 1892, but the agreement that had been intended to last 999 years was terminated by a second Reading bankruptcy in 1893. In 1901, the Reading purchased a controlling stock interest in the CNJ, and the two lines subsequently were operated independently though in close cooperation. During this time period, the CNJ expanded its Pennsylvania trackage and its connections with the Reading, giving Scranton-area residents their most direct option for reaching Philadelphia.

The Baltimore & Ohio Railroad's trains reached New York via Reading lines from Philadelphia to Bound Brook and Jersey Central tracks to the CNJ Jersey City ferry terminal. Passengers taking the B&O Royal Blue Line of sleeping and parlor car trains from Washington, D.C., then boarded CNJ ferries to Manhattan, where the B&O for some years operated a bus to various hotels.

Modern tourists visiting Ellis Island or the Statue of Liberty can buy a ferry ticket in the old Jersey City CNJ passenger terminal and gaze at both destinations while they wait in line for their boat. After the United States opened its immigration processing center on Ellis Island in 1892, the same CNJ terminal became the first American experience for millions of immigrants heading west to other cities once they were formally permitted to enter the country. In 1944, the CNJ capitalized on its terminal's proximity to Lady Liberty by adopting a new emblem featuring her silhouette.

Like many other railroads, the CNJ developed a resort to tempt city dwellers to ride a train on their days off. In the 1890s and early 1900s, residents of New York City and urban northern Jersey could ride the CNJ to High Bridge and thence to Lake Hopatcong for an outing on property that the railroad had developed at Nolan's Point on the lake's eastern shore. The resort had a dance pavilion and woodland paths, as well as hotels for those who could afford to remain overnight.

In 1939, the CNJ entered receivership brought on by the Depression as well as the decline in 'the use of anthracite coal. A decade of bankruptcy ended in 1949, but by the 1950s, the railroad was facing a new kind of competition for freight and passengers from the New Jersey Turnpike and the airport at Newark. The CNJ filed for its final bankruptcy in 1967, ceasing operations in Pennsylvania in 1972. It became part of Conrail in 1976.

Part of the CNJ's old main line continues to serve passengers today as NJ TRANSIT's Raritan Valley Line from Newark to Raritan with limited service to High Bridge, and connections from Newark to Lower Manhattan via PATH, or Penn Station in New York City via NJ TRANSIT's Northeast Corridor Line. A number of vintage CNJ passenger stations remain in use, including those at Cranford and Westfield, dating from the 1930s, as well as Victorian structures in Fanwood, Raritan, and Netherwood, the hometown of president John Taylor Johnston, where the station was constructed in 1894.

In 1967, the state of New Jersey instituted its Aldene Plan, rerouting CNJ trains into Newark's Penn Station and leaving the railroad to abandon its Jersey City Terminal. The site became strewn with debris until local activists agitated for an urban park to serve as a beautiful backdrop for the Statue of Liberty. Jersey City deeded 156 acres of land to the state, and in 1972, New Jersey passed the Green Acres Bond Act, which provided significant funding toward the purchase of the remaining land. On Flag Day 1976, Liberty State Park opened as New Jersey's Bicentennial gift to the nation.

Those interested in the history of the CNJ can contact the Central Railroad of New Jersey Historical Society in Dunellen, New Jersey, or the Anthracite Railroads Historical Society in Lansdale, Pennsylvania (contact information can be found at the back of this book). The New Jersey Transportation Heritage Center planned for Phillipsburg is also expected to reflect the history of this railroad.

Liberty State Park has recently become the scene of the annual Jersey Central Railroad Heritage Festival, an autumn gathering when veterans of this railroad get together to educate and entertain the public. Visitors can examine artifacts, documents, and model layouts on display; take guided tours; and ride miniature trains. Recent supporters of this event included the Tri-State Railway Historical Society, United Railroad Historical Society of New Jersey, Stevens Institute of Technology, Phillipsburg Railroad Historians, West Jersey Chapter of the National Railway Historical Society, and Friends of the New Jersey Transportation Heritage Center.

The Lehigh Valley Railroad

Inspired by the early success of the Reading Railroad, a number of Philadelphia businessmen joined forces to incorporate the Delaware, Lehigh, Schuylkill & Susquehanna Railroad in 1846. They planned to ship coal being mined in the area surrounding the Lehigh Valley to markets in New York and Philadelphia faster and more efficiently than was being done on the canal owned by the Lehigh Coal & Navigation Company, which had long protected its monopoly on through transportation in this region.

By the time construction was under way in 1853, the railroad's name had been changed to the Lehigh Valley Railroad Company, and two New Jersey railroads had managed to get representation on its board. To prevent the Lehigh Valley from extending its tracks to New York City and endangering its monopoly on traffic between Philadelphia and New York, Commodore Robert Field Stockton of the Camden and Amboy Railroad lent $200,000 in exchange for three board seats. CNJ financiers interested in developing the Lehigh Valley as a coal feeder for their own railroad purchased stocks and bonds, and CNJ president John Taylor Johnston took a seat on the Lehigh Valley's board.

By 1855, Asa Packer, president of the Lehigh Valley, had completed the railroad's construction from Mauch Chunk to Easton on the Delaware River, but its success depended on a bridge over which Pennsylvania coal could reach Phillipsburg, New Jersey. The problem was that the CNJ and the Belvidere Delaware Railroad (then controlled by the Camden and Amboy monopoly) had been constructed at two different elevations. Robert H. Sayre, chief engineer for the Lehigh Valley, came up with a double-decker bridge design in which the top level connected the Lehigh Valley with the CNJ, while a curving span allowed Lehigh Valley trains to descend to the tracks of the Bel-Del. Construction persisted—through floods and outbreaks of cholera among the workers—until 1856, when the first coal train crossed the Delaware, to be followed by many more in the course of the Civil War.

The spot where the Lehigh River flowed into the Delaware, where the towns of Easton and Phillipsburg faced each other on scenic bluffs overlooking the water, became a hub of transportation systems. Railroads terminating in this general area included Pennsylvania's Lehigh Valley, Lackawanna, Lehigh & Susquehanna, and North Pennsylvania railroads; and New Jersey's CNJ, Belvidere Delaware, and Morris and Essex railroads. The Lehigh and Morris canals both terminated there too.

Each of these business concerns remained independent and competitive until 1869, when the Lackawanna leased the Morris and Essex. Two years later, the CNJ leased the Lehigh & Susquehanna. This left the Lehigh Valley to compete with two through routes and fewer connection options to get the coal its trains carried to markets in New York.

It also coincided with a time when Asa Packer and his associates planned to expand the Lehigh Valley into upstate New York and Buffalo on Lake

According to *Historical Collections of the State of New Jersey*, this is where the Lehigh River enters the Delaware. Phillipsburg is on the right.

Erie. If they could stretch their railroad from the Great Lakes to the Hudson, the Lehigh Valley would also become an important through route potentially handling many different kinds of freight.

Packer purchased the Perth Amboy & Bound Brook Railroad, which had been chartered in 1858 but never built. He obtained his own New Jersey charter for the Bound Brook & Easton Railroad Company and consolidated both entities as the Easton & Amboy Railway Company in 1872. This would allow Packer to ship coal to docks in Perth Amboy and his railroad's passengers to change trains in Bound Brook and reach Newark or Jersey City via the CNJ. Passengers later would get a second option when the Lehigh Valley built a connection to the Pennsy at Metuchen.

Difficulty in constructing a tunnel through New Jersey's Musconetcong Mountain cost time and money, but the sixty-mile Easton & Amboy opened for business in 1875. By December, hundreds of thousands of tons of coal had been hauled over the line that Jersey residents called "the Packer Road" to the coal and freight piers the Lehigh Valley had constructed on marshland at the mouth of the Raritan.

Back in 1871, before building the Easton & Amboy, the Lehigh Valley had guaranteed itself a backup route to tidewater by leasing the Morris Canal. When the facilities at Perth Amboy proved inadequate to handle all the freight the railroad could carry, the railroad's managers discovered that they owned a very valuable sixty acres of Hudson River waterfront in the canal's Jersey City basin. Just north of the CNJ terminal, the Lehigh Valley constructed its own terminal in the "Big Basin," which remained in use until 1976 but never offered passenger service to Manhattan.

After Asa Packer's death in 1879, his nephew Elisha P. Wilbur leased the Lehigh Valley to the Reading prior to its 1893 bankruptcy. Wilbur relinquished his presidency in 1897, and financier J. P. Morgan gained control, making many needed improvements to the railroad's physical plant and moving the railroad's executive offices to New York.

World War I gave the Lehigh Valley a significant boon when changes made for the war effort routed its passenger trains directly to Pennsylvania Station in New York. In the 1920s, the Lehigh Valley built its massive Claremont Terminal on unoccupied land in the Greenville section of Jersey City. That same decade, the Lehigh Valley cooperated with the Pennsy in constructing a new bridge across Newark Bay, connecting the Claremont Terminal with the Lehigh Valley's Oak Island classification yard. World War II further improved business for the Lehigh Valley, thanks to the military supplies shipped through its tidewater terminal facilities and the troop trains proceeding from Camp Kilmer near South Plainfield, New Jersey.

With the market for anthracite coal shrinking, the Lehigh Valley tried to reinvent itself in the 1950s as an industrial carrier with modernized freight cars, but it could not compete with trucks and interstate highways. In 1962, the Pennsylvania Railroad Company, which had maintained a controlling interest in the Lehigh Valley's stock since 1928, took full control. The Lehigh Valley Railroad still lived on with its own corporate identity as part of the Penn Central system when the Pennsy merged with the New York Central in 1968.

In 1972, the bankrupt CNJ eliminated all its operations in Pennsylvania, and its employees went to work for the Lehigh Valley. The following year, the Lehigh Valley proposed a complete shutdown but was rescued by Congress, which was reviewing America's overall railroad situation. The Lehigh Valley was incorporated into Conrail in 1976.

Today the Lehigh Valley main line through New Jersey is still operated by Conrail and used by Norfolk Southern and CSX. Its history is preserved in the Lehigh Valley Railroad Historical Society in Manchester, New York. The Cornell Railroad Historical Society of Ithaca, New York, a chapter of the National Railway Historical Society, takes particular interest in the history of the Lehigh Valley and the Lackawanna, two railroads that brought many college students to its town.

Rail Stories of the Region

The Morris Canal

While on a fishing trip at Lake Hopatcong in the rugged northern interior of New Jersey, a Morristown resident named George P. McCulloch envisioned a canal that would unite the upper Delaware River with the sea. Farmers could ship their produce through such an artificial waterway, but even more important, coal mined in the area around the Lehigh Valley could make its way directly across the state. Not only was there a huge market for coal in and around New York City, but cheap and readily available coal also might revive Morris County's iron industry, whose forges and furnaces were being abandoned for want of fuel.

In December 1824, New Jersey's legislature chartered the Morris Canal and Banking Company to build a canal between the Delaware and Passaic rivers. It was to be a public thoroughfare for toll-paying customers. McCulloch became a member of its original board empowered to sell its stock.

It took until 1836 for all 102 miles of the Morris Canal to open. Construction began in 1825 but was delayed by a lack of funding and the difficulties in constructing inclined planes to haul canal boats over northern Jersey's mountains. The project also required additional capital after the decision was made that a terminus in the more distant Jersey City on the Hudson, rather than either Paterson or Newark on the Passaic River, would get cargo to New York much faster.

The canal's summit was Lake Hopatcong, which was 914 feet above tide level and 760 feet above the Delaware River, an elevation sufficiently high to require canal boats to negotiate twenty-three inclined planes. Each plane was in itself a tiny railroad from 500 to 1,500 feet long, incorporating water-powered winches to hoist canal boats that had been loaded onto railroad cars up a hill. The chains attached to the cars frequently broke, causing a car to roll back down, its velocity increasing until it hit the water with a cannonball splat that was sometimes forceful enough to send the boat flying out of the canal altogether.

The canal was 32 feet wide and 4 feet deep, a size that would limit its usefulness. Coal being shipped to New York from Pennsylvania had to be transferred from large barges that plied the canal on Pennsylvania's Lehigh River to smaller boats in Easton. Before the Morris Canal's Jersey City extension was opened, cargo had to be transferred again to sloops in Newark because the Morris Canal boats were too small to be towed the rest of the way.

Some improvements came after 1844, when a new group of Essex County businessmen purchased the Morris Canal, which had gone up for sale under foreclosure proceedings following its first bankruptcy. They enlarged the canal and bought new boats with greater capacities. They also remodeled the inclined planes and double tracked some of them, replacing the troublesome chains with more reliable iron wire cable.

Business improved in the 1850s, when the canal's management made deals to serve as a connection with the Lehigh Valley and Lackawanna railroads. It peaked in the 1860s, when the Civil War increased the demand for iron and coal. The Ogden Mine Railroad was built in 1865 as a feeder to the Morris Canal for iron ore from the mines of Jefferson Township.

When the Lehigh Valley Railroad went looking for a route through Jersey that it could call its own, it leased the Morris Canal in 1871. By that time, the canal was facing new financial difficulty as a result of competition from the Morris and Essex Railroad. The Lehigh Valley tried to operate the Morris Canal profitably, but once the state authorized it to build a Jersey railroad, it began seeking permission to abandon the canal. But despite two commissions endorsing abandonment, the canal lived on until the 1920s. A new set of commissioners agreed that the Lehigh Valley Railroad could retain Morris Canal property in Phillipsburg and Jersey City while the state of New Jersey acquired the remainder of its real estate and water rights. The canal was drained and largely dismantled by 1929.

At Waterloo Village, you can walk along what is left of the Morris Canal.

Remains of the Morris Canal at Waterloo Village. The collapsed bridge leads to an old inclined plane awaiting restoration.

The best place to learn about the canal and its railroad associations today is Waterloo Village. Open to the public since 1964, this historic village's restored structures are manned by costumed docents, who interpret life in a Jersey village that started as an ironworks and became a busy port on the Morris Canal, still later the terminus of the Sussex Mine Railroad. The museum of the Canal Society of New Jersey is located in a late-1800s Waterloo Village house where a canal boatman once lived.

Visitors can stroll along a stretch of the canal across a lane from an operating Methodist church and a Victorian home called the Nathan Smith House, both dating from the mid-nineteenth century, as well as a structure identified as the Canal House, but which actually dates from the village's iron-manufacturing era before the Morris Canal existed. A guard lock and inclined plane nearby are both scheduled for restoration.

The tracks of the Sussex Mine Railroad once ran to an ore dock on the canal, roughly between the church and the Nathan Smith House. The tracks were later extended over a bridge across the Musconetcong River to an ore dock and icehouses on the other side, where the railroad added shops and a station. The bridge's abutments and the foundation of the icehouse still exist, but by 2005, the footbridge to the opposite side of the river had collapsed, making them inaccessible.

The Bel-Del

The Belvidere Delaware Railroad, or the Bel-Del, was conceived as a subsidiary of the Camden and Amboy system, a feeder line stretching 64 miles up the east bank of the Delaware from Trenton through Phillipsburg to Belvidere. It would keep freight flowing from the upper Delaware and Lehigh river valleys south to Trenton in the winter when the Delaware and Raritan Canal was closed.

The Belvidere Delaware Railroad Company was incorporated in March 1836, but the depression of 1837 made its stock a hard sell. In the 1840s, this railroad, which existed only on paper, survived attacks by the promoters of the Somerville & Easton Railroad, which would become part of the Jersey Central system, and found new support and backing from the Trenton Iron Works.

Construction got under way in the 1850s after New Jersey's legislature allowed the C&A to buy half the stock for the proposed Bel-Del. The C&A also guaranteed its bonds and lent the railroad its chief engineer, Ashbel Welch. Commodore Robert Field Stockton and Edwin Augustus Stevens took seats on the Bel-Del's board of directors.

Welch designed the riverbank railroad after examining the bark of trees growing on the banks for evidence of how high the waters of the Delaware might rise in late winter and early spring. He came up with a railroad where trains easily managed the grade at fairly high speeds. The Bel-Del was open from Trenton to Lambertville in 1851, to Phillipsburg in 1854, and to Belvidere in 1855. In 1864, the Bel-Del was extended to Manunka Chunk for a junction with the Lackawanna.

Official opening day for the Bel-Del occurred on February 3, 1854, when a train bearing a thousand businessmen and political leaders who had boarded in Philadelphia's Kensington Station and the city of Trenton reached Phillipsburg's downtown Union Square. The parades, banquets, and speeches continued until the following morning.

About ten months later, the Bel-Del's 12-mile spur between Lambertville and Flemington, called the Flemington Railroad and Transportation Company, celebrated a more modest opening day. The Camden and Amboy Railroad had also financed this agricultural line, but the Flemington Railroad maintained its own corporate identity until 1885, when it merged with the Bel-Del and became known as its Flemington Branch.

When the Lehigh Valley Railroad was planning to construct a double-decker bridge across the Delaware between Easton and Phillipsburg, the Bel-Del cooperated. In 1856, a train ran over the span connecting to the bridge's lower level, or Bel-Del level, on its way from Mauch Chunk to Trenton. Thus the Bel-Del became part of a new coal-hauling route through Trenton to Philadelphia.

The Bel-Del earned its keep hauling standard freight and passengers. It had an extraordinary number of stations, and its trains stopped on average just over every 2 miles. When the late-summer peach harvest was especially plentiful in Hunterdon and Mercer counties, the Bel-Del ran special peach trains to haul the fragile fruit to Trenton and thence to Jersey City or Philadelphia. The Bel-Del also cooperated with the Lehigh

Valley and Lackawanna railroads to offer tourists a particularly scenic summer excursion trip to the Delaware Water Gap and Pocono Mountains or to Mauch Chunk, the "Switzerland of America," with its rugged terrain, waterfalls, and exciting switchback passenger railroad.

When the Pennsylvania Railroad Company leased the United Companies in 1871, the Bel-Del became part of the Pennsy system. In the ensuing decades, the Bel-Del's redundant shops, roundhouse, and other facilities in Lambertville were torn down.

The Pennsy carried the Bel-Del into the Penn Central system and then into Conrail. Both railroads abandoned parts of the Bel-Del's roadbed, but Conrail retained others to serve industrial customers from Phillipsburg south to Milford and north to Belvidere.

In the same years that some railroads were dying, new ones were being born. A group of steam railfans that would later incorporate as the Black River & Western Railroad Company leased the Flemington Branch from Ringoes to Flemington in 1964 and began operating steam passenger excursions in 1965. This railroad later purchased more trackage in this area and now serves sixty thousand excursion passengers per year, as well as several large freight customers as a handling line for Norfolk Southern. It is affiliated with the Belvidere & Delaware River Railway serving the Phillipsburg area.

The Warren Railroad

In 1851, the Warren Railroad Company obtained a charter to construct a railroad between New Hampton, on the Central Railroad of New Jersey (CNJ) line, and a point since named Delaware Station, on the Delaware River near where the Lackawanna Railroad was under construction. Some sources indicate that both the CNJ and the Lackawanna purchased stock, but for two years, no real construction was done.

Some mystery remains over exactly who intended to control this railroad: the powers that controlled the CNJ, those at the Lackawanna, or the prominent citizens of Warren County who actually formed the majority of its original board. In any case, businessman John I. Blair took over the Warren Railroad on March 4, 1853, when he and some supporters purchased most of its stock, and Blair assumed the presidency.

The takeover preceded by a few days one of the most famous incidents in New Jersey railroad lore. At that time, the rival Morris and Essex Railroad was trying to secure a right-of-way through the same gaps in the mountains that would be the best route for the Warren. On March 8, 1853, carrying a survey that had been made by Edwin McNeill, chief engineer of the Lackawanna, Blair boarded a train to Trenton, where he intended to file it with New Jersey's secretary of state. Blair must have known that a representative from the Morris and Essex was on the same train for precisely the same purpose. The legend, as recounted in an 1881 history of Sussex and Warren counties compiled by James P. Snell, states that "while the latter [the Morris and Essex representative] was attending to some matters of toilet, preparatory to make his debut before the secretary, Mr. Blair slipped in and transacted his business." For good measure, Blair requested that the time of receipt be recorded on his survey so that there would be no doubt which document had been filed first.

The Morris and Essex obtained a court injunction that delayed construction of the Warren through the route in question until 1855. The Warren was completed the following year. On opening day, guests left New York City via the CNJ and halted at the town of Washington, where celebrations began. The train rolled on through the Poconos and ended up in Scranton, where the travelers feasted at a hotel.

The Warren Railroad was less than 19 miles long, but the engineering features required by the topography it traversed made it an extremely expensive short line. Its trains ran over several embankments, a trestle spanning the Musconetcong Valley, and a stone-arch bridge across the Pequest River. The trains used a temporary route until a 3,000-foot-long tunnel through Van Nest Gap was finally completed in 1862.

The Lackawanna leased the Warren, which became its southern outlet. A massive engineering project called the Lackawanna Cutoff, which ran across New Jersey from Port Morris to the Delaware River, was intended to eliminate some of the Warren's curves and grades and also did away with two of its tunnels.

The Sussex Railroad

The citizens of prosperous Sussex County had been agitating for a local railroad since the early 1830s, but they had to wait until 1851 for the Sussex Mine Railroad to open. The Sussex was chartered in 1848 by Abram S. Hewitt and his partner Edward Cooper, who wanted to transport iron ore from the Andover Mine, which they had purchased, to their Trenton Iron Company. The railroad was conceived as a mule-drawn narrow-gauge line 7 miles long that would connect the mine with the village of Waterloo, a port on the Morris Canal, from which iron ore could be barged to Phillipsburg. It became the model for a number of other small iron railroads constructed in northern New Jersey.

The railroad went into service in 1851, and the next year Hewitt made a deal with the Morris and Essex for a drawback, or refund, on the freight and passenger business that continued to destinations on that line. The

Sussex was able to extend its tracks in the standard gauge to Newton, where the residents turned out on December 11, 1854, as the first passenger train entered town to the roar of cannons. But the railroad was not particularly profitable for Cooper and Hewitt, precipitating negotiations that briefly placed it under the control of local citizens who did not want to lose their transportation link.

John I. Blair purchased the Sussex in 1864 and expanded it to Branchville and Franklin. In 1881, he wrote to inform his general manager that he had sold control of a short portion of the Sussex to the Lehigh and Hudson River Railway Company and the bulk of it to the Lackawanna.

The Lackawanna upgraded and modernized its Sussex Branch, and the railroad's freight gradually evolved from iron ore to milk and anthracite coal. After the Lackawanna merged with the Erie, its new Erie-dominated management downgraded the Sussex Branch with the intention of eliminating it.

The last Sussex Branch train ran in 1969, and the branch was not merged into Conrail with most of the rest of the Erie Lackawanna in 1976. The Sussex Branch was scrapped in 1977, and portions were later sold to New Jersey's Department of Environmental Protection.

The Lehigh and Hudson River Railway

The Lehigh and Hudson River Railway Company (L&HR) operated in northwestern New Jersey and into New York, where it long served as an important bridge line between New England and the large railroads of the Mid-Atlantic states. It got its start in 1860 as the Warwick Valley Railroad Company when the farmers of a village called Warwick in New York State sought a connection to the Erie, whose main line terminus had by then been moved from Piermont, New York, to Jersey City. The railroad opened in 1862, and it used the Erie's locomotives and rolling stock until 1880.

The Warwick Valley Railroad moved agricultural commodities, mainly dairy products, from Orange County in New York and Sussex County in New Jersey to customers in New York City. A farm equipment company in the town of Warwick patented the now familiar milk can design for this purpose, and the Warwick Valley Railroad was the nation's first to run refrigerated milk cars. The Warwick Valley Railroad obtained a new source of freight revenue when iron ore mines were opened in the general area it served following the Civil War.

In 1881, an entrepreneur named Grinnell Burt obtained a charter to build a line called the Lehigh and Hudson River Railroad from Belvidere on the Delaware to Great Meadows in New Jersey. It soon absorbed another railroad called the Pequest and Wallkill Railroad Company, connecting Belvidere and the New York state line. These interests merged with the Warwick Valley Railroad Company, becoming the Lehigh and Hudson River Railway in April 1882. Because construction was already under way, the new railroad celebrated opening day very shortly, on July 11, on the shore of a picturesque pond. President Grinnell Burt drove in the final spike and poured water drawn from the Hudson and Delaware rivers into the lake, which was to be known thereafter as Lake Grinnell.

The connection at Belvidere made the L&HR one of the Pennsylvania Railroad's options for getting freight to New England. When the Pennsy extended trackage rights to the L&HR over the Bel-Del to Phillipsburg in 1889, it put this railroad in position to make deals with the CNJ and the Lehigh Valley Railroad for their New England–bound freight. The railroad constructed its Hudson Yard with offices, a shop, and a turntable along the Delaware outside Phillipsburg.

To become a genuinely effective bridge line to New England, however, the L&HR still needed a bridge across the Hudson River. Its Poughkeepsie Bridge opened in 1888, and the railroad's first coal train bound for New England crossed it in August 1889.

By 1892, eleven railroads joined forces to form the Central States Dispatch, a 600-mile freight route between Maryland and Boston with its own management that used the L&HR and its Poughkeepsie Bridge. The L&HR also attracted a new major partner when the Lackawanna began sending its New England trains over this railroad and its Hudson River bridge in 1905.

The merger that created the Erie Lackawanna in 1960 was not good news for the L&HR, because the new railroad avoided it, preferring the Erie route into New York. The merger of the Pennsy with the New York Central proved to be even worse after the Penn Central began using the New York Central's West Shore line to send freight to New England via two other connecting railroads.

Despite setbacks, the L&HR remained solvent until 1970, when the Penn Central and its other connecting lines were being forced into bankruptcy. The railway entered receivership in 1972, and all hope for successful reorganization ended in 1974, when arsonists allegedly ignited the ties of the deck of the Poughkeepsie Bridge.

The L&HR was officially included in Conrail, which declined to fix the bridge and petitioned to abandon the line, ripping up some of its tracks in 1986. Today the L&HR remains abandoned between Belvidere and Sparta Junction near old Lake Grinnell. The New York, Susquehanna & Western Railroad acquired and rehabilitated a northern section, renewing service in 1985. The company's historic documents were transferred to the Railroad Museum of Pennsylvania.

The New York, Susquehanna & Western Railroad

The New York, Susquehanna & Western Railroad Company, sometimes called the Susie Q, but more generally the Susquehanna or the NYS&W, was incorporated in 1881, fairly late in New Jersey railroad history. Its main precursor, the New Jersey Midland Railway Company, had gone bankrupt in 1880 after years of struggling for passenger and freight business. Investors purchased and extended it with the intention of building west and creating a mine-to-tidewater route. In 1882, the NYS&W consolidated with its recently purchased Blairstown Railway, a short passenger line for residents of the Paulinskill Valley, which service they continued to provide.

The NYS&W began hauling Lackawanna coal cars from a town north of Stroudsburg called Gravel Place to a location in Jersey City, from which Lackawanna locomotives hauled them the rest of the distance to Hoboken. In 1893, the NYS&W extended its Pennsylvania tracks from Stroudsburg to Wilkes-Barre and built a Hudson River waterfront terminal on land it purchased in Edgewater.

The railroad made most of its money hauling coal. Another important source of freight revenue was milk produced by the creameries that were located in nearly every Paulinskill Valley town. As the tourism industry grew in Sussex and Warren counties, the NYS&W took summer vacationers to hotels and boardinghouses as well as to steamboat landings on the Delaware.

The NYS&W could also ship freight to New England via a station in New York called Maybrook, where another railroad continued the journey over the Poughkeepsie Bridge. Another coal carrier, called the Lehigh & New England Railroad, also provided service from Pennsylvania's southern anthracite region to Maybrook, but it coexisted peacefully with the NYS&W for many years, even sharing 19 miles of NYS&W's single track.

The lower rates for hauling coal charged by the NYS&W forced its competitors to lower their rates and angered financier J. P. Morgan, who thought too much competition was not good for the railroad and mining industries. Morgan arranged for the Erie to take over the NYS&W in 1898 through acquisition of a majority of its stock. In 1901, the Erie purchased the Erie & Wyoming Valley Railroad and chose to route most of its coal traffic over that railroad's lower grades. The Erie also assigned the NYS&W its most dated rolling stock. But the railroad survived this persecution, and thanks to a court decision, it became independent of the Erie in 1940.

The Lincoln Tunnel boosted business for the NYS&W when the railroad opened its Susquehanna Transfer. Residents of northern Jersey could board an air-conditioned passenger car to the transfer where they could get on a bus and be in Times Square ten to fifteen minutes later.

The railroad had been reducing its services and abandoning tracks since the 1930s, however. In 1966, the NYS&W discontinued its no longer profitable passenger service. The Pennsylvania and New York Central railroads considered including the NYS&W in Penn Central but then declined, and the railroad went bankrupt in 1976.

In 1980, it saw new life and a new owner in the Delaware Otsego Corporation, which reopened the tracks between Butler and Sparta Junction. Today a new New York, Susquehanna & Western Railway, headquartered in Cooperstown, operates more than 400 miles of track in New York, New Jersey, and Pennsylvania, where it serves many freight customers and makes connections with CSX, Norfolk Southern, and Canadian Pacific railroads. The New York, Susquehanna & Western Technical & Historical Society preserves this railroad's history and operates excursions in New York and, most recently, New Jersey. The New Jersey Midland Railroad Historical Society is dedicated to New Jersey railroad history, particularly that of its namesake, its successor the NYS&W, and connecting and affiliated lines.

Mark Twain Travels

In 1866 and 1867, Samuel Clemens, writing as Mark Twain, published a number of travel sketches in a San Francisco newspaper called the *Alta California*, which were later collected and published as a book titled *Mark Twain's Travels with Mr. Brown*. Critics have speculated that Clemens invented Mr. Brown as an alter ego through whom he could express frontier humor and colorful vulgarities while his persona Twain grew increasingly sophisticated. Clemens describes a trip across New Jersey on the Jersey Central in March 1867:

> I began to feel crampy a little, and then chilly—and presently I noticed that the fire was very low, and remembered that I had seen no one doctor it for over three hours. I got up and tried to open the stove door, but could not do it. A drowsy neighbor said it was locked, to keep the passengers from burning too much coal! I looked again, and found the keyhole—so it was true. The man said this was done "on all them d—d Jersey monopoler [*sic*] roads." I grew chilly fast, then, and gradually grew peevish and fretful, also. I observed that the furniture was mean and old, and that the train moved slowly, and stopped to land a passenger every three hundred yards. After that, every time we stopped I cursed the railroad till we started again, and that afforded me some little satisfaction. I observed, also, that the usual mean man was aboard, who kept his window a little open to distress his fellows. After that I noticed how fearfully dismal and unhappy the passengers looked, doubled up in uncomfortable attitudes on short seats in the dim, funereal light—like so many corpses, they looked, of people who had

died of care and weariness. And then I said I would rather walk than travel that route again, and I wished the Company would burst up so completely that there wouldn't be money enough left to give the Directors Christian burial, but I hoped they might need it shortly.

I shall never be able to express how glad I was when the gray dawn stole over the plain, and the sun followed and cheered the scene, and the train stopped and I gave my limbs a grateful stretch, and steeped my sorrowful soul in inspiring coffee.

The conductor was pompous and discourteous, as natural wood-sawyers in office are apt to be. Your dog with a brass collar with his master's name on it, is ever prone to snub the undecorated dog. Brown plied the fellow with questions at every opportunity, and scorned all rebuffs. He asked him with fine irony, if that train ever ran by a town before they could stop it; and when he was fiercely answered "No," he said he thought such a thing might be possible, but he had not gone so far as to consider it probable. And he wanted to know if this was the country where the "Jersey lightning" of history came from, and if they had any of it aboard that train. When we finally ran over a cow, he felt better satisfied about the speed of the train, because, as he said, he knew we must be going along tolerably lively else we could not have overtaken the cow.

Local Chapter of the National Railway Historical Society

Headquartered in Morristown, the Tri-State Chapter of the National Railway Historical Society has added a number of pieces of railroad equipment to the collections of the Whippany Railway Museum, including a restored Lackawanna caboose and a baggage car. The group has a number of other equipment restorations in progress, including a diesel locomotive and other cabooses. A CNJ Blue Comet observation car was recently transferred to the Cape May Seashore Lines, where it will be used for excursions following its restoration.

The Tri-State Chapter is also accepting donations for the restoration of a railroad station in Sparta. Built as a passenger and freight station by the NYS&W, the structure will be placed on the National Register of Historic Places and eventually house a museum interpreting the town's history and the importance to the town of railroads.

The chapters' members organize rail excursions, including caboose hops; rail-trail hikes; and the holiday season's Santa Train. They host an annual picnic, and their regular meetings include presentations. They publish a quarterly newsletter called the *Block Line* and post news about events and activities on their website at www.tri-state-rail-history.org.

In addition, a group called the New Jersey Live Steamers has been operating its miniature steam railroad in Liberty Corner in New Jersey's

Somerset Hills since 1961. Those interested can join as associate or junior members by submitting an application, found on the group's website at www.njlivesteamers.org/index.html.

The Region's Railroad Giants

John I. Blair (1802–1899)

Although several of John I. Blair's eighteenth-century ancestors were charter faculty members of Princeton University, Blair was born into a modest family in a New Jersey town called Foul Rift. His family moved to a farm on Beaver Brook, and John worked on the farm and went to school until the age of ten or eleven, when his formal education ended. Blair was a born entrepreneur, and the author of his biographical sketch in the *National Cyclopaedia of American Biography* observes, "His wonderful business foresight made a success of every undertaking, and also enriched all who were associated with him." At nineteen, he opened a general merchandise store in a town called Gravel Hill, which was later renamed Blairstown. Less than a decade later, he owned four mills and five general stores in neighboring towns, operated by his brothers and brothers-in-law. He was also Gravel Hill's postmaster and the founder and president of the Belvidere Bank.

John J. Blair
NATIONAL CYCLOPAEDIA OF AMERICAN BIOGRAPHY

George and Selden Scranton of Pennsylvania sought Blair's advice when they purchased the Oxford Iron Furnace in New Jersey's Warren County. The Scrantons' initial attempts at manufacturing iron with anthracite coal were successful, and soon their Oxford facility was turning out railroad car wheels. Blair's guidance helped the Scrantons expand their business into the Scranton Coal and Iron Company.

Blair became a director and one of the oldest stockholders of the Delaware, Lackawanna and Western Railroad, which evolved from two smaller railroads that the Scrantons built. In a move meant to stymie the rival Morris and Essex Railroad, Blair took over the yet-to-be-constructed Warren Railroad in a single day on March 4, 1853, by acquiring a majority of its stock and booting any potential enemies off its board. He then raced to Trenton to file a survey made by the Lackawanna's chief engineer, just beating the Morris and Essex representative, thus securing the best route through Warren County. This route was later ushered into the Lackawanna system.

By 1880, Blair was or had been president or major stockholder of fourteen railroads, including New Jersey's Sussex Railroad. He also assisted in getting the Union Pacific Railroad chartered. When he died in 1899, Blair left a fortune estimated in excess of $60 million.

Ashbel Welch (1809–1882)

Ashbel Welch spent his early years in Madison and Oneida counties in the state of New York, where he was schooled in Utica. He also attended Albany Academy for one year.

He spent several years working on the canal on Pennsylvania's Lehigh River before joining the engineering staff of the Delaware and Raritan Canal Company in 1830. Welch was assigned to the canal's upper division, also known as the Feeder Canal, which ran between Trenton and Bull's Island. This job brought him to Lambertville, New Jersey, where he spent the rest of his life. He served as chief engineer for the canal company for thirty-nine years following his appointment to that position in 1835.

Among Welch's many innovations and accomplishments on the D&R, he constructed a wooden lock on quicksand in Bordentown. In 1852, he managed to enlarge the entire Delaware and Raritan Canal in three months. In 1868, he equipped the locks with steam power, doubling their capacity.

Welch simultaneously worked on the Belvidere Delaware Railroad, surveying its route from the canal to Belvidere in

Ashbel Welch

1836. He later supervised construction of the Bel-Del as well as the Flemington Railroad and served as chief executive for both from 1878 until his death.

In 1862, Welch was appointed vice president of the Camden and Amboy Railroad. In this position, he promoted a plan for telegraphic safety signals, which became the forerunner of railroad block signaling.

When the Delaware and Raritan Canal Company, Camden and Amboy Railroad and Transportation Company, and New Jersey Railroad and Transportation Company became the United Canal and Railroad Companies, Welch became their president. He negotiated the lease of their properties to the Pennsylvania Railroad Company in 1871.

As a consulting engineer, Welch also worked on the steamship *Princeton*, the Chesapeake and Delaware Canal, and floating batteries constructed in Hoboken during the Civil War.

John Taylor Johnston (1820–1893)

John Taylor Johnston grew up in New York City and graduated in 1839 from what is now New York University, then the University of the City of New York. He studied law at Yale and was admitted to the New York bar but gave up the profession to travel abroad for several years.

He became involved with the Elizabethtown & Somerville Railroad, a small New Jersey line, and was elected its president in 1848. In 1849, Johnston combined his railroad with the Somerville & Easton, creating the Central Railroad of New Jersey. He later leased the Lehigh & Susquehanna Railroad between Easton and Wilkes-Barre, providing his rail system with access to Pennsylvania's anthracite coalfields.

Unsatisfied with his railroad's original boat connection from Elizabethport to New York City, Johnston envisioned a terminal directly opposite Lower Manhattan. He secured a right-of-way and the land for CNJ's future yards in Jersey City. In 1860, New Jersey's legislature authorized the railroad's extension to Jersey City by means of a bridge across Newark Bay. Johnston conducted opening ceremonies

John Taylor Johnston
LIBRARY OF CONGRESS

in 1864 on a double-tracked drawbridge that measured almost 10,000 feet in length and cost about $250,000. In his *History of Essex and Hudson Counties*, published in 1884, William H. Shaw comments, "By this route, the distance from Elizabeth to New York is eleven miles; by way of the New Jersey Railroad it is fifteen miles."

Johnston is also remembered as an art collector and a man interested in aesthetics. He brought America the convention of neat uniforms for the men who worked on his trains, and he offered an annual prize to the CNJ stationmaster whose station had the best landscaping. Johnston also saw to it that the CNJ had low grades and few grade crossings. With its frequent and convenient passenger service, his railroad fostered the development of attractive suburbs between Jersey City and Somerville.

Johnston constructed art galleries attached to his home in New York City and opened them to the public in order to share his unrivaled collection of paintings. In 1870, he became the first president of the Metropolitan Museum of Art. Following a financial panic in 1873 and financial reverses for the CNJ, in which he was primarily invested, Johnston lost his personal fortune. He resigned from the CNJ and sold his art collection in 1876 in New York City's first great art sale.

Sampling the Region's Railroad History

The Black River & Western Railroad

The Black River & Western Railroad Company was incorporated in 1961 but actually got its start in the 1950s, when founder William Whitehead began collecting rolling stock and looking for a place to operate a tourist railroad. For a time, he kept the equipment on a branch of the Central Railroad of New Jersey (CNJ) near Chester, where the nearby Black River lent the operation its name.

After the managers of this new railroad moved their equipment to a siding in Flemington, they negotiated with the Pennsylvania Railroad Company to repair and operate a section of track between Flemington and Lambertville. In the spring of 1965, the Black River & Western's first tourist train pulled out of Flemington.

By 1970, the Black River & Western had purchased the Flemington-Lambertville line, assuming its freight service and emerging as a genuine short line. When Conrail was created, the Black River & Western expanded in Lambertville and purchased the track between Flemington and Three Bridges from the CNJ.

Locomotive 752 pulls into the historic station at Ringoes while conductors wait to board the train.

Today the Black River & Western operates between Three Bridges and Lambertville as a handling line carrier for Norfolk Southern, with commercial interchanges with CSX and the Canadian Pacific Railway. It shares a president and general manager with the affiliated Belvidere & Delaware River Railway, which operates in the Phillipsburg area.

The Black River & Western continues to serve about sixty thousand passengers per year on its tourist trains, which run back and forth between Ringoes and Flemington. The railroad extends their excursions to Three Bridges on winter weekends and runs special holiday trains, such as the Santa Express and Easter Bunny Express, as well as the Great Train Robbery.

Volunteers handle the tourist operations with a great deal of enthusiasm. While uniformed engineers and conductors waited for the train to pull up to the Ringoes station for its first trip one summer morning in 2004, a volunteer picked up a screw from the ground and offered it to a colleague who works on Black River & Western equipment during the week, joking, "Hey, when you guys put these things back together, make sure you use all the parts!"

The locomotive that day was #752, a GP9 officially called the Harold T. Filskov, but known to the crew as Harry. One of the passenger cars had been built circa 1923 for the CNJ and had an interior decorated with mahogany inlay. Another car was furnished with armchairs and a bar and

The station at Ringoes is said to have been constructed in 1854.

Additional Black River & Western Railroad equipment at Ringoes.

could be chartered for BYO parties. According to a conductor, it is popular for birthdays and had once been the scene of a railfan wedding.

The train ran through New Jersey farm country, passing a golf course and some marshy meadows, where grazing deer fled the sound of its diesel horn. It passed a home with a mailbox shaped like a locomotive and an operating garden-scale railroad visible to passengers. It crossed the Copper Hill Trestle, which is about 50 feet high. Legend has it that the original wooden trestle in this location survived a flood, only to collapse under the weight of the next locomotive that crossed it. The locomotive was recovered, but its bell was never found and is thought to remain somewhere in the bed of the shallow stream beneath the trestle.

The ride terminates in the parking lot of a large retail outlet complex in Flemington, where passengers can shop and return on a later run or watch the locomotive being switched for the return trip. Those who begin their round-trip in Flemington can spend the corresponding time in Ringoes exploring the equipment in the rail yard or touring the station, which the railroad claims was constructed in 1854. This would make it older than the railroad station in Berlin, purportedly New Jersey's oldest, but its history has not been documented yet for a place on the National Register of Historic Places.

The Black River Railroad Historic Trust cooperates with the Black River & Western Railroad to restore and preserve railroad equipment, documents, and objects. Membership is open to people of all ages.

Railfan Sites in Phillipsburg

Once Phillipsburg was New Jersey's western gateway and a key transportation hub. Besides its five railroads, turnpikes and trolley lines converged there, and canal boats and ferries crossed the river to Easton, Pennsylvania.

Today about twenty-five freight trains come through Phillipsburg daily on Norfolk Southern's Lehigh Line. The short-line Belvidere & Delaware River Railway also operates out of Phillipsburg. Cars cross the Delaware on either the Route 22 toll bridge or what the locals call the "free bridge," a national historic civil engineering landmark.

Across the river in Easton, every weekend brings so many visitors to the Crayola Factory Discovery Center and the mule-drawn canal boat rides at Hugh Moore Park that parking can be a real problem, but Phillipsburg's downtown square remains relatively quiet. Some nineteenth-century buildings are being renovated and new upscale restaurants have opened, including the Wardell Steakhouse and Raw Bar, which offers "train car dining experience like nowhere else"–the option of eating your steak at a table in a renovated passenger railcar. This eatery is constructed on the site

Two railroad bridges still span the Delaware between Phillipsburg and Easton. The piers of an older bridge are visible on the eastern shore.

where three Pennsy cars once derailed, crashing into and burning the old Wardell Hotel in 1967.

In the spring of 2004, Phillipsburg was decorated with banners reading, "The Past Is Our Future," and a large sign spanning one of its main streets pointed the direction to "Train Rides." Passenger rail service had returned to Phillipsburg, thanks to the efforts of the Belvidere & Delaware River Railway; the New York, Susquehanna & Western Technical & Historical Society; the New Jersey Department of Transportation; and various local agencies.

The first of Phillipsburg's twenty-first-century rail passengers rode a 1930 self-propelled Brill Model 55 railcar, popularly called a doodlebug, named the Delaware Turtle. It had been renovated and operated on a scenic railroad in Florida after spending some time in a railroad museum following a career of service in New England.

The real excitement came to Phillipsburg when the New York, Susquehanna & Western Technical & Historical Society brought in locomotive #142. This hand-fired coal-burning steam locomotive was built in China in 1989 from an American design engineered in 1918. American tourist railroads were among the final customers for the Tang Shan Locomotives

Phillipsburg has one attraction that Easton lacks: a terrific view of the Lehigh flowing into the Delaware.

In the summer of 2004, the New York, Susquehanna & Western Technical & Historical Society brought #142 to operate out of Phillipsburg. The steam locomotive was built in China, based on an early-twentieth-century American design.

& Machine Works, and #142 was one of the last steam locomotives to be built in the world.

On a humid day in July 2004, #142 arrived at a small reconstructed station, pushing several restored passenger cars built in the 1950s for the Long Island Railroad. Since the train rides had commenced very recently, the eager passengers were holding tickets that had actually been printed for the Black River & Western Railroad's Ringoes to Flemington run. The train filled quickly with railfans whose vehicles had already overflowed the parking lot on the hill above the Bel-Del tracks.

The train passed some remains of the Morris Canal and went under the old railroad bridges across the Delaware. At first there wasn't much scenery because of foliage on both sides of the tracks, so dense and so close that the conductors warned passengers to keep their hands and their children's heads inside the open windows.

The scenery improved as the train approached the Route 78 bridge across the Delaware River, where passengers could see the Delaware and admire how the Bel-Del tracks had been constructed along its banks. The train proceeded to a burg called Carpentersville, containing little more than a few tract houses overlooking the river, before making the return trip to Phillipsburg.

Phillipsburg has another train ride, though it operates less frequently than the Bel-Del. A group incorporated as the Phillipsburg Railroad His-

Phillipsburg's ticket office.

torians, which operates a small museum behind a funeral parlor, acquired a miniature 2-inch-scale railroad called the Centerville & Southwestern in 1993. This little railroad was originally constructed by the Becker family on their dairy farm in Roseland in 1938. They named it after the southwesterly direction in which it ran toward the town of Roseland, which had originally been called Centerville. Its builders opened it to the public in 1948 and operated the railroad for many years on summer Saturdays. Its miniature trains ran on its main line over tiny trestles and past signals and stations, keeping to a strict schedule and making it perhaps the only miniature railroad in America to do so.

The Becker farm was sold in 1972, and the railroad's steam engine was donated to the Henry Ford Museum. When the remainder of the railroad failed to attract a buyer, its diesel locomotives and other cars were stored in a warehouse belonging to the Monmouth County Park Commission, where they remained for about two decades.

The Phillipsburg Railroad Historians refurbished and installed part of the Centerville & Southwestern and began running trains again in 1997. The historians operate the railroad and offer rides several times a year; check the organization's website for a schedule. They also maintain one of two small railroad museums currently operating in Phillipsburg.

The town will place a great deal more railroad heritage on view if the Friends of the New Jersey Transportation Heritage Center are successful in

Formerly Phillipsburg's Union Station, now the Welcome Center for the prospective New Jersey Transportation Heritage Center.

Among other exhibits at the Welcome Center is a model of what Phillipsburg could look like once the New Jersey Transportation Heritage Center is constructed.

their mission. This organization was formed in 1989 after various railroad technical and historical societies joined forces to explore the idea of a major transportation museum in New Jersey. In the early 1990s, a museum commission studied several possible sites for such a museum, narrowing the field down to Plainfield, Netcong–Port Morris, and Phillipsburg. The commission selected Phillipsburg for a master plan study, which was completed on schedule in 2000.

The master plan called for not only a roundhouse with an operable turntable, railroad equipment exhibits, and train excursions, but also exhibits and attractions celebrating all kinds of surface transportation, including ferries, trolleys, trucks, buses, and horse-drawn carriages. The planned Transportation Heritage Center would also house the archival collections of several transportation organizations, making them available for research and education.

It was estimated that this museum on the east bank of the Delaware, coupled with the attractions in Easton and the National Museum of Industrial History proposed for Bethlehem, would eventually draw up to 150,000 visitors each year. But such a facility would cost a lot of money, and though New Jersey's state senate passed legislation allowing Phillipsburg to establish a fund-raising foundation, similar legislation stalled in the state's Assembly Appropriations Committee in 2002.

In 2003, the Friends of the New Jersey Transportation Heritage Center opened a small museum and information center in the town's Union Station, where visitors can inspect a model of what Phillipsburg could look like if the Transportation Heritage Center ever materializes. Visitors can also examine this historic building, which was shared by the Lackawanna and the Jersey Central after the Lackawanna built it in 1914. The group continues to support the project and now numbers over five hundred members.

The Whippany Railway Museum

On a Saturday early in December 2004, the parking lot of an adjacent church was overflowing as parents abandoned their vehicles and hurried their children to the Whippany Railway Museum for the next departure of the Santa Claus Special. The little stone train station tucked behind a highway jug handle was nearly obscured by crowds purchasing hot pretzels and other snacks. Some who failed to order tickets in advance were disappointed to see a sign in the ticket office stating that most trains were already sold out. A diesel horn announced the train's return, and the crowd briefly doubled as those getting off the Santa Claus Special joined the folks waiting to board.

A regular ticket purchased a seat on a regular NJ TRANSIT commuter car. A couple more dollars admitted a passenger to the Morristown &

Visitors wait to board the Santa Claus Special at the Whippany Railway Museum.

This is not the Santa Claus Special at the Whippany Railway Museum, but a 1940s steam locomotive dressed up for the holiday season.

Erie Railroad's parlor car. The train pulled out for its 10-mile trip with Santa and his elves safely on board and prepared to start handing out holiday treats. Left behind at the station was the museum's steam locomotive #4039, built in the 1940s and decorated for the holiday with a giant grinning bearded Santa face. It posed patiently for photographs with all comers.

The Whippany Railway Museum runs other equally popular excursion trains to celebrate Easter and Halloween. Located inside a restored freight house, their museum is open on Sunday afternoons from April through October. Its collection includes a wealth of railroad and ocean liner artifacts, as well as the Whippanong Valley Railroad, one of the largest O-gauge model train layouts in New Jersey. Out in the rail yard, visitors can examine a water tank formerly used by the Morristown & Erie Railroad and other restored railroad equipment and rolling stock.

Founder Earle Richard Henriquez-Gil grew up in Morristown, the son of a man who worked for the company that made Erector Sets and American Flyer model trains. Fascinated with steam-powered railroad operations, in the early 1960s Gil contemplated running steam-powered excursion trains in northern New Jersey. He purchased a Baldwin steam engine and restored it, obtaining permission to run it on the Morristown & Erie line between Whippany and Morristown. He added four passenger cars from the New Jersey Central and a Pennsy caboose, incorporating his railroad as the Morris County Central. Gil's tourist railroad began running in 1965.

Some of Gil's employees and volunteers mounted a railroad artifact exhibition in part of the Morristown & Erie freight house, which they named the Morris County Central Railroad Museum. In 1967, the freight house was moved to the other side of the tracks, opposite the passenger station, where it remained open to excursion railroad passengers until 1973.

That year, Gil decided to move his railroad to some tracks no longer used by the New York, Susquehanna & Western near Newfoundland, New Jersey. The railroad reopened the next year, and the museum moved into an old railroad refrigerator car at the new site, where it became known as the Pequannock Valley Transportation Museum.

The Morris County Central shut down in 1980, and the museum moved back to Whippany, where the Morristown & Erie Railroad permitted its supporters to refurbish their original building, which by then had been earmarked for demolition. Renamed the Whippany Railway Museum, the operation reopened in 1985. It has since attracted the donation of the rolling stock displayed at the site. The museum cooperates with the Morristown & Erie Railway, now a short-line freight railroad serving customers in Morris and Essex counties.

Northlandz in Flemington

About a mile north of Flemington's outlet centers and the big-box retailers flanking Route 202, just where the scenery again becomes rural, there's a large gray building that purportedly houses the "world's largest miniature railway." Its founder, Bruce Zaccagnino, who is also known as a computer game developer and publisher, spent a lifetime building this model train layout, which he named the Great American Railway. The larger site where it is located is known as Northlandz.

Like many model train layouts, the Great American Railway was originally housed in its builder's basement. When he ran out of room, Zaccagnino expanded the basement. Like many layout builders, Zaccagnino and his wife occasionally opened their masterpiece to the public. It grew to be so popular that they bought land and constructed a warehouse. Starting in the mid-1990s, Northlandz opened to the public all year long.

According to its website, the Great American Railway incorporates 8 miles of track and sufficient lumber to construct "42 large houses." It includes HO-gauge, O-gauge, and G-gauge equipment. The website also states that visitors may walk a mile-long one-way path, going up and down ramps and winding their way through what appear to be two huge canyons that they view from many different angles. Strategically posi-

The steeply vertical surreal world of the Great American Railway at Northlandz.

tioned mirrors make the layout seem more vast and far deeper than it actually is.

Most large model train layouts sprawl horizontally, but the Great American Railway instead sprawls vertically, making visitors wish they had brought along binoculars, not to see what lies in the middle of the layout, but to view what teeters on distant mountain ledges. Call it X-treme model railroading. Or the Salvador Dali layout.

Like most other layouts, the Great American Railway includes some visual jokes, many playing on the layout's verticality, and others involving one of its tiny residents whom visitors never actually see, identified on labels as Grandma. Grandma refused to sell her homestead to the developers of a quarry, and after they quarried all around her place, Grandma's house ended up on a steep island reached only by a bridge. When the project destroyed Grandma's indoor plumbing, she constructed an outhouse on a ledge over the quarry, where she daily takes her revenge. The Great American Railway also includes the world's tallest outhouse and an outhouse-manufacturing operation.

The layout's vertical nature tends to isolate some of its communities, such as a monastery near the top of the canyon, connected to a tiny railroad station and the rest of the layout only by the flimsy kind of pedestrian suspension bridge one sees in Tarzan movies. A community called

Northlandz Village is built into the side of a cliff, and its residents' houses are connected to one another by a precipitous winding drive. On yet another mountainside, tiny players are putting steeply uphill or down on a very demanding miniature golf course.

Although the website promises "100+" trains, they appear to be almost an afterthought, or perhaps an excuse for constructing this surreal landscape, which indeed suggests the fantastical scenery of some computer games. The Great American Railway makes an interesting contrast with what's on view at the Union Model Railway Club in Union, New Jersey, or the impressive layout in Shartlesville, Pennsylvania, called Roadside America.

The structure housing the Great American Railway also contains a pipe organ and concert hall, which visitors enter several times on their way along the path through the model layout. Signs indicate the time of the next concert.

Outside, visitors can ride the Raritan River Railroad, with a miniature diesel locomotive gaily painted in bright colors to look like the kind of steam engine a toddler would prefer under the Christmas tree. The ride proceeds through a wooded area, over a curving trestle, and through a "tunnel," actually the building where the train is housed at night.

The Raritan River Railroad at Northlandz.

Clinton Station Diner

Among the eateries beckoning drivers to pull off I-78 and take a break, the Clinton Station Diner is a standout. The striking sand-colored building is located practically on top of the highway. Off to one side of the restaurant, as if it were pulling into a railroad station, stands a genuine Blue Comet observation lounge car.

Locals say that the Blue Comet car was there for many years, surviving a succession of owners who operated different sorts of roadhouses at the site. Most recently, the restaurant and railroad car survived years of abandonment before getting an extreme makeover from the current owner.

Today the main part of the restaurant is not actually a diner, but it has all the classic elements a traveler might expect to find at one, including a counter to sit at and a refrigerated bakery display case stuffed with cakes, pies, and oversize muffins and cookies. The dining area

The Clinton Station Diner.

looks more like a gentleman's library, with its wood paneling and stone fireplace. The day we visited, the restaurant was festooned with little flags imprinted with its logo, featuring a steam engine, along with advertisements for an upcoming event in which contestants would compete at consuming the world's largest burger.

The food was great, the portions were enormous, and the coffee was deliciously fresh and hot. No one minded when we toured the Blue Comet car, not even when we started taking pictures. The car had been painted inside and out, and its interior woodwork had been polished. Patrons accommodated at small tables and chairs were observing passing traffic through the car's large windows.

Lorett Treese Travels

With good weather predicted for Memorial Day weekend 2005, my husband and I decided to leave the Jersey shore to our fellow Pennsylvanians and spend some time on the shores of New Jersey's Lake Hopatcong. On

The Delaware Water Gap. The Lackawanna's former railbed is on the opposite (Pennsylvania) shore.

the way to our hotel, we left I-80 in order to search for artifacts of the famous Lackawanna Cutoff and other operations of this railroad in New Jersey's Skylands region.

The brainchild of Lackawanna president William H. Truesdale, the Lackawanna Cutoff connected the railroad's highest point in New Jersey with its main line in Pennsylvania, replacing a whole lot of curves with what was pretty much a straight line. Hills, valleys, rivers, and other geographic obstacles were summarily overcome with marvels of human engineering.

We abandoned I-80 at the first exit in New Jersey to see what we could learn at the Kittatinny Point Visitor Center, operated by the National Park Service in the Delaware Water Gap. It was closed, its parking area rendered inaccessible by yellow crime scene tape, but we found another place where we could park the car, admire the view, and spot the tracks once used by the Lackawanna on the Pennsylvania side of the river.

Back on I-80, we had our first cutoff sighting when we passed under the Lackawanna's Delaware River Viaduct. One does not stop on I-80 for anything trivial, so there was no time to compose a good photograph, and I was left with only a fleeting impression of graceful arches within arches in our rearview mirror.

I had directions to the Paulinskill Viaduct from the town of Columbia, but we drove through the tiny town of Hainesburg several times before we found the backroad that would take us to its piers. This unmarked road crossed a one-lane trestle bridge over the Paulinskill River. Lots of cars were parked on the river's opposite side, and the river, which is stocked with trout at that time of year, was filled with fishermen.

We couldn't see the Paulinskill Viaduct until we had actually passed underneath it. Then we spotted a dirt path leading down to the water, where several more cars were parked. We left our car and headed down the trail, not without some trepidation. I knew that the viaduct was said to be haunted. There are stories of murders and suicides at this isolated spot,

The Paulinskill Viaduct—deserted, said to be haunted, and currently waiting for new trains.

not to mention all the workers who are said to have perished during its construction, including one who supposedly sank into wet concrete and whose remains still constitute part of a pillar. Rumor has it that his ghost can be seen at night haunting this spot. This reputation attracts some very strange characters who come to practice satanic rituals or other nonsense, and we preferred not to run into them. As if to confirm the rumors, as we drew near the river, we found a sofa placed in the viaduct's shade.

We discovered the owners of the parked vehicles innocently fishing, however. After a brief acknowledging nod, they ignored us while I flitted about seeking a good angle from which to photograph the viaduct. Note to fellow photographers and railfans: Visit in early spring or late autumn, when the trees have fewer leaves to obstruct the view.

The Paulinskill Viaduct was much higher than the Delaware River Viaduct, or at least it seemed so from where we were standing. Its massive piers stretched impossibly high to arches that had been disfigured with graffiti, confirming that there are ways to climb around inside the arches. We decided not to go looking for them. A plaque attached to one of the viaduct's piers memorialized a fisherman at what must have been his favorite spot. Beneath it, a graffiti artist had painted a large fish with a caption in ghostly lettering that read, "He sleeps with the fishes."

We continued along Route 94 to Blairstown, the town named for John I. Blair, a Lackawanna director. This charming town climbs a steep hill, where its nicest Victorian houses are still located. One of its most striking historic structures is the old Waterworks, bearing a stone marker with a tribute to Blair.

The waitress who served our lunch directed us to Blairstown's Foot Bridge Park, which that afternoon was being groomed for Memorial Day activities. The footbridge for which it is named crosses the Paulinskill to a park with a picnic shelter and some military memorials. This general area once held the yard and sta-

John I. Blair's Blairstown, where a marker on the waterworks building acknowledges his local fame.

This looks like merely a tunnel through a hill, but it is part of the Pequest Fill, built by the Lackawanna to carry trains over preexisting roads.

tion for the Blairstown Railroad, built by John I. Blair, which connected Blairstown with Columbia. We found no memorials to the railroad or any traces of it, except possibly some overgrown concrete foundations near the parking area.

Farther east, we left Route 94 in the village of Yellow Frame and began driving through some very pretty Jersey countryside where horses were grazing in the fields. In the village of Greendell, protected by a chain-link fence, we found a Lackawanna railroad station constructed of concrete, but missing its doors and windows, and also defaced by graffiti. Behind it and mostly obscured by foliage, the roof of an old interlocking tower was just barely visible.

We had planned a route to Andover that would introduce us to the Pequest Fill, a man-made 3-mile ridge that the railroad constructed through a valley south and west of the town. The Pequest Fill is 110 feet high at some points and purportedly still holds the record of being the world's largest railroad fill.

We first spotted the Pequest Fill on rural Route 603, where the trees growing on it made it look like nothing more than a hill pierced by a concrete tunnel for cars to drive through. We found a similar tunnel through the fill on Route 517, where there was also a marker explaining the historic importance of the Lackawanna Cutoff. A longer tunnel ran through the fill on Route 206. It takes several encounters with the Pequest Fill to appreciate just how big it is and how remarkable that all these roads through its tunnels were here before it was constructed so that trains could run over them.

We stopped on Cranberry Lake's South Shore Road and located the parking area for the Sussex Branch Rail Trail, a pleasant shaded lane. We drove around the lake looking for some trace of the Lackawanna's Cranberry Lake Resort, a resort destination for many passengers before World

A deserted station along the old Lackawanna Cutoff.

War I, but found instead a lot of waterfront vacation homes. One resident out walking his dog explained that the resort hotel had been on the lake's northern shore. "But there's nothing left now," he told us. "Not a thing. You want to see what it looked like, maybe go on the Internet and look for some old postcards."

The New Jersey Department of Transportation purchased the Lackawanna Cutoff in 2001, and for years there have been reports of joint efforts with a Pennsylvania short-line railroad called the Lackawanna County Railroad Authority to reestablish train service from Scranton over the cutoff to Hoboken, from which commuters would have several options for reaching Manhattan. The benefits would be many, including less congestion on I-80 and development opportunities in and around Scranton, but the project has been slow to start. According to the Greater Scranton Chamber of Commerce, it is unlikely that trains will run before 2007 or 2008. In the meantime, railfans will just have to wait to take pictures of trains crossing the striking concrete viaducts or enjoy what will surely be one sweet ride across the sky.

The Region's Rail Trails

At more than 27 miles in length, the Paulinskill Valley Trail in Sussex and Warren counties is one of New Jersey's longest rail trails. It traverses farmland and wooded areas roughly parallel to the Paulinskill River as it follows the route of the New York, Susquehanna & Western Railroad (NYS&W) and its predecessors, the Midland and Blairstown railways.

After the NYS&W abandoned it in 1962 and removed its rails and ties, the city of Newark purchased the right-of-way with the idea of creating a water conduit, but this was never completed. The New Jersey Department of Environmental Protection proposed a rail trail in 1985. Considerable controversy ensued, with antitrail locals forming a group called the Railroad Right of Way Repurchase Association, and those who liked the trail idea organizing the Paulinskill Valley Trail Committee. Polls conducted by a local publication showed that the vast majority of people favored the trail, and several New Jersey freeholders signed a resolution supporting the state's purchase of the land. New Jersey Green Acres bought the right-of-way, and it became a state park in 1992.

Trail users will discover the remains of several former railroad stations, as well as the icehouses and creameries that were important customers for the railroads whose trains once traveled this route. The trail crosses the Paulinskill River several times, with bridges where fishing is allowed. In Blairstown, the trail passes through Foot Bridge Park near the site of the yard for the Blairstown Railway.

Railfans hiking the trail will want to tour the nearby Paulinskill Viaduct, a magnificent artifact of the Lackawanna Cutoff constructed in 1909. This reinforced concrete bridge is more than 1,100 feet long, supporting a deck 115 feet over the Paulinskill River. For a brief time following its construction, it was the largest such structure in the world.

The Paulinskill Valley Rail Trail intersects with the Sussex Branch Rail Trail, another one of New Jersey's longer rail trails, at a place called Warbasse Junction, just south of the town of Lafayette. The Sussex Branch Rail Trail stretches 21 miles through Sussex County from Byram to Main Street in Branchville.

The earliest portion of this right-of-way first saw rail traffic in 1851, when it was built by the Sussex Mine Railroad to link the iron ore mines around Andover with a port on the Morris Canal called Waterloo. John I. Blair acquired the railroad in 1864 and extended it. The Lackawanna renamed it the Sussex Branch when this railroad took over in 1881.

When the Erie and Lackawanna merged, new management policies caused traffic to decline. Some of the Sussex Branch tracks were removed in 1966, and the remainder was scrapped in 1977. New Jersey's Department of Environmental Protection purchased the right-of-way in two transactions completed in 1979 and 1982.

Very near the official end of the trail, hikers can find the restored village of Waterloo, which is open to the public in spring, summer, and fall.

The Columbia Trail passes through the town of High Bridge.

Outside of Andover, hikers use a concrete tunnel to pass under the Pequest Fill, an embankment constructed by the Lackawanna as part of their massive cutoff engineering project.

The Columbia Trail is another long trail in the Skylands region of New Jersey, running for 16 miles through Hunterdon and Morris counties between the towns of High Bridge and Flanders. For part of its length, the trail curves above the south branch of the Raritan River. It is constructed on the right-of-way of the High Bridge Branch of the Jersey Central (CNJ), a line that connected other northern New Jersey iron ore mines with the town of High Bridge, named after its railroad trestle over the Raritan (later replaced by an embankment). This line also carried a great deal of ice cut from the frozen surface of Lake Hopatcong and stored in icehouses along the route.

Genuine commuter trains still arrive at the High Bridge station on the NJ TRANSIT Raritan Valley Line. The Columbia Trail starts farther up Main Street, however, across from the parking lot for what is now a public recreation area. Park near the entrance and your front bumper may nearly touch some overgrown tracks connecting this former rail yard with the NJ TRANSIT main line.

As hikers leave the town of High Bridge, the asphalt paving of the Columbia Trail turns to crushed stone and fenced backyards yield to wooded surroundings. A few miles away, hikers emerge in Califon, which has a historic district on the National Register of Historic Places.

The trail runs directly past the old Califon passenger rail station, a stone edifice that now houses the Califon Historical Society. Its historical function is memorialized by a weathervane shaped like the profile of a train and a small portion of reconstructed track near the door. Hearsay has it that the residents of prosperous Califon disdained the standard-issue frame station provided by the CNJ and provided at their own expense the stone to build a much nicer station. The station houses a gift shop and some local memorabilia that can be examined on the two Sundays a month that it is open.

Hikers through Califon will also pass a building that was once a creamery, now occupied by the town's fire department. A freight door on its upper level faces the trail and once would have been used to load freight cars on the tracks below.

Although it is not a continuous railroad right-of-way, the Patriot's Path will provide 50 miles of recreational trail in Morris, Sussex, and Hunterdon counties when all its pieces are finally connected. The Patriot's Path connects parks and historic sites along the Whippany, Black, and Raritan rivers. The few miles of trail that once were traveled by trains were part of a short line called the Rockaway Valley Railroad, which ceased to operate before World War I. It ran between White House and Watnong near Morristown.

Most history-seeking visitors to Morristown head for the Ford Mansion on Morris Avenue, where a widow named Mrs. Jacob Ford Jr. offered her home to General and Mrs. George Washington in 1779 when the Continental Army encamped in Morristown. Those who walk around the mansion to the sidewalk in front of it, perhaps to take a photograph, are standing on a portion of the Patriot's Path. From here, they can proceed down the avenue to a supposedly haunted Italianate mansion called Acorn Hall, headquarters of the local historical society.

The stone passenger station at Califon.

Those who would rather spot trains can walk on to the railroad station and watch the commuter traffic on the NJ TRANSIT Morristown Line. An upscale steak house called Sebastian's has window seating facing the tracks that seems tailor-made for railfans.

In the 1880s, a daily train called the Morristown Bankers' Express ran between Hoboken and Morristown. It provided rapid transportation to New York City for residents of Morristown and Madison who held the sort of executive positions that enabled them to leave work and make it by ferry to Hoboken in time to board this express train, which left at 4:15 P.M., hence its association with bankers' hours. Ridership on this train, as well as the population in the suburban area it served, grew after the Hudson and Manhattan Railroad tubes opened in the early twentieth century, making it no longer necessary for commuters to New York City to brave the weather on a Hudson River ferry.

The Morristown railroad station is really a detour from the Patriot's Path, however. Those interested in serious hiking should obtain a map of this still-developing network of trails from the Morris County Park Commission and learn to recognize its markers.

In Morris County's Chester Township, there are two other rail trails with iron-mining heritage. The Black River County Park Trail was once part of the CNJ system. The Black River WMA (Wildlife Management Area) Trail was once the Chester Branch of the Lackawanna system.

The Traction Line Recreational Trail runs from Morristown to Madison, originating across the street from the Ford Mansion. It is about 3 miles long and used to be a right-of-way for the trolleys run by the Morris County Traction Company, which fell prey to competition from automobiles during the 1920s. The trail runs parallel to the NJ TRANSIT line, separating hikers from trains with a fence.

Several New Jersey state and local government agencies and private organizations have joined forces to promote the Morris Canal Greenway Project to convert remains of the canal into recreational paths. They are currently concentrating on a path between Ledgewood and Saxton Falls, where sections of the canal remain intact. The remains of two inclined planes and a canal basin can be found at Canal Park in Ledgewood. Lake Hopatcong Historical Museum is located in a lock tender's house at Hopatcong State Park, where Lake Hopatcong once supplied most of the canal's water. Restored Waterloo Village contains half a mile of well-restored canal and the sort of buildings that a working canal port would have had.

The Mahlon Dickerson Reservation has about 8 miles of trails, including the 2 miles forming the Ogden Mine Railroad Path. Abandoned in

1935, it once connected mines north of Lake Hopatcong to the lakeshore, where iron ore could be transferred to canal barges. Another segment of the same railroad is preserved as the Berkshire Valley Management Area Trail in Roxbury Township.

A trail winding along Capoolong Creek in Hunterdon County's Capoolong Creek Wildlife Management Area was once the Pittstown Railroad and now connects Pittstown with active rails in Landsdown. Nearby, the Landsdown Trail runs to Clinton and was once a spur of the Lehigh Valley Railroad.

In Warren County, the Pequest Wildlife Management Area Trail between Buttzville and Townsbury was part of the Lehigh and Hudson River Railroad, which became a bridge line over which much anthracite coal reached New England. In Pahaquarry, also located in Warren County, the Karamac Trail runs from the I-80 bridge to some old railroad bridge abutments and offers hikers pleasant views of the Delaware.

The Hamburg Mountain Wildlife Management Area in Sussex County includes about 3 miles of trail constructed as a branch of the NYS&W to support zinc mines in Ogdensburg and Franklin. The modern NYS&W operates in this area, and the trail runs parallel to the railroad's active line for most of its length. In Ogdensburg, interested visitors can take a two-hour tour at the Sterling Hill Mining Museum, which includes a visit to this zinc mine and much interesting information on the relationship between the mining and railroad industries in this area.

Other recreational trails in the Skylands region of New Jersey include the Oxford Bikeway, the Loantaka Trail, the Bedminster Hike & Bikeway, and the Wood Duck Nature Trail.

Gateway Region

Great Railways of the Region

The Pennsy in Northern Jersey

The New Jersey Railroad and Transportation Company, fated to become part of the Pennsy system, was chartered by the state legislature in 1832. It would be New Jersey's third railroad, and another project that the controlling interests at the Camden and Amboy did not regard as a threat. That was because this railroad would run from a ferry in Jersey City through Newark, Elizabeth, and Rahway to New Brunswick, where it would connect with a branch proposed for the Camden and Amboy, bringing all its traffic to the monopoly. Its charter also empowered the new railroad to construct branches to other ferries opposite New York City, particularly the one operated by the Stevens family in Hoboken.

Its builders faced some daunting geographic challenges. They had to keep the roadbed from sinking into the tidal marshes called the Hackensack Meadows and cut through 40 feet of solid rock known as Bergen Hill, an extension of a row of cliffs in northeastern New Jersey called the Palisades. The New Jersey Railroad joined forces with the Paterson and Hudson River Railroad to share the cost of the Bergen Cut, and in 1834, while the cut was still under construction, it opened from Jersey City to Newark with a temporary track around Bergen Hill.

By midcentury, the New Jersey Railroad was running fifty trains per day between Newark and its Hudson River ferries, making it possible for commuters to live in New Jersey and work in New York. In 1853, the New Jersey Railroad purchased the boats and buildings of a ferry company it had leased since 1841 and soon opened its own new terminal at the foot of Montgomery Street in a location called Exchange Place. But when the New Jersey Railroad tried to extend its tracks from New Brunswick to the Delaware River, the Camden and Amboy eliminated this threat of competition by gathering the New Jersey Railroad into its fold. In 1867, the New Jersey Railroad and Transportation Company became part of the United Companies of New Jersey. Four years later, when the Pennsy leased the United Companies, the New Jersey Railroad was part of the deal.

The Pennsy made some improvements to the Exchange Place terminal, realizing that it would have to be replaced in order for the railroad to compete with the New York Central in providing upscale service for the wealthy patrons of its "limited," or express trains, to Chicago. A devastating fire in 1884 caused by a gas explosion at the ferry house made this project a necessity, despite the efforts of the Jersey City Fire Department

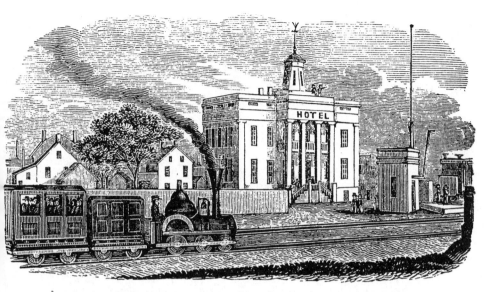

The New Jersey Railroad and Transportation Company trains stopped in Rahway in 1845, the year John W. Barber and Henry Howe first published *Historical Collections of the State of New Jersey.*

and the fire boats rushed in from New York City. The Pennsy lost its entire ferry house, together with its float bridges, as well as the offices and waiting room of its railroad depot.

The Pennsy's new train shed was designed by Charles Conrad Schneider, who had designed a bridge over the Niagara River. Schneider's train shed had a curving glass roof 86 feet high in the center without a single pillar to support it, and it stood at Exchange Place from 1890 until 1941, when the railroad razed it. Just north of the Exchange Place passenger terminal, the Pennsy developed a tract of marshland called Harsimus Cove, which had been purchased by the United Companies, adding piers, freight houses, a grain elevator, and stock yard that could handle five hundred cars daily. Around the same time, the railroad constructed new repair shops in Jersey City and embankments and viaducts so that it could elevate its Jersey City tracks, improving the life expectancy of pedestrians and horses, which previously had to negotiate grade-level crossings.

By the turn of the twentieth century, when the Pennsy had exhausted the possibilities for expansion in the Exchange Place neighborhood, the railroad started building its Greenville freight-handling terminal at the south end of Jersey City, which was connected with Newark by a Pennsy short line called the New York Bay Railroad. The Greenville terminal opened in 1906 and handled more than two thousand railroad cars per day at its peak.

Jersey City as seen from New York in 1845, from *Historical Collections of the State of New Jersey.* The caption reads, "The Car House of the New Jersey Railroad is on the right."

Despite all the improvements, Pennsy passengers arriving in Jersey City were still separated from Manhattan by a wide river, meaning that they and their bags had to move from train to ferry, resulting in delays that New York Central passengers did not have to endure. Had the idea not been vetoed by America's Department of War, the railroad might have constructed a huge bridge across the Hudson River.

In 1900, the Pennsylvania Railroad Company's innovative and forward-looking president, Alexander J. Cassatt, purchased the Long Island Rail Road and began work on a plan to link it with the Pennsy's operations in New Jersey through an elaborate passenger station in Manhattan. After Cassatt examined underwater railroad tunnels in France and Baltimore, the Pennsy established an engineering board to look into the possibility of tunnels under the Hudson and East rivers and Bergen Hill.

The Pennsylvania Railroad Company built a total of six underwater tunnels, under the direction of Charles Jacobs. It employed a multinational crew of experienced tunnel workers, whom their contemporaries called "sandhogs." The East River tunnels opened in September 1910, and the first Pennsy passenger train to pass beneath the Hudson was a local departing from Manhattan on November 27 of that year. After the Seventh Avenue subway opened in 1917, passengers arriving at Pennsylvania Station in New York City had easy access to rapid transit to other parts of the metropolis.

Railfans and architectural historians still mourn that the classical architecture of Pennsylvania Station, the crown jewel of Cassatt's plans, met the wrecking ball in 1965. Yet most of what the railroad constructed below street level at Thirty-third Street and Seventh Avenue remains in place and in use by three modern-day railroads: Amtrak, NJ TRANSIT, and the Long Island Rail Road. This includes tracks, platforms, and Sunnyside Yard, the railroad's Manhattan storage and service yard, with turntable and shops.

The steam engines that hauled Pennsy trains over the Allegheny Ridge could not take them through the underwater tunnels, so the railroad created the Manhattan Transfer, where they could be exchanged for electric locomotives. Located in the swamps just over the Passaic River from Newark, Manhattan Transfer shared its elevated platforms with the Hudson and Manhattan tubes. Passengers could reach it and depart only by train, and many a humorous story was told about yokels who got off the train by mistake, thinking they were already in New York City when they heard the conductor use the word *Manhattan* in calling the stop.

In 1935–36, in cooperation with the city of Newark, the Pennsylvania Railroad Company built a multimillion-dollar Newark depot as part of its main-line electrification project. The passenger station, built of Indiana limestone with pink granite trim, was designed by the famous architectural firm McKim, Mead, and White. The railroad closed Manhattan Transfer in 1937, as any locomotive switching that was still required could be handled at the Newark depot. Today Newark's recently refurbished Penn Station is a busy transportation hub serving Amtrak, NJ TRANSIT, PATH, and the Newark City Subway. A community has grown on the

The Raritan River, the Delaware and Raritan Canal, and a railroad bridge in New Brunswick in 1845, as depicted in *Historical Collections of the State of New Jersey.*

Newark's Penn Station, where you can arrive by subway, NJ TRANSIT, Amtrak, or PATH.

site of the Manhattan Transfer, and its residents can now use the PATH system's Harrison Station to quickly reach Newark or New York.

Exchange Place and its ferries continued to function as another way for commuters to reach Manhattan until passenger service to the facility was discontinued in 1961, but the Penn Central continued floating railroad cars to New York from Exchange Place until 1969. Now a popular new hotel occupies the site. Its guests and the residents of Jersey City can easily reach Lower Manhattan via PATH's Exchange Place station, located practically adjacent to the hotel, or via a water taxi that they can catch nearby.

The New York Central on the Western Shore

Unlike every other major railroad with a terminal on the Hudson's western shore, the New York Central Railroad did not need to lay tracks through Jersey to get its freight and passengers to New York City. Yet it too became a New Jersey railroad when it leased the bankrupt short-lived line called the West Shore.

The giant New York Central Railroad was born late in American railroad history, when New York's legislature permitted a collection of short lines linking cities along the Erie Canal to merge in 1853. Little railroads, such as the Schenectady & Troy and Buffalo & Rochester, became part of a system linking Albany and Buffalo, which had a chance of competing with developing east-west systems such as the New York & Erie and the Pennsy.

The name Vanderbilt will forever be linked with the New York Central thanks to this railroad's second president. Cornelius Vanderbilt added an important connection to New York City when he consolidated his operation with two other railroads, creating the New York Central & Hudson River Railroad in 1867. He later extended the railroad's reach to Chicago by taking over the Lake Shore & Michigan Southern Railway and Michigan Central Railroad. His son William Henry Vanderbilt continued the westward expansion by acquiring the Pittsburgh and Lake Erie and the New York, Chicago, and St. Louis railroads, as well as leasing the Canada Southern.

After many entrepreneurs tried and failed to compete with the New York Central in the state of New York, in the 1880s a group took over a small railroad called the New York, West Shore and Chicago Railroad, renaming it the New York, West Shore & Buffalo Railroad, commonly known as the West Shore. In New Jersey, the project was greeted with great enthusiasm by contemporaries. According to William H. Shaw in his 1884 *History of Essex and Hudson Counties:*

> The line promises to become one of great importance to this State, as it makes another great thoroughfare to the West. The road-bed, extending from Weehawken to Buffalo, a distance of four hundred and twenty-five miles, with all its appurtenances, has been constructed in a first-class manner, was opened for public travel in the summer of 1883, passengers being taken from Buffalo to Jersey City by way of Bergen Junction. Aside from its important share of through business between the points named, it is believed that no line of road in New Jersey has more important connections or better prospects for local traffic, both east and west.

Between 1881 and 1883, the West Shore constructed a tunnel nearly 4,000 feet long through the Palisades, and by 1885, the railroad completed a new passenger and freight terminal at Weehawken, New Jersey. Although it was hardly lavish, the facility looked a lot better than the other then-decaying railroad terminals on the Jersey side of the river. "The depot building and ferry house surpasses in size and beauty of design any railroad structure in New Jersey," Shaw says. "Passengers since the middle of May 1884, have been brought direct to the Weehawken Ferry, excepting those who are traveling through to Philadelphia or points further South, and these are still taken to the Pennsylvania Railroad Company's terminus at Jersey City." It may have been this traffic pattern that caused William Henry Vanderbilt to suspect that the West Shore was being assisted and controlled by the New York Central's arch rival, the Pennsylvania Railroad Company. Vanderbilt decided to do something about it.

His solution was to organize and begin construction of the South Pennsylvania Railroad, intended to run parallel to, and compete with, the Pennsy's main line in Pennsylvania. Financier J. P. Morgan stepped in to end the competition, which he feared would depress profits for both

New Jersey's scenic Palisades, a headache for railroad engineers, from *Historical Collections of the State of New Jersey.*

railroads and kill the market for their securities. In July 1885, he invited executives from both railroads to a meeting on his yacht, the *Corsair.* There he negotiated the famous Corsair Compact, in which each railroad would gain control over the line that threatened competition. The Pennsy sold its West Shore stock to buyers who leased the railroad to the New York Central Railroad. Construction abruptly ceased on the South Pennsylvania Railroad.

The few miles of West Shore tracks in New Jersey might have seemed redundant to the New York Central Railroad, but they soon proved to be a great advantage. When business increased and the railroad could not expand its freight operations directly into the city, it was able to divert traffic to Weehawken and float freight cars across the river, as the other railroads did.

The New York Central's rivalry with the Pennsy continued into the twentieth century. Both railroads offered high-speed luxury train service between New York City and Chicago, giving passengers a choice between the mountain scenery of the Pennsy's Broadway Limited and the New York Central's Water Level Route through river valleys and along the shores of the Great Lakes. In 1913, the New York Central

Railroad opened its Grand Central Terminal in Manhattan to compete with Pennsylvania Station.

Both railroads also shared a decline in business following World War II, as they faced competition from automobiles, trucks, and airplanes, whose industries were aided by federally funded highways and airports. The rivals eventually were forced to merge as the ill-fated Penn Central in 1968, which gave up its long-distance passenger service to Amtrak in 1971 and became part of Conrail on its creation in 1976.

Commuter service via ferry to Manhattan on the old West Shore ceased to operate in 1959. CSX continues to run freight trains on the line between Selkirk Yard in Albany and Oak Island Yard in Newark.

The National New York Central Railroad Museum was founded in 1987 in Elkhart, Indiana, to preserve the histories of the New York Central, the Lake Shore & Michigan Southern Railway, and other affiliates. Cleveland, Ohio, also has a New York Central System Historical Society.

The Lackawanna, the Erie, and the Erie Lackawanna

Since the early 1840s, the Scranton family had been manufacturing iron in the Lackawanna Valley, a place blessed with coal and iron ore deposits but sufficiently distant from any existing canals or railroads to make shipping a problem. Once they got an order for T-rails from the New York & Erie Railroad, under construction not that far away, they purchased a charter for their own railroad, an unfinished line called the Ligetts' Gap Rail Road. In 1851, they built their railroad from Scranton to the New York state boundary and a junction with the New York & Erie, renaming it the Lackawanna & Western Railroad.

Possibly at the urging of John I. Blair, the Scrantons chartered another railroad, called the Delaware & Cobb's Gap Railroad Company, between the Delaware Water Gap and Cobb's Gap on the Lackawanna River. In 1853, the two railroads merged into the Delaware, Lackawanna & Western Railroad, also called the DL&W, or simply the Lackawanna. George Scranton became its first president.

Planning to haul coal and iron ore to market in New York, the Lackawanna's directors proceeded to seek good connections with other railroads. They leased the Warren Railroad when it was completed in 1856, putting their line in touch with the Morris and Essex and the Morris Canal; contracted with the Central Railroad of New Jersey (CNJ) to run trains over their rails; and made a similar deal with the New Jersey Railroad. The Lackawanna made a lot of money hauling coal during the Civil War, enabling the railroad to purchase land with some of the best coalfields in the anthracite region.

Before the 1860s were over, the Lackawanna was looking for a route eastward to tidewater that it could control. The successful CNJ was too expensive to purchase, and the Morris Canal was yesterday's transportation system. On the other hand, the Morris and Essex was in debt, it had extensions to Hoboken and Phillipsburg, and it was constructing a new freight line called the Boonton Branch.

On December 10, 1868, the Lackawanna leased the Morris and Essex and thus made an enemy of the CNJ. The CNJ used the terms of its old contract with the Lackawanna to sue but backed down when Lackawanna executives proposed a merger.

Suddenly New Jersey's entire business landscape changed. The CNJ retaliated by extending its own reach into Pennsylvania anthracite country by leasing the Lehigh & Susquehanna Railroad. The Lehigh Valley Railroad crossed the Delaware by purchasing the Morris Canal and later building its own line.

The Lackawanna originally had been constructed as a broad-gauge railroad to match the gauge of its original connection with the New York & Erie Railroad. As it developed connections to other railroads, its managers made plans to switch to standard gauge, and in 1876, they made the switch on the entire roadbed within a period of forty-eight hours.

Besides coal, the Lackawanna became known in the late nineteenth century for the roses that it hauled over its Morris and Essex line to cus-

Rear of the Hoboken terminal where train passengers could board ferries.

The arresting interior of the Lackawanna Hoboken terminal.

tomers in New York. By 1895, the railroad had a daily rose train used by growers around the town of Madison. Because the roses were grown in greenhouses heated with coal, the rose growers were Lackawanna customers in more ways than one.

In 1899, the Lackawanna got a new president to replace the aging and highly conservative Samuel Sloan, who had been in charge for thirty-one years. William H. Truesdale's name became synonymous with change and modernization for the railroad.

The Lackawanna Cutoff, one of Truesdale's greatest achievements, was a series of construction projects designed to straighten out the Lackawanna's New Jersey line. When completed, it was 11.12 miles shorter, with fewer curves, reduced grades, and engineering features that conquered geography with drama and style. The Lackawanna Cutoff's Paulinskill Viaduct was built of reinforced concrete and measured 1,100 feet long and 115 feet high, making it the world's largest concrete bridge in its day.

Truesdale was also responsible for the magnificent new ferry terminal and railroad depot that opened in Hoboken in 1907, whence Lackawanna passengers could depart for Manhattan or a 400-mile trip to Buffalo on a long-distance train named the Phoebe Snow after the railroad's successful advertising icon. Modern-day passengers can still reach Manhattan from this same Hoboken terminal, as well as Port Jervis, Philadelphia, and a whole lot of towns in New Jersey. According to the Greater Scranton Chamber of Commerce, before 2011, trains should be able to go via a reinstated Lackawanna Cutoff from Hoboken to a new transportation hub in Scranton.

The Lackawanna ran excursions to a resort the railroad developed at New Jersey's Cranbury Lake, where one of the key attractions was a miniature railroad featuring a steam locomotive just 28 inches high. Cranbury Lake's hotel burned in 1910, and the resort never really did recover as a tourist destination.

The New York & Erie Railroad, commonly called the Erie, was conceived as a trunk line between Dunkirk on Lake Erie and Piermont, the closest town to New York City on the western shore of the Hudson that was still in New York State. The Erie's first train ran in 1851.

Since Piermont was still 24 miles upstream, Erie passengers were intended to reach Manhattan by steamboat, but they soon discovered they could disembark in Suffern and reach the city via two New Jersey railroads that ran through Paterson: the Paterson and Ramapo and Paterson and Hudson River. In 1852, the Erie leased these two lines.

The Erie purchased waterfront property between Jersey City and Hoboken in 1855, creating the Long Dock Company and the Pavonia Ferry Company. The next year, the railroad began blasting a new tunnel through the Palisades, which went into operation in 1861. The Erie's original Jersey City terminal soon had more passenger traffic than it could handle, and the railroad opened a new terminal in 1886.

Business setbacks were prompting railroad mergers in the mid-twentieth century, and the Lackawanna and the Erie merged to form the Erie Lackawanna Railroad Company in 1960. The new railroad moved the Erie's Jersey City passenger operations to the Lackawanna's terminal in Hoboken.

The merger seemed logical and cost-effective, but it failed to save the railroad. In 1968, the Erie Lackawanna became part of a holding company called Dereco, together with the Delaware & Hudson, Boston & Maine, Reading, and Jersey Central. The railroad continued to operate until 1972, when Hurricane Agnes washed out portions of roadbed along 200 miles of its main line. In 1976, most of the remaining Erie Lackawanna became part of Conrail. Properties abandoned by Conrail were sold by trustees to pay taxes and creditors.

Considerable Jersey portions of the Erie Lackwanna system live on in NJ TRANSIT. The Pascack Valley Line, with its northernmost stations in New York State, requires diesel locomotives and is also used by Conrail. The Main Line and Bergen County Line both terminate in Port Jervis. The Bergen County Line separates from the Main Line, hitting different

Jersey towns and bypassing Paterson and Passaic. NJ TRANSIT's Morris and Essex Lines comprise four routes, including the original Morris and Essex route, M&E's Boonton Branch, the Lackawanna's rural Gladstone extension, and a railroad chartered in 1852 that first was a Morris and Essex branch, then became a Lackawanna branch, and now is called the Montclair Line.

Today the Erie Lackawanna Historical Society maintains a website at www.erielackhs.org and conducts annual meetings each fall at a site along the former Erie Lackawanna Railroad. The organization retains a portion of the railroad's documents on deposit at the University of Akron in Ohio. The Anthracite Railroads Historical Society in Lansdale, Pennsylvania, also interprets the history of the Lackawanna.

Rail Stories of the Region

Hoboken, Castle Point, and John Stevens's Demonstration Railroad

Following the American Revolution, during a time when a great deal of confiscated Tory real estate was placed on the market, the newly married John Stevens crossed the Hudson from New York City to examine some land in New Jersey and decided he liked the view. In 1784, he purchased a large estate, which he proceeded to develop as an upscale English "park." Its highest elevation was a cliff, which Stevens named the Point of Castile. The name became popularly corrupted as Castle Point, and its command of the river was sufficient for its consideration as a military garrison during the War of 1812. In this general location, Stevens built a mansion that came to be called the Stevens Villa, where his family entertained the elite of New York City.

Below his personal compound, Stevens surveyed building lots, which he offered at public auction in New York City. He named his real estate development the New City of Hoboken. Stevens also developed hillside walks and drives for the enjoyment of Hoboken residents and visitors. Called the Elysian Fields, these pleasure grounds evolved into one of America's favorite leisure destinations.

In 1825, late in John Stevens's life, in an effort to prove to the world that railroads were the future of transportation, he added another attraction to the sights of Hoboken, a demonstration railroad with a steam locomotive that could move carriages back and forth. Its tracks were laid out in a circle near the Hoboken Hotel, and its four-wheeled locomotive had a boiler shaped like a tube. The tracks were constructed with a grade to demonstrate

One of the buildings of the Stevens Institute of Technology, legacy of the Stevens family in Hoboken.

that steam railroads need not be perfectly level. Contemporary newspaper accounts reported that Stevens's trains moved at about 6 miles per hour. Guests at the villa were encouraged to try riding the carriages, and the railroad was said to be a favorite amusement for courting couples.

In the course of Hoboken's nineteenth-century history, a second Stevens family mansion replaced the old villa and piers, and warehouses multiplied on the town's wide strips of beach. Another railroad came to dominate the town as the buildings of a growing city obliterated the site where John Stevens constructed the first operating steam railroad in America.

The Paterson and Hudson River Railroad

While the Camden and Amboy Railroad was being proposed and planned, the citizens of Paterson were dismayed to learn that its main line was being routed to bypass their thriving industrial city. Some Paterson entrepreneurs proposed constructing their own railroad between Paterson and Jersey City and began making surveys. Morris Canal executives balked, but those in charge at the Camden and Amboy Railroad did not regard the project as serious competition, so in January 1831, the Paterson and Hudson River Railroad was chartered, making it New Jersey's second railroad and northern Jersey's first.

The railroad was constructed in phases; its first segment between Paterson and Passaic opened in 1832. Horses provided the motive power for the first train, composed of three double-decker cars each capable of holding thirty passengers. It completed the trip in about fifteen minutes.

The most difficult construction work for this railroad still lay ahead. In order to lay rails through the tidal marshes east of Passaic known as meadows, workers had to construct embankments by driving piles surprisingly deep into the muck before reaching bedrock, and then hauling in tons of fill. They also had to construct bridges over the Passaic and Hackensack rivers strong enough to withstand river tides.

The biggest obstacle between Paterson and Jersey City was the Bergen Hill, part of the ridge of cliffs called the Palisades. The Bergen Hill was made of basaltic rock, a real challenge for the drills and black powder of the day. The Paterson and Hudson River Railroad formed a joint venture with the New Jersey Railroad and Transportation Company and finally conquered the Bergen Hill by blasting a cut along the course of an old riverbed, but they created a path with many turns that took six years to complete. In the meantime, passengers on the Paterson and Hudson River Railroad had to switch to stagecoaches that could handle the hill's grade. In 1838, trains first passed through the Bergen Cut; six railroads would eventually use it. Today, PATH trains still pass through the cut at a Jersey City station called Journal Square on their way from Newark to the Hudson River tunnels.

The railroad fostered growth in both Paterson and Passaic and was instrumental in the development of Paterson's locomotive industry. In fact, the Paterson and Hudson River Railroad's first locomotive, constructed in England and named the McNiell, became the model for Paterson's famous engineer and locomotive manufacturer Thomas Rogers.

The New York & Erie Railroad Company leased the Paterson and Hudson River Railroad in 1852, together with another short line called the Paterson and Ramapo Railroad. In the 1940s, the Erie acquired additional stock, increasing its control.

By the time John W. Barber and Henry Howe published an updated edition of *Historical Collections of New Jersey* in 1868, Paterson was known for its many factories.

The Morris and Essex roars through Madison in 1845, the year John W. Barber and Henry Howe first published *Historical Collections of the State of New Jersey.*

The Morris and Essex Railroad

The Morris and Essex Railroad (M&E) was another early Jersey railroad. It was chartered by local capitalists in 1835 to connect the town of Morristown with Newark and thence New York City, primarily responding to the needs of farmers in Morris and Essex counties. By 1836, horses were drawing its cars from Newark as far as Orange. The horses were phased out the following year, and by 1838, the line was completed to Morristown.

Passenger fares made up most of the railroad's initial revenue, but in the 1840s, the M&E was among the first of many New Jersey railroads to do significant business transporting milk from country to town. Farmers were charged by the quart to load fast early-morning trains with their milk cans, which the railroad returned free of charge in the evenings.

The M&E's founders had always intended to eventually expand into New Jersey's iron ore region and on to the Delaware River across from Pennsylvania's coal country. In 1848, they opened an extension to Dover, and two years later, the railroad began making surveys for a route to the Delaware Water Gap. A Morris and Essex representative lost the famous 1853 race to Trenton with John I. Blair to file their companies' surveys, and the M&E subsequently tried to stop the rival Warren Railroad with an injunction. Work was delayed for years while lawyers for each railroad charged its opponent with corporate espionage and fraud. Blair and his Warren Railroad were vindicated, and the Morris and Essex had to settle for another route to Phillipsburg, which the railroad completed in 1865.

In 1867, the M&E built a branch between Denville and Boonton, which it expanded as the Boonton Line in 1870. Its grades were more freight-friendly than the M&E's main line, and the railroad soon double tracked it. The Boonton Line provided an alternate route for heavy, slow-moving freight trains as well as express trains, keeping the railroad's passenger trains on its main line running on time.

The Morris and Essex was leased by the Lackawanna in 1868, becoming that railroad's route east to tidewater.

The Locomotives of Paterson

Within walking distance of the train station in Paterson, visitors can view one of America's natural wonders at the Great Falls, a national historic landmark. At 77 feet in height, the Great Falls, or Passaic Falls, is one of the largest waterfalls east of the Mississippi. George Washington's secretary of the treasury, Alexander Hamilton, regarded the Great Falls as a superb source of water power. Together with other American leaders, he established the Society for the Establishment of Useful Manufactures in 1791, intended to encourage business entrepreneurs to build factories that could take advantage of what nature had provided. In 1792, a city was chartered at this location, named after New Jersey governor William Paterson.

Silk weaving became an important early-nineteenth-century Paterson industry. In 1835, Paterson's Patent Arms Company was organized to manufacture the revolvers invented by Samuel Colt in 1829.

The Great Falls at Paterson, one of America's natural wonders, became a power source that made this New Jersey town an ideal place for manufacturing. The building in the foreground is one of America's earliest hydroelectric plants, built in 1913–14.

It was also in 1835 that Thomas Rogers, a partner in an expanding manufacturing concern, was hired by the Paterson and Hudson River Railroad to assemble its first locomotive, which was being delivered from England. Like the first locomotive for the Camden and Amboy Railroad, it arrived unassembled, with its various pieces packed in crates. And like Isaac Dripps, Rogers had never seen a locomotive, but he also succeeded in putting it together and used his experience to later build a locomotive of his own, and subsequently a successful locomotive-manufacturing business.

By the time the Civil War started, the locomotives produced by Rogers's company were recognized as some of the best in the world. During the war, the Rogers plant constructed ten to twelve locomotives per month. Business was so good that Rogers joined forces with two other manufacturers to build the Paterson Horse Railway, whose sole purpose was hauling completed locomotives over the streets of Paterson to the tracks of the Erie rail yard. Moving the huge locomotives sometimes required up to forty horses, and the spectacle drew quite a crowd.

Other Paterson manufacturers also produced locomotives, including the Grant Locomotive Works and Danforth, Cooke and Company. In the 1920s, the locomotive manufacturers of Philadelphia surpassed those of Paterson, but the factories where locomotives were made remained intact, and they became part of Paterson's historic district during a revitalization effort in the 1970s.

Since 1982, the Paterson Museum has been located in the Thomas Rogers Locomotive Erecting Shop.

Inside the Paterson Museum, many exhibits interpret the town's industrial and railroad history, including this garden-scale model railroad.

After spending many years at the public library and the carriage house of a former Paterson mayor, the holdings of the Paterson Museum were moved to Thomas Rogers's old Locomotive Erecting Shop in 1982. The red brick building is located on Market Street, and its former function is acknowledged by the rolling stock parked outside its front door. The Paterson Museum interprets the history of the entire city and all its industries, including the life and work of Paterson's favorite son, comedian Lou Costello. Railfans might be particularly interested in a large garden-scale model train layout, with up to three trains running through a landscape depicting life around 1900. It numbers among its denizens a group of hobos hanging out around a boxcar.

Outside its factory district, Paterson's attractions include a number of late-nineteenth-century and early-twentieth-century commercial buildings constructed in the opulent Revival styles of their day. Paterson's city hall has a Beaux Arts design and a clock tower that is a copy of the one on the city hall in Lyons, the silk-manufacturing center of France. The staff at the Historic District Cultural Center opposite the Great Falls will provide a visitors' guide and map free of charge.

Joel Cook Travels

In 1882, the Philadelphia publisher J. B. Lippincott & Company presented in book format a series of newspaper articles that travel writer Joel Cook had produced for the summer issues of Philadelphia's *Public Ledger.* The book's title was *Brief Summer Rambles Near Philadelphia,* and each of its essays covered a destination that could be reached from Philadelphia in a single day, many of them by train.

After taking a trip from Philadelphia to New York on the Pennsy, here's what Cook had to say about Bergen Hill and Jersey City:

The train passes the village of Marion and runs into the deep and crooked rocky cutting through Bergen Hill. The railway zigzags through on short curves, swinging the cars from side to side, but work is progressing at straightening the line by making a broad new cutting southward of the present line. It is a task of great difficulty, however, for the roadway has to be bored through the solid rock. Here in the heart of the hill the railway divides, the lines for the freight traffic going northward towards the extensive wharves and docks at Harsimus Cove. Plenty of trains pass, showing how busy the line is, and we run out of the cutting and curve around on the side of the hill and enter the suburbs of Jersey City. Here the meadows to the southward extend down to Communipaw, with vacant land between, and over in the lower part of the Hudson River can be seen Ellis's Island and Bedloe's Island. We are now fairly in Jersey City, and run along between rows of houses, whose little back-yards border the railway; and where they seem to have a perpetual wash-day, the different families in each story and even each room of these temement-houses rigging the wash clothes upon lines extended on pulleys between the upper windows. There they flutter in the wind like so many flags of truce, regardless of the soot flying from the locomotives. As we gradually come down to the level of the street the road is fenced in on both sides, with gates for the street-crossings, past which the train rushes at almost full speed. Huge factories line the streets, for Jersey City, too, is a great manufacturing town, and has been mainly built up by the overflow from New York. Here the great railways from the west come out upon the Hudson, and are connected by ferries with the metropolis. Here are the capacious Pennsylvania and Erie Railway docks and elevators, where vast amounts of freight are transshipped to vessels for export to Europe. The immense stock-yards and abattoir, where meat is slaughtered for the New York market, are in the northern part of the town. The largest ferryboats in the world carry the enormous passenger traffic of these great railways over the Hudson from Jersey City, and the railways have huge terminal stations communicating with the ferry-slips. Jersey City is only a modern town. The neck of land on which it stands is the old Paulus Hook, where barely a dozen persons lived at the beginning of the present century, and it was not until 1820 that the settlement became of any size, while thirty years ago it was still only a village. Since then the overflow of New York, and especially the vast growth of the railways, have made it a very large place, and the second city of New Jersey.

Local Chapters of the National Railway Historical Society

Established in 1937, the North Jersey Chapter is one of the oldest in the National Railway Historical Society. Some of its members sport pins commemorating twenty-five and even fifty years of continuous membership.

The chapter sells photos from an extensive collection of black-and-white negatives, many of them images of trolleys, compiled by one of the organization's members. Members conduct regular meetings in Bloomfield with programs on various aspects of railroad operation, publish a newsletter called *The Marker Lamp,* and host a website at www.nojersey nrhs.homestead.com. An index to the chapter's photo collection can be viewed online.

The Jersey Central Chapter is affiliated with the United Railroad Historical Society, and its members have restored or donated funds toward the restorations of rolling stock owned by both organizations as well as those done elsewhere. The chapter provided financial support for the restoration of the miniature Centerville & Southwestern Railroad operating in Phillipsburg. An Erie caboose restored by chapter members is on display at the Whippany Railway Museum.

The chapter holds regular meetings with special presentations. Popular annual events include a train show and sale in March and a Santa Excursion using NJ TRANSIT cars over the Raritan Valley Line, formerly the CNJ main line from Raritan and Westfield, as far as High Bridge. The chapter publishes the *Jersey Central News* and has a website at www.jcrhs.org.

The Bergen-Rockland Chapter's activities include regular meetings with guest presentations, an annual banquet, and special tours and outings. Members participate in the Jersey Central Railroad Heritage Festival in the autumn, conduct an annual slide contest in March, and publish *The Stoker.*

The Region's Railroad Giants

John Stevens (1749–1838)

John Stevens was born in New York City and studied at what is now Columbia University. He served as a captain under George Washington during the American Revolution.

John Stevens
NATIONAL CYCLOPAEDIA OF AMERICAN BIOGRAPHY

His fascination with steam-driven transportation is said to have begun in southern New Jersey, where he saw a steamboat being tested on the Delaware River by an inventor named John Fitch. Stevens had been on his way to visit his future wife, Rachel Cox, who lived near Trenton, but he decided to detour and follow the boat to its landing where he could study it.

Years later, Stevens established the world's first scheduled steam ferry between Hoboken and New York City, on a vessel called the *Juliana.* When New York City's transportation monopolists forced him out of business, he decided to put his larger steamship, the *Phoenix,* into ferry service on the Delaware. To get it there, his son Robert had to take it onto the Atlantic Ocean, where the *Phoenix* became the first steamboat to survive the open sea.

In 1812, Stevens addressed a prophetic pamphlet titled *Documents Tending to Prove the Superior Advantages of Rail-Ways and Steam-Carriages over Canal Navigation* to a New York State transportation commission. He proposed a steam railroad between Albany and Lake Erie, rather than a canal, and envisioned railroad transportation pretty much the way it would evolve: carriages on iron wheels moving over a timber railway propelled by a steam engine that moved with the train.

Stevens obtained charters to build railroads from the state of New Jersey in 1815 and the commonwealth of Pennsylvania in 1823, but in neither case was he able to raise sufficient funds to build. To convince government officials and potential investors that railroads were feasible, he constructed a circular railroad track in Hoboken and built a model steam locomotive. His demonstration railroad opened in 1825, the same year as the Erie Canal.

Stevens lived long enough to see the Camden and Amboy Railroad chartered in 1831, and he celebrated when its first locomotive arrived in Bordentown. Within another century, the evolution of American technology made possible a few more of John Stevens's visions, including bridges and tunnels conquering the Hudson.

William Gibbs McAdoo (1863–1941)

William Gibbs McAdoo was born in Georgia during the Civil War. After attending the University of Tennessee, he studied law while working as a deputy clerk of the U.S. Circuit Court in Chattanooga.

He entered the railroad industry as a lawyer for the Richmond & Danville Railroad, later becoming president of the Knoxville Street Railway Company, in which he was heavily invested. He secured funds to make it possible for Knoxville to electrify its horsecar lines and become one of America's first cities with electrified street railways.

After moving to New York to work as a railroad bond salesman, McAdoo discovered the crowded ferries that took commuters to jobs in Manhattan. He also learned that an abandoned segment of tunnel lay under the Hudson. McAdoo began gathering investors and revived the project as the successful Hudson and Manhattan Railroad Company, also called the Hudson and Manhattan tubes, or sometimes the McAdoo Tunnels. The $70 million project was completed in eight years, revolutionizing commuter transportation in this region and making McAdoo a local celebrity.

McAdoo became known as a business reformer. Among other innovations, he paid male and female employees equally. Whether or not William Henry Vanderbilt ever really exclaimed, "The public be damned!" McAdoo made his company's policy "The public be pleased," offering safe and efficient public transportation. He invited complaints and suggestions from the public, boasting that fewer than fifty complaints were ever received.

He later became a prominent business and political leader. He was appointed secretary of the treasury under President Woodrow Wilson, for whom he had campaigned when Wilson was running for governor of New Jersey and later president of the United States. McAdoo was one of the architects of the Federal Reserve system. In 1932, he was elected to the Senate representing California, a state he by then had made his home.

William Gibbs McAdoo
LIBRARY OF CONGRESS

Thomas Rogers
LIBRARY OF CONGRESS

Thomas Rogers (1792–1856)

Thomas Rogers settled in Paterson after a common school education in Groton, Connecticut, where he was born. He also served apprenticeships that introduced him to the trades of carpentry and blacksmithing.

After working in a shop that made wooden looms, he joined with John Clark and Abram H. Godwin to manufacture looms and spin cotton. In 1831, Rogers sold out of this business to join with Morris Ketchum and Jasper Grosvenor to form Rogers, Ketchum & Grosvenor (later Rogers, Ketchum & Co.), which initially also produced cotton-manufacturing machinery.

The company expanded into railroad car wheels and other metal castings. Railroad executives began urging Rogers to construct locomotives. He got a chance to study the first locomotive purchased by the Paterson and Hudson River Railroad when he was asked to assemble the vehicle after it arrived from England. Rogers built his first locomotive in 1837, and it immediately found a buyer once it was successfully tested. In 1839, he produced a locomotive for the New Jersey Railroad that outperformed anything English manufacturers had yet produced.

Rogers built many more locomotives, often incorporating improvements that he should have patented, as they were later widely adopted by other locomotive manufacturers. Eventually his firm employed twelve hundred people, and his locomotives were shipped all over the United States, as well as Cuba and South America. In 1905, the firm, which survived him, was taken over by the American Locomotive Company.

Sampling the Region's Railroad History

PATH

John Stevens's idea for a railroad tunnel beneath the Hudson River became increasingly popular in the 1860s, as Manhattan grew congested and the idea of commuting to work from Jersey became increasingly attractive. In 1874, DeWitt Clinton Haskins organized the Hudson Tunnel Railway Company and began construction. After the Lackawanna briefly halted these efforts with an injunction, work resumed until an accident took the lives of twenty workers. William Gibbs McAdoo expanded the project when he created the Hudson and Manhattan Railroad (popularly called the Hudson and Manhattan tubes), a two-tunnel system linking Manhattan with the western-shore waterfront terminals of three major railroads (the Lackawanna, the Erie, and the Pennsy) and stops farther west in Jersey City, as well as Newark and subsequently the Pennsy's Manhattan Transfer.

Tunnel construction began in 1902 under chief engineer Charles Jacobs, whose work crews employed a mechanical shield to bore through the mud at a relatively rapid pace. When the first tube was completed in 1904, Jacobs and McAdoo walked from New Jersey to New York through the tunnel.

Opening day came on February 25, 1908, when invited dignitaries gathered at a station on the New York side of the Hudson. A telegraph operator sent a message to the White House, where Theodore Roosevelt pushed a button on his desk that turned on the station's power and illuminated its waiting trains. Guests boarded and rode beneath the river to a point at the boundary between New York and New Jersey, where the states' governors shook hands. Crowds waiting in Hoboken cheered when the trains arrived and the guests emerged from the underground station.

McAdoo made sure that the stations were attractive and efficient. To eliminate the confusion of passengers both boarding and exiting when the doors opened, his busiest stations were constructed so that passengers getting on the train used one platform and those exiting used another. Passengers entered New York stations through retail stores, not stairways from the sidewalks, and the Sixth Avenue stations had display windows where merchants could encourage window shopping. McAdoo preferred to hire women to staff the ticket windows and paid his female and male employees equal wages. He made certain employees knew that the railroad's priority was its passengers' safety and convenience.

The Hudson and Manhattan system served about 59 million passengers in its opening year, and into the late 1920s, as many as 113 million passengers per year rode its steel cars. The tubes drew ridership from the railroad ferries, but they were eclipsed by the Holland and Lincoln tunnels and the opportunity they offered to drive or ride a bus directly into New York City. The tubes also lost business as passenger traffic declined for the railroads whose Jersey terminals connected with them. In 1954, the Hudson and Manhattan Railroad filed for bankruptcy.

In 1962, the Port of New York Authority purchased and took control of the Hudson and Manhattan Railroad, renaming it the Port Authority Trans-Hudson Corporation, or PATH. The port authority was not so anxious to operate the then-deteriorating rapid-transit system as it was to acquire McAdoo's Hudson Terminal and its office complex in lower Manhattan. At one time the world's largest, this complex had four thousand offices and an exclusive restaurant on its top floor. The plan was to knock it down and replace it with the twin towers of the World Trade Center.

The port authority invested in new cars but kept the fares low, thus winning back much ridership. It also upgraded the stations, tunnels, and tracks. Rather than expand the system that ran at capacity during rush hour, however, in the 1980s the port authority offered commuters the new option of an older transportation system: ferries across the Hudson operated by a contractor called NY Waterway.

Service between the World Trade Center and Exchange Place shut down for a week when the World Trade Center was bombed in 1993. It was suspended for several years following September 11, 2001, when the towers fell, destroying the Lower Manhattan PATH station. More than $500 million was spent to restore PATH service to Lower Manhattan, and the trains were running again in late 2003 from an expanded Exchange Place to a new and still improving World Trade Center station.

The Newark City Subway

By the 1920s, the portion of the Morris Canal that flowed into Newark held little but stagnant water, which posed a health problem for the city. The city considered transforming the canal bed into a right-of-way for trolleys but opted to build the Newark City Subway instead.

Construction began in 1929, and the trains started running between Broad Street and Heller Parkway in 1935. Downtown, the line was covered by a new street called Raymond Boulevard, named for a former Newark mayor. In 1937, the line was extended so that its trains could run to the city's new Pennsylvania Railroad station. The system was extended to the north in 1940.

For many years, the Newark City Subway was a great favorite with railfans because it was still operating rolling stock from the 1940s. Its cars were President's Conference Committee (PCC) trolley cars acquired from the Twin Cities Rapid Transit Company in the 1950s, when Minneapolis was abandoning its trolley system. These were not replaced until the 1990s (after NJ TRANSIT assumed control), when the decision was made to upgrade the subway so that it could be integrated into any future light rail system planned for this area. The Newark City Subway now employs the same sort of vehicles used by the Hudson-Bergen Light Rail line.

These new cars are clean and quiet, and they run frequently, but overall the Newark City Subway has seen better days. Riders transferring from Newark's Penn Station pass some vintage Art Deco mosaics and a more modern sculpture group depicting subway riders in days gone by, but art can't distract passengers from noticing the tiles peeling off the walls along the steps to the platform. The downtown stations nearest Newark's New Jersey Performing Arts Center are in no better condition, their uneven stairs cracked and stained.

The New Jersey Historical Society, located near the Military Park Station (formerly the Broad Street Station), houses some interesting mementos of the subway and its predecessor, the Morris Canal. A collection of photographs made by local commercial photographer William F. Cone illustrates Newark in the late nineteenth and early twentieth centuries. In 2003, the society mounted a Cone exhibit, with an enlarged photo of what was left of the Morris Canal in 1919, shortly before its demise, as well as earlier glimpses of other portions of the canal when it still held water and the Newark City Subway while it was under construction. A map of Newark drawn in 1915 showed what the city looked like before the canal became a subway and there was still a place called Manhattan Transfer across the Passaic River.

NJ TRANSIT

By the early 1970s, many New Jersey residents depended on commuter rail service to reach their jobs, and a number of Jersey railroads continued to provide it, including the Central Railroad of New Jersey (CNJ), Erie Lackawanna, Penn Central, Reading, and Pennsylvania-Reading Seashore Lines. But the heavily taxed railroads, which were witnessing the demise of their more important freight business, tended to defer maintenance on their passenger operations. Deteriorating coaches and rail infrastructure became the inevitable result.

In 1959, New Jersey created a railroad division in its state highway department, and in the 1960s, the state began offering some modest assistance to railroads operating in its northern counties, including the CNJ, Erie Lackawanna, and Penn Central. Because the new entities of Conrail and Amtrak had no commuter divisions, in 1979 the New Jersey Transit Corporation was created to acquire, control, maintain, and operate public transportation. In 1982, NJ TRANSIT Rail Operations was established as a subsidiary of NJ TRANSIT, and by the following year, it was fully in charge of the commuter trains.

Within a relatively short time after NJ TRANSIT's first train left the station at Hoboken, the agency was running new coaches and locomotives on lines that had seen significant structural improvements and repairs. Before the end of the 1990s, it operated 591 weekday trains with more than 100 locomotives and 700 passenger cars serving 161 stations, including some in New York and Pennsylvania. A $61 million project originally known as the Kearny Connection made the old Morris and Essex lines on the Erie Lackawanna system compatible with the electrification system used by the former Pennsy lines. This made it possible for additional NJ TRANSIT lines to offer a ride into Manhattan via the tunnels built by the Pennsylvania Railroad Company, giving commuters more options and saving them time.

Today NJ TRANSIT operates eleven commuter rail lines in three divisions: the Hoboken Division, Newark Division, and Atlantic City Rail Line. The agency's most recent projects include a new station at Newark International Airport and Secaucus Junction, which makes it possible for passengers to transfer among all lines except the Atlantic City Rail Line. Its largest and busiest stations are operated as transportation hubs where rail, bus, subway, and even ferry lines converge. The agency's current mission is luring drivers off New Jersey's crowded highways and out of its notoriously nerve-wracking traffic.

Secaucus Junction

In New Jersey's marshy meadows about halfway between the stations that the Pennsylvania Railroad Company built in Newark and New York City, there rises a huge new $450 million train station. While under construction, it was known as Secaucus Transfer, not Secaucus Junction, and its purpose was no less than revolutionizing the NJ TRANSIT system.

Built in the shape of an enormous cross, it connects NJ TRANSIT's Main Line–Bergen County Line, Pascack Valley Line, Montclair-Boonton Line, Morris and Essex Lines, Northeast Corridor Line, and North Jersey Coast Line, effectively linking most of NJ TRANSIT's stations. The monitors mounted above its platforms displaying information on arriving and departing trains occasionally flash the slogan "You can get there through here."

Passengers on incoming trains exit onto long platforms and make their way to wide halls with stone walls and flooring. To get to the heart of this structure, they insert NJ TRANSIT tickets to their final destinations through turnstiles; a helpful NJ TRANSIT employee quickly materializes to help those who cannot figure out how to do this, preventing the clueless from holding up foot traffic.

The Secaucus Transfer, or Secaucus Junction, is constructed around a huge rotunda.

On the concourse level, passengers enter a rotunda 75 feet high, topped with a skylight and clerestory windows that illuminate a centrally located sculpture titled *Twentieth First Century Cattail,* which looks like the marsh reeds they might find outside, only much larger. In the rotunda, they also find waiting areas, ticket-vending machines, restrooms, customer service windows, and retail stores. Eventually Secaucus Junction will also include office towers, plus a hotel and conference center. The size and grandeur of the place recall the major urban railroad stations built a century ago.

One thing that passengers will find a bit more difficult to locate is a door that leads outside. The rotunda is ringed with

An NJ TRANSIT train approaches Secaucus Junction on its lower level, which is criss-crossed by the elevated tracks overhead for Northeast Corridor trains.

directions to the proper tracks for each line that runs through the junction, but just like the old Manhattan Transfer, it's difficult to get to or leave this place by any vehicle other than a train. It will eventually accommodate some automobile access, but Secaucus Junction will have no sprawling commuter parking lot. Secaucus Junction is just that: a junction of rail lines, not a park-and-ride.

The construction of Secaucus Junction was a public-private partnership engaging seventeen engineering, fourteen architectural, and eleven construction firms. Although it was built directly on one of the world's busiest rail corridors, construction crews worked during off-peak hours and did little to disrupt the schedules of the four hundred passenger and freight trains that daily passed through the construction site.

Secaucus Junction immediately reduced the time it took to commute from Bergen County to Manhattan and enabled NJ TRANSIT to run more trains between Newark and New York City at peak travel times. It also enabled Amtrak and NJ TRANSIT trains to stay out of each other's way. New Jersey transportation officials hope it will take more than fifteen thousand vehicles off the state's congested roads each weekday and keep ten thousand cars and five hundred buses out of the perpetually slow-moving traffic in the tunnels under the Hudson River.

Hudson-Bergen Light Rail

Looking at the profitable Newark City Subway as a model, a citizens' group encouraged politicians to consider a light rail public transportation system connecting Hoboken and Jersey City that ultimately could be extended as far north as Tenafly and as far south as Bayonne. After fifteen years of planning, a portion of the Hudson-Bergen Light Rail line (HBLR) opened in April 2000 and immediately became a working model for similar systems throughout the nation.

Long in planning, the initial portion of the Hudson-Bergen Light Rail system was actually built in less than three years. New Jersey's commissioner of transportation instituted an approach called Design-Build-Operate-Maintain (DBOM), in which owners assign responsibility for designing, building, operating, and maintaining a system to a single entity, in this case a consortium called Twenty First Century Rail, mainly Raytheon Infrastructure and a Japanese firm called Kinkisharyo, which built the light rail vehicles for this transportation system.

The system's route is complex, linking the former Lackawanna terminal in Hoboken with the sites of the former Erie and Pennsy terminals in Jersey City. At each of these locations, passengers can easily reach a PATH station. The system's Bayonne Branch is constructed on a former CNJ

A Husdon-Bergen Light Rail train arrives at Liberty State Park.

line and includes a station near a highway with a large commuter parking lot.

On the system's opening day, New Jersey governor Christie Whitman joined the state's U.S. senators and transportation executives on a maiden voyage to the station at Liberty State Park for festivities. Trains then began running about seven minutes apart, and ridership has since increased steadily. In 2002, riders made about sixteen thousand trips each day.

Perhaps more important, Hudson-Bergen Light Rail has stimulated growth in Bayonne and transformed the waterfront in Jersey City and Hoboken. Abandoned warehouses and rail yards have been quickly replaced by new office buildings, condo complexes, large retailers, and even a mall. Property values have increased to the point where Jersey City is sometimes referred to as New Jersey's Gold Coast.

Following September 11, 2001, PATH closed its Exchange Place station, and Hudson-Bergen Light Rail became the only mass transit to this destination. The system also provided support to Ground Zero rescue teams by placing cars at their disposal.

The system will be expanded in phases until the trains can cover more than 20 miles of track and serve thirty-two stations. By 2010, the Hudson-Bergen Light Rail line is expected to accommodate a hundred thousand daily trips.

Maywood Station

A new destination for railroad enthusiasts opened in 2004, when the restored station at Maywood became a museum. Constructed in 1872 by the New Jersey Midland Railway Company, one of the ancestors of the New York, Susquehanna & Western Railroad, it was located on an old country road between Hackensack and Paramus. It predated the official creation in 1894 of the borough of Maywood, which subsequently developed as a residential community in an industrial area.

The railroad no longer needed Maywood Station after 1966, when it ceased providing passenger service on these tracks. It failed to lease the station to Maywood, and the station deteriorated until the borough ordered its demolition.

In 2002, volunteers formed the Maywood Station Historical Committee. The station was identified as one of the state's oldest to retain much of its original character, and it was deemed worthy of New Jersey's Register of Historic Places. That same year, the local committee joined with the New York, Susquehanna & Western Technical & Historical Society and began raising funds to restore the station as a meeting place and museum of local and railroad history. Volunteers removed tons of stucco from the exterior walls, added a new roof, and made improvements to the flooring, lighting, and landscaping. To restore the original interior color scheme, they took paint samples from what lay beneath the stucco. The samples showed that the station had originally been painted in the signature colors of the New Jersey Midland Railway, and these colors were restored to its walls. Maywood Station was added to the National Register of Historic Places in 2003.

Today the station is furnished with local railroad artifacts. It is open to the public several days each year.

The Union Model Railroad Club

Behind a Home Depot off a highway in Union, New Jersey, the Model Railroad Club, better known as the Union Model Railroad Club, occupies a nondescript, barnlike building. The club was founded as the Summit–New Providence HO Railroad Club in 1949 by several hobbyists, including master model railroader Paul Mallery, the author of many books and articles, who housed the club's layout in his basement for a number of years. Mallery worked hard to secure permanent quarters for the club, ultimately resulting in an arrangement with the Union County Department of Parks and Recreation. Members funded and built the club's structure and currently maintain it, but they donated it to the park system when it was completed around 1972. They now open the club to the public a certain number of hours each year.

The annual sound and light show held on several weekends between Thanksgiving and Christmas is popular with the public. Visitors get a good look at the 40-by-40-foot HO-scale layout from a catwalk built above two sides of this large space. Below them, engineers are positioned here and there in the aisles getting ready for show time. Other engineers work the control center, which is curtained off from the rest of the viewing balcony.

The main attraction at the Union Model Railroad Club.

The show features the recorded recollections of three narrators who talk about their experiences on the three operational model railroads of the layout. While they discuss different kinds of journeys, the little trains stop and start, their progress illuminated by lights. The show is a sophisticated combination of history and stagecraft well worth negotiating a Home Depot parking lot at Christmastime.

The first narrator recalls her childhood on a Jersey dairy farm and the many trips she took on the Trenton Northern, a mythical interurban railroad centered in Ringoes, illustrating the importance of this kind of transportation to area farmers. The second talks about working around the time of World War II on the Rahway River, a fictitious short line modeled on the genuine Rahway Valley Railroad, which once operated in this general area. A third brings visitors back to the present day with information on the Hudson, Delaware and Ohio Railroad, which hauls make-believe freight between Hoboken and Pittsburgh. Club members have gone to considerable trouble to ensure that the buildings in their layout are historically correct for the region and periods that the narrators describe.

While waiting for the show to begin, visitors are corralled in the club's N-scale layout, where trains operate at two elevations around a 30-by-27-foot room. Club members are on hand to answer questions, and they proudly point out the tiny details of the world where their railroad, the Jersey Shore and Western, runs.

The club's newest layout is its expanding garden-scale railroad, which operates both inside and outside the building. Visitors to the club's website can watch a video of a garden-scale train equipped with a snowplow clearing its tracks of real snow. Its occasional derailments are amusingly righted by a member's hand.

Lorett Treese Travels

My husband and I set off for Jersey City on the worst possible travel day (or maybe the best, if you like to see transportation systems working at capacity) of the year—the day after Thanksgiving. We would be traveling the route of the Pennsy and its earlier components—the Philadelphia and Trenton Railroad, United Canal and Railroad Companies, and New Jersey Railroad—across Jersey to Newark, where we planned to pick up the old Hudson and Manhattan tubes. In terms of today's transportation systems, that translates to SEPTA's R7 to Trenton, the NJ TRANSIT Northeast Corridor Line, and PATH.

An awful lot of people with luggage were waiting for the R7 on the platform at Philadelphia's Thirtieth Street Station. We felt peculiar standing among them, because we were on the same platform where we usually board the R5 for our home in Paoli, and the R5 had just deposited us in the city.

The R7 pulled in on a different track, however, and we headed out of town on tracks much closer to the Philadelphia Zoo than the R5 route takes us. We crossed the Schuylkill River on a viaduct above the zoo's front gate, and soon the scenery changed from North Philadelphia row homes to industrial buildings and freight cars idle in a rail yard, and then to a view of I-95. Shortly before we arrived in Trenton, we rode parallel to the Delaware River shore, where sheds and lawn furniture told us we might have seen people picnicking in warmer months. Then we spotted Trenton's famous bridge with its familiar slogan, "Trenton Makes, the World Takes," as we crossed the Delaware.

SEPTA schedules its R7 so that the train hits Trenton a few minutes before a NJ TRANSIT Northeast Corridor train leaves for New York City, usually from the same track. However, you will not make this connecting train unless you were wise enough to buy your NJ TRANSIT ticket from the vending machines at Thirtieth Street Station and already have it in hand or are willing to pay the steep surcharge added to tickets purchased on NJ TRANSIT trains. The line at the ticket window in Trenton is usually pretty long, but it still moves faster than the line of people waiting for some amateur to push the right buttons on the NJ TRANSIT vending machines. Luckily Northeast Corridor trains depart from Trenton so frequently that you won't need to wait long for the next one. New Yorkers and New Jersey residents face a similar problem traveling to Philadelphia, though SEPTA does not add the surcharge to the onboard ticket price if the few SEPTA vending machines in Trenton are not working.

I heard from a transit system maven that SEPTA and NJ TRANSIT are contemplating through trains between New York and Philadelphia. Simply offering through ticketing would be a vast improvement.

Our Northeast Corridor train stopped at Princeton Junction, Monmouth Junction, and a relatively new station called Jersey Avenue. We had a nice view of New Brunswick before we crossed the Raritan River. The station named for New Jersey's favorite son, Thomas Edison, was identified as Stelton on some of my older maps. We stopped at Metuchen and then MetroPark, a huge park-and-ride surrounded by office complexes.

By the time our train made stops in Rahway, Linden, and Elizabeth, it was packed, with people standing in the aisles and restrooms. People heading for shows and holiday shopping in Manhattan had even piled into the drafty connections between cars, and we began to fear we would not be able to get out the door in Newark. Right after the stop at Newark International Airport, we managed to get our bags off the luggage rack, and I used my well-practiced SEPTA snow-day "Excuse me, please" plus shoulder thrust to clear a path to the nearest exit. While yet more passengers attempted to board in Newark, we burst through the throng and were free on the platform with all our bags intact.

PATH trains boarded from the same platform we arrived on, so we missed Penn Station that trip, but we had plenty of time to explore it on a stay in Newark the following month. We found it to be busy at all hours of the day. The waiting room with its vintage wooden benches and architectural ornamentation illustrating the history of transportation reminded us of Thirtieth Street Station in Philadelphia. The rectangular shape of the waiting room with its high ceiling recalled Thirtieth Street Station too, though Penn Station is smaller and the ceiling is decorated with simple stars on a blue background, whereas Thirtieth Street has elaborate gilded coffers. The Newark station had fewer food vendors, though the merchandise in the concourse bakery and the shop selling panini looked a lot more tempting than anything I've seen at Thirtieth Street Station's larger Food Court.

The best part of Newark's Penn Station would have to be the enclosed information kiosk positioned conveniently near the center of the waiting room, with a patient attendant equipped to answer a host of transportation questions, including those about bus routes and taxis. One of them even provided us with walking directions to nearby Ferry Street, where we made our selection from the many inviting Spanish and Portuguese restaurants in the city's Ironbound District, so called because it was once surrounded by railroad tracks. We greatly admired the kiosk attendants for so capably handling what at times must be a very frustrating job. At one point, we stood in line behind a woman with a heavy foreign accent who had trouble comprehending that Newark was not the city where she was going to find Times Square.

That Friday after Thanksgiving, we each shoved $1.50 into the PATH turnstile and boarded the waiting train. All PATH trains leaving Newark are headed for the World Trade Center, but it takes less than a minute or two to comprehend the system diagram posted in each car and plan the appropriate connections if you want to go to Hoboken or elsewhere in Manhattan.

We crossed two bridges and the site of the former Manhattan Transfer, and soon we arrived at Journal Square. This new station was rebuilt around the time the World Trade Center was originally constructed, when PATH had recently become the new owner of the Hudson and Manhattan tubes. It is located on historic ground—or, rather, historic rock—in the old Bergen Cut excavated through this hill in 1838. The steep faces of the cut blocked the sun as our train approached the station, whose concrete walls appeared to rise out of the very rock.

Our stays in Jersey City and later Newark exposed us to many more PATH stations, and we can recommend Hoboken and Pavonia-Newport for railroad history buffs. Hoboken retains a turn-of-the-last-century look, with hooded stairs to the street that appear original. The columns supporting the station's ceiling have been painted bright blue, and their original capitals are decorated with the letter *H* in period typeface. Pavonia-Newport has been redecorated, and its columns are bright salmon with green capitals each bearing the letter *E,* as the station was called Erie back when it connected with the waterfront terminal for the Erie system. It now offers easy access to the Newport Centre Shopping Mall.

In contrast, PATH stations in New York looked sterile, faced with graying ceramic tiles. At Thirty-third Street, we had to ask a security guard how to exit. He directed us up into the Manhattan Mall, where, just like passengers of McAdoo's day, we had a chance to glimpse at retail merchandise and enter New York City through a store.

Our destination that day was Exchange Place, which had recently been renovated, expanded, and reopened following restoration of PATH service to lower Manhattan in 2003. Here we discovered just how far underground the tunnel in which we had been riding was, as we stood on an escalator for a seemingly endless ride to the street. We observed that the name Exchange Place now applied not to a place where people switched from Pennsy trains to ferries, but to a pristine waterfront promenade with a breathtaking view of the Hudson, the Manhattan skyline, and down-river, the Statue of Liberty.

Back in the seventeenth century, this general area was called Paulus Hook, a piece of farmable land jutting into the Hudson east of the salt marshes. Just to the south, Dutch settlers constructed a fortified village around 1660 at a place the Indians had named Communipaw. As early as 1669, its residents could board a ferry and sail to Manhattan Island. To the north was a tract of land called Pavonia, a word derived from the Latinized name of its absentee Dutch owner, Michael Pauw. Farther north was a swampy island that the Indians referred to as Hopoghan.

In 1834, the New Jersey and Paterson and Hudson River railroads opened, significantly expanding the ferry business in this general location. An 1867 map shows the Hoboken Ferry connecting with the Morris and Essex Railroad near Twelfth Street; the Erie system ferry operating from the foot of Pavonia Avenue; the Jersey City and New Jersey Railroad ferries roughly at the current Exchange Place; and the Central Railroad of New Jersey Ferry connecting with a track along a long pier extending out into the water.

Between 1870 and 1900, Hudson County's population nearly tripled as the major railroads of the day established their beachheads. The New York Central's West Shore Division terminated in Weehawken. The Lackawanna built a freight, commuter, and warehousing complex at the southern end of Hoboken. The Erie shared its Jersey City Pavonia terminal with the New York, Susquehanna & Western Railroad. The Pennsy's Exchange Place terminal was near its own freight complex at Harsimus Cove. The Lehigh Valley Railroad's freight terminal was just south of Exchange Place, on the Morris Canal basin above CNJ's massive riverfront complex, which also served the Baltimore & Ohio Railroad.

Serving all these railroads was Jersey City's Central Stockyard and Transit Company, commonly called the abattoir (slaughterhouse). Cattle, sheep, and hogs arrived in ventilated railcars, some of the animals coming from New Jersey farms, but far more of them from America's western states.

Except for the cry of gulls, the noises and smells of a century past are gone now, as are the masses of commuters in a hurry, though Jersey City probably seems more crowded when the tall office buildings around Exchange Place are open for business. On a regular workday, the atmosphere probably is dominated by the sounds of construction work, since everywhere new apartment complexes are rising and vintage brownstones are being renovated. Plastic Now Renting! signs are flapping all over Jersey City in the river breeze.

As usual, my husband and I managed to obtain a lot of local information by chatting with bartenders and restaurant employees. The manager of an Italian restaurant just a few blocks from Exchange Place recently relocated to Jersey City and told us the experience was like "coming home." He added that his Jersey City apartment cost about half as much in rent as similar lodgings in Manhattan. A bartender in a nearby tavern who grew up in Brooklyn spoke of his amazement at the speed of development in Jersey City. The building in which he works had been scheduled for destruction before a pair of brothers snapped it up and turned it into an elegant dining and drinking establishment. "Nobody waits for zoning or nothing around here," he explained. "They just go right ahead."

We decided to explore this peninsula on one of the key contributors to its transformation—the Hudson-Bergen Light Rail line. Passengers purchase tickets from the same sort of vending machines used for the River-LINE, which were just as reluctant to accept our perfectly good dollar bills. During our long weekend in Jersey City, there were times when we just gave up, succumbed to temptation, and got onboard an approaching train without a ticket, trusting that any transit police would believe we had made a good-faith effort. The Hudson-Bergen's cars are similar to those of the RiverLINE, but they travel more frequently and seem to have a pretty healthy ridership at all hours, including predawn.

Near the Marin Boulevard and Essex Street stations, we found the outlet of the old Morris Canal. Its historic importance is honored by a statue, and its watery remains now serve large pleasure craft as a marina. New office towers stand where the old Colgate Palmolive Company operated for more than a century, but the beloved old Colgate clock, which perched atop the building, has been restored and pointed toward the river.

Riding north through Harborside and Harsimus Cove, we did not see much left of the old Pennsy freight yards, but we did see an old brick

This Jersey City inlet and marina are fragments of the Morris Canal.

A sculpture honors the Morris Canal in Jersey City.

industrial building that looked to us like a power plant. I later learned that it was the 1906 powerhouse for the Hudson and Manhattan tubes. The Newport Centre Mall housed a Macy's and a J. C. Penney, and north toward Hoboken, we saw strip malls with big-box stores such as Target and Linens-N-Things.

Also like the RiverLINE, Hudson-Bergen Light Rail stations are decorated with works of art, whose significance sometimes was lost on me. One station had weathervanes that depicted a tortoise and a hare, but why? Had I missed some inside joke? I understood the art I found at the Liberty State Park Station, though. After passing under a viaduct where a CSX locomotive was hauling a long freight train, we got off and noticed that the glass blocks

Like the RiverLINE stations, the stations of the Hudson-Bergen Light Rail line are decorated with works of art. This one is at Liberty State Park.

forming the station's wall were etched with the logos of railroads and other transportation systems. The title of this work of art was *Riding the Rails.*

We found ourselves in a large park-and-ride near an exit of the New Jersey Turnpike. A waiting shuttle bus gave us a clue that we needed to take one more ride on NJ TRANSIT to actually reach the park. The driver will ask if you are headed to the Liberty Science Center or the ferries. If you really want to see the CNJ terminal, the correct answer is the ferries. Chances are that your youthful bus driver has never heard of the Jersey Central.

The shuttle bus travels down a long, cobbled causeway to what remains of the Central Railroad of New Jersey terminal, a brick structure built in 1889 and enlarged between 1912 and 1914, when its ferry and train sheds were added. Today visitors use a side entrance to this building, which is oriented to face the river. Walk around it and get as close as you can to the water's edge for the best view of its front facade, where a large clock beneath its dominant gable still offers those leaving or arriving by ferry the correct time.

Most people hurry through the terminal's entrance, looking for the right place to buy a ferry ticket to Liberty Island. Train buffs linger to examine the concourse, still decorated with signs saying, To Trains and To Ferries. The concourse once accommodated twenty tracks beneath a Bush-type train shed. Named for A. Lincoln Bush, its designer, the shed is built of concrete and wire glass and designed to admit as much daylight as possible while protecting passengers and platforms from rain and snow. One of the largest of its type ever built, this train shed has earned a place on the National Register of Historic Places. Signs still indicate the proper platform for various trains that once departed every few minutes for Philadelphia or destinations in New Jersey, including the Blue Comet to Atlantic City.

The waiting room is still decorated with original cream-colored glazed bricks and is illuminated by the building's Palladian-

Trains no longer arrive at the CNJ Jersey City terminal at Liberty State Park, but ferries still run to Ellis and Liberty islands.

The train shed at the CNJ Jersey City terminal.

style windows. Since the trains stopped running and Liberty Park opened, it has become furnished with souvenir kiosks where visitors can purchase the green foam headbands with protruding rays so popular as mementos of a visit to the Statue of Liberty.

The terminal used to have a ferry shed on its waterfront side. Its float bridges are still in place and fenced off from the people queued up waiting on the dock for a ride on the Circle Line–Statue of Liberty and Ellis Island Ferry.

The railroad terminal, the Statue of Liberty, and the museum now open on Ellis Island together tell the story of arriving in America for millions of immigrants in the late nineteenth through mid-twentieth century. After glimpsing the statue that meant their ocean voyage was over, most immigrants were transported to Ellis Island to be processed. For most of them, the next stop was a New Jersey waterfront railroad terminal. One enlarged photo on display at Ellis Island shows immigrant children with railroad tickets to their ultimate destinations pinned to their garments for safekeeping.

The CNJ terminal doors were closed in 1967 when the railroad went bankrupt. State and federal funding purchased the property, and the state of New Jersey opened the first section of Liberty State Park in 1976, just as restoration work on the terminal building began. Today the CNJ terminal is open every day except Christmas, with guided tours available in the summer. It is the scene of many special events, including the recently initiated Jersey Central Railroad Heritage Festivals.

The Lackawanna Terminal in Hoboken opened to the public in 1907, just two years after its predecessor was destroyed by a fire originating in a ferry resting in a nearby berth. The simultaneous loss of both ferry and railroad terminals left the railroad free to build a consolidated facility for its patrons, estimated at a hundred thousand daily. A. Lincoln Bush, chief engineer for the Lackawanna at the time, designed the 5-acre train shed. Kenneth Murchison, educated at the Ecole des Beaux Arts in Paris, designed the combined terminals at Hoboken, positioning the buildings for the greatest convenience of commuters. The thirty-five thousand passengers arriving by train, almost all of whom were heading for Manhattan, could reach the vessels easily, but so could the estimated sixty-five thousand that arrived by trolley, on foot, or in a horse-drawn vehicle or automobile that they expected to take onboard the boat. Pedestrians used an upper concourse to the ferry's upper decks, while wheeled vehicles drove onto the lower decks, eliminating a great deal of curbside confusion.

The upper concourse was nearly 500 feet long and has been compared to the Hall of Mirrors at Versailles in its magnificence. It was furnished with columns and chandeliers and housed a fine restaurant with a great river view.

Ferry traffic in Hoboken began falling off in the 1930s, after the George Washington Bridge and the Lincoln Tunnel opened. The ferries were running at a loss by the 1960s, and the Erie Lackawanna halted service in 1967.

Today Hoboken's remarkable ferry terminal is closed even though Hoboken once again has ferry service to Manhattan, thanks to NY Waterway. This transportation system operates from a temporary facility just off the Hoboken train shed, and its printed schedules hail the service as "the cure for the common commute." Additional NY Waterway ferries are located elsewhere in Hoboken and Jersey City, often within easy reach of the Hudson-Bergen Light Rail stations.

In 2003, New Jersey's transportation commissioner announced a plan to restore the ferry terminal at Hoboken. NJ TRANSIT will cooperate with the Port Authority of New York to rebuild six ferry slips and remodel the building's historic facades and interior spaces.

The waiting room at the Hoboken terminal was restored in the 1980s, enabling visitors to experience the understated elegance of Murchison's Beaux Arts architecture. Pale limestone walls rise to a Tiffany glass ceiling skylight. An impressive stair with a decorative cast-iron railing once led to the upper ferry concourse. Architectural ornamentation abounds, but it delights rather than overwhelms the modern visitor. One example is a lion's head sculpture still identified as an ice-water fountain.

The Hoboken Terminal also has a large clock on a tower outside, and its exterior copper facade has aged to a spruce patina. A sign still proclaims the building as property of the Lackawanna Railroad, and standing guard not far away is a statue of the Lackawanna's longtime president, Samuel Sloan.

We skipped Hoboken's waterfront promenade and headed for Washington Street, which was thronged with people, reminding us of Greenwich Village or the Chelsea District of Lower Manhattan. We located the corner of First and Washington, where we found two restaurants and a grocery store where John Stevens once operated his circular demonstration steam railroad. After stopping for refreshment, we found Castle Point on the campus of the Stevens Institute of Technology. A tall building called the Howe Center occupies the ground where Stevens's villa used to stand.

We liked Hoboken. We liked the view from the curving boulevard called Sinatra Drive. We liked the Italian food and the friendly people, including the guy who volunteered directions at the PATH station. And even though an alert police officer stopped to inquire why we were taking notes and so many pictures of a busy transportation hub, we liked the Hoboken Terminal, clearly one of the most beautiful train stations of America's Northeast.

The Region's Rail Trails

The West Essex Trail covers about 3 miles between the towns of Little Falls and Verona in Essex County. Built as a local railroad called the Caldwell Railway Company to foster real estate development, the line became part of the Erie system in 1898. Passengers could use the Erie's Caldwell Branch until 1966. Green Acre funding purchased the right-of-way in 1985.

The Middlesex Greenway runs nearly 4 miles, from Middlesex Avenue in the city of Metuchen to a village called Fords in Middlesex County. It was once a branch of the Lehigh Valley Railroad used to get coal to docks at Perth Amboy. Conrail abandoned the line in 1986 and pulled out the tracks in 1993. Community activists, including the Middlesex Greenway Coalition and the Edison Greenways Group, cooperated to open the trail to the public. Middlesex County purchased the right-of-way in 2002.

This region also includes the Ramsey Bike Path, built on an old trolley right-of-way between Paterson and Suffern, and the Rochelle Park–Saddle Brook Area Bike Path, both in Bergen County. Great trails with scenic views can also be found in the New Jersey section of Palisades Interstate Park.

State park or superhighway? Controversy currently rages over the fate of Jersey City's Erie Cut and Bergen Arches. Constructed between 1906 and 1910, these engineering features are adjacent to the tunnel that the Erie had completed through the Palisades in 1861. The Erie Cut forms a canyon where passenger trains once ran to the Erie's Jersey City terminal under the Bergen Arches, which preserved existing roads. This right-of-way, once hailed as an engineering marvel, is now overgrown and defaced with graffiti. Some government officials want to turn it into a waterfront expressway, whereas preservationists would prefer to create Bergen Arches State Park. Members of the Jersey City Landmarks Conservancy have championed the preservationist cause and conducted tours through the Erie Cut in the recent past.

Shore Region

Great Railways of the Region

The Central Railroad of New Jersey's Southern Division

When the New Jersey Southern Railroad Company became the Central Railroad of New Jersey's Southern Division in 1879, the CNJ faced the question of what to do with a second route between New York City and Philadelphia. The railroad did most of its business in northern Jersey, its passengers and freight reaching Philadelphia by means of the railroad's already well-established route via the Reading's lines. The CNJ eventually expanded all the railroad's southern, or shore, facilities conservatively, seeking to profit from the growth potential its management recognized along the Jersey coastline.

Times were prosperous, and new resorts south of Long Branch, such as Point Pleasant, were beginning to develop, so the CNJ extended its New York & Long Branch (NY&LB) line south in 1880 and 1881. The Pennsy, which by then had branches terminating in Bay Head and Sea Girt, appeared prepared to construct a parallel line all the way to Long Branch. In 1882, these railroads agreed that both could use the tracks of the New York & Long Branch. They renewed this agreement in 1888, when the CNJ formally promised not to build south of its Bay Head junction with the Pennsy, while the Pennsy promised not to build a line that would compete directly with the NY&LB.

The NY&LB made it possible to travel to the northern Jersey coast resorts completely by rail from Jersey City, but the CNJ continued to operate its Sandy Hook Route, a fleet of steamboats, during the summer. Passengers could board a steamboat called the *Asbury Park*, the *Monmouth*, or the *Sandy Hook* at the foot of West Forty-second Street and enjoy what the railroad's advertisements described as "a splendid marine spectacle" as they took in "the grim forts that guard the entrance to the Narrows, the interesting harbor lights with their suggestion of evasive mystery; [and] the passing craft of every type and tonnage." The steamboats served meals, featuring a special lobster dinner and cocktails called the Blue Comet and the Sandy Hook. In a little over an hour, passengers were in the New Jersey town of Atlantic Highlands, where their trains were waiting.

Between 1883 and 1893, the Reading leased the CNJ twice, a relationship complicated by the Reading's intermittent bankruptcies and J. P. Morgan's appearance in the management picture. Beginning in 1887, when both railroads were under the direction of Morgan's bankers' trust, the CNJ underwent a financially beneficial corporate reorganization,

The bluff overlooking the beach at Long Branch, from the Pennsy's 1885 *Summer Excursion Routes.*

acquiring the Vineland Railroad in southern Jersey. In 1901, on behalf of the Reading, Morgan purchased a controlling interest in the CNJ, and the two lines were operated independently but in close cooperation until 1920, when the Supreme Court ordered their separation.

The CNJ had provided through service between Jersey City and Atlantic City since 1889, but by the 1920s, it was seeing business to Atlantic City drop off. An increasing number of tourists preferred to get there by bus or automobile or else use the easier connections of the competing Pennsylvania Railroad Company. CNJ president R. B. White tried to increase passenger revenue by initiating deluxe coach service on its Blue Comet trains, which began running in 1929.

The CNJ painted all its Blue Comet rolling stock blue, including the locomotives, which were also decorated with nickel-plated fittings and gold lettering. The cars had blue seats and carpets, and even the tickets and the porters' uniforms were blue. Each car was named after a known comet. Each train included an observation car plus a diner if it ran at lunch- or dinnertime.

The CNJ operated two Blue Comet round-trips each day in the summer, and these trains covered the 136 miles between Jersey City and

Atlantic City, stopping at Elizabethport, Red Bank, Lakewood, Lakehurst, and Winslow Junction. Before the creation of the Pennsylvania-Reading Seashore Lines, the Blue Comet used the Reading's tracks between Winslow Junction and Atlantic City. Later, the Blue Comet ran on the rails of the former West Jersey and Seashore Railroad Company.

Yet even the classy Blue Comet could not overcome the Depression's effect on vacation passenger business, nor could it stand up to the competition that the Pennsy continued to offer, with trains that departed from Penn Station in Manhattan and ran more frequently. By the late 1930s, the famous Blue Comet was operating at a loss, and in 1939, the CNJ petitioned to abandon the service, which finally ended in September 1941.

The seashore's vacation business suffered further in the era after World War II, when more widespread automobile ownership and the Garden State Parkway gave the shoregoing public new options at different beaches. By the mid-1960s, the CNJ's NY&LB line was the only passenger line still serving New Jersey's northern shore towns, which by then had evolved into residential communities and suburbs of New York. Conrail acquired the CNJ in 1976, and New Jersey's Department of Transportation now operates all that remains of the old Southern Division as part of its North Jersey Coast Line.

Rail Stories of the Region

The New York & Long Branch

Long Branch, named for a branch of the South Shrewsbury River, had long been welcoming Native Americans seeking good fishing grounds when a member of the Perot family of Philadelphia opened a boarding-house in a cottage confiscated from a British officer following the American Revolution. By the 1840s, the town was dominated by hotels that attracted those who had the cash it cost and the time it took to travel there. An anonymous travel account published in 1834, titled *Things as They Are; or, Notes of a Traveler,* described the situation at the time:

> Long Branch is a favourite resort to the citizens of New-York, and still more so to those of Philadelphia, although they have to perform a monotonous ride, over a sandy path, across a pine plain to reach it, while the route from New-York is by steam[boat], excepting four of the last miles. A description of the place may be given in a few words; yet nothing short of a visit to it, and a long familiarity with its aspect in different states of weather, will give any person an adequate idea of its attractions.

After Ulysses S. Grant was elected president, some supporters purchased a cottage for him in Long Branch, which he used as a summer White House. President James Garfield also spent some time in a cottage near Long Branch, where physicians thought the ocean breezes would aid his recovery following an assassination attempt.

By the time the New York & Long Branch Railroad (NY&LB) was chartered in 1868, the Raritan & Delaware Bay and Long Branch & Sea Shore railroads were already serving this resort, but both included steamboat connections with New York City. The NY&LB's proposed all-rail route from Jersey City would get summer visitors to the resort faster and provide reliable service in the winter.

John Taylor Johnston of the CNJ visited Monmouth County to examine the route proposed for the NY&LB, and he made its promoters the generous offer of constructing it in exchange for a long-term lease. The railroad's charter empowered it to construct a bridge or ferry over the Raritan River, but the Pennsylvania Railroad Company objected to any kind of structure that would interfere with traffic on the Delaware and Raritan Canal. The two railroads compromised on the proposed bridge's dimensions, and the CNJ granted the Pennsy trackage rights. The NY&LB engi-

Ocean Grove from the sea, as published in the Pennsylvania Railroad Company's 1885 edition of its promotional *Summer Excursion Routes.*

neers had to construct two other bridges over the Navesink River and Matawan Creek, but the railroad opened for business in June 1875. Ulysses S. Grant came along for the opening train ride in his private railroad car.

The NY&LB immediately extended its tracks south to a station south of Long Branch that would serve growing Asbury Park and Ocean Grove, a village known for its Methodist Tabernacle and city of tents that sheltered its vacationing faithful. Another bridge brought its trains into Belmar and Sea Girt by 1876.

After some initial squabbles early in the 1880s, the CNJ's NY&LB began allowing the Pennsy's trains to run over its tracks. This privilege made it possible for the Pennsy to offer a genuine all-rail route from Manhattan to New Jersey's northern seaside towns after the railroad built its Hudson River tunnels and electrified its lines from Rahway to South Amboy.

The Raritan & Delaware Bay

Unlike most of New Jersey's other longer railroads, the Raritan & Delaware Bay Railroad (R&DB) was supposed to cross Jersey from north to south rather than east to west. It was planned to connect the Raritan Bay with Manchester, Egg Harbor City, and Cape May. It may have seemed unproductive to build a railroad through the undeveloped Pine Barrens in the mid-nineteenth century, but this railroad's promoters intended it to be part of a larger system extending from the New York to Norfolk, with ferries across the Delaware and Chesapeake bays.

In 1853, the Camden and Amboy (C&A) monopolists had prevailed on New Jersey's legislators to rescind a charter for a similar railroad project, but they created so much resentment in southern New Jersey that the legislators felt compelled to approve the next such project proposed. The R&DB was chartered in 1854, but because of fund-raising problems, it was not until 1856 that ground was broken in Port Monmouth, and not until four years later that trains were placed in service to Red Bank. Later that year, the R&DB built tracks to Eatontown and a spur to Long Branch, already popular as a summer resort.

The C&A operators created a little competition for the emerging R&DB with their Long Branch & Sea Shore Railroad Company, chartered in 1863 to run from Sandy Hook through Long Branch and farther down the coast. The two railroads' Long Branch depots were not very far apart, but the Long Branch & Sea Shore had a shorter, more direct route to its pier at Sandy Hook.

In the meantime, the Civil War made it impractical to build a railroad between Yankee New Jersey and Confederate Virginia, putting the managers of the R&DB in the market for a new southern terminus. Hoping for a connection to Philadelphia, they built tracks southwest toward Atco and a connection with the Camden and Atlantic Railroad that linked Philadelphia with Atlantic City. Trains were running along this route by 1862, many cars carrying Union soldiers and military supplies. R&DB management claimed they were not violating the C&A's monopoly between New York and Philadelphia by advertising their route as one that connected Brooklyn and Camden. In 1867, however, a court ruling stopped the R&DB from running trains from its own tracks through to Philadelphia, and that year the R&DB filed for bankruptcy.

In 1870, the R&DB was absorbed into a new system called the New Jersey Southern Railroad Company, together with its old rival the Long Branch & Sea Shore Railroad. The New Jersey Southern spent a great deal on improvements during the next two years, placing it heavily in debt. After the C&A monopoly had become a thing of the past, speculator Jay Gould acquired a majority of New Jersey Southern's stock and bonds, as well as the bonds of the Vineland Railroad, which the New Jersey Southern had leased. In 1873, he replaced the railroad's senior managers and tried to revive plans to extend the New Jersey Southern to the Delaware Bay via Vineland and Bridgeton to a new city (now Bayside). The depression that began in 1873 interfered with these plans, and the New Jersey Southern went bankrupt in 1879. That year, Jay Gould reorganized the railroad and leased it to the CNJ.

The Tuckerton Railroad and Its Artifacts

Like many of New Jersey's earliest towns, Tuckerton, founded in 1699, was nowhere near the pounding surf of the Atlantic, even though it was an important port in colonial days. Located on the Tuckerton River, Tuckerton developed as a whaling community and a place from which southern Jersey's lumber, tar, and turpentine were exported to American shipyards. Tuckerton also became a point of departure for those who wanted to reach Long Beach Island, such as fishermen, duck hunters, and hay fever sufferers seeking the relief of ocean breezes.

Local landowners chartered a precursor to the Tuckerton Railroad in 1866 to be constructed from Tuckerton to Whiting, where it would connect with other rail lines. It was not until 1871 that the Tuckerton Railroad opened for full revenue service. By 1886, the railroad had been extended to Long Beach Island across a wooden trestle from Manahawken, an old Jersey town settled in 1743. From Ship Bottom, its tracks ran north to Barnegat Light and south to Beach Haven.

Manahawken's old train station has been moved but can still be visited in a town park.

The railroad suffered greatly from the Great Depression and a devastating northeaster in 1935 that damaged the roadbed. The government permitted abandonment of the Tuckerton in 1936, and despite attempts to revive the railroad, by the early 1940s most of its tracks had been removed and sold for scrap metal.

Throughout its history, the Tuckerton Railroad carried a great many oysters harvested in Tuckerton and Manahawken to Whiting, and thence to Philadelphia and New York. Today both Tuckerton and Manahawken offer visitors a chance to study the few remaining fragments of this short line, still very fondly remembered in this area.

Manahawken remains a major gateway to Long Beach Island, and those traveling there pass Stafford Township's Historical Society's Heritage Park, where the Manahawken train station has been moved. It is open a few hours each week and houses books and artifacts, a vintage ticket window, and a potbellied stove, as well as several model train layouts.

We drove through Tuckerton several times, passing numerous marinas, looking in vain for some trace of the Tuckerton Railroad's depot and railbed. Finally we pulled in at the local library, where a framed map hanging on the wall identified their former location. We found nothing at the site except a street called Railroad Avenue, but we had better luck at Tuckerton Seaport, a re-created maritime village of buildings representing the trades of those who once made a living on Barnegat Bay. In a reconstructed lighthouse, we found museum exhibits acknowledging the importance of the Tuckerton Railroad in promoting beach and sporting vacations, featuring advertisements touting travel between Philadelphia and Sea Haven, a former resort on the southern end of Long Beach Island. Exhibits in an "oyster house," a commercial building where oysters were processed, also admitted the importance to the industry of the Tuckerton Railroad and informed us that those harvesting oysters didn't always get along with the watermen harvesting clams. A building called the Hotel DeCrab showed us the rustic and primitive kind of accommodations that would have been all that was available to the earliest visitors to Jersey's barrier islands.

When I was planning our trip, I took a look at the Tuckerton Seaport website and mistakenly assumed we'd find good eats at its Parson's Clam House and Napoleon Kelley's Oyster House. The museum exhibits in these two buildings were great, but we had to look elsewhere for fresh seafood. Good thing I did not try to book reservations at the Hotel DeCrab.

Catherine Drinker Bowen Travels

Catherine Drinker Bowen is best known as a biographer of American and British historical figures who promoted constitutional government, including John Adams, Sir Edward Coke, and Benjamin Franklin. Her most famous and popular book is probably her story of America's Constitutional Convention called *Miracle at Philadelphia*. In 1970, Little, Brown and Co. published her autobiography and family history, titled *Family Portrait*. In it, Bowen described summer vacations in Monmouth County's Beach Haven during her childhood at the family summer home, Curlew Cottage.

> Curlew Cottage was a frame house, painted a drab olive brown and perfectly hideous. A wide porch ran all round. A captain's lookout crowned the roof, enclosed in colored glass, bright greens and reds and yellows; you reached it by a ladder from the boys' dormitory. Only one cottage lay between us and the dunes, so that the sound of the surf came loud all day, and at night we went to sleep by it. Not counting the third floor dormitory, there were seven bedrooms, always occupied—and one bathroom with a tin-lined tub, the inside of which I painted white every summer, receiving ten cents for the job.

Prior to World War I and the advent of the automobile, the shore region around Beach Haven was fairly isolated and undeveloped. Only two hotels existed in the area, and Bowen remembers that one was run by a Quaker, who would not allow liquor on the premises. Each June, the family made the trip out on the train, even freighting the family dogs and carrying the cat in a basket.

The trip down for us began in a ferryboat from Philadelphia to Camden, then the dusty, cindery cars, very stuffy until we reached the bridge and the bay, when a life-giving air came suddenly, as if someone had opened a door. When we smelled the sea we used to break into hallelujahs. Each child had his lunch in a paper bag; a hard-boiled egg, a sandwich and a banana, to be eaten on the train. . . . Beach Haven was the end of the railroad line. Mount Holly–Barnegat–Tuckerton–West Creek: the conductor sang out the names. Mamma always took a cab from the Beach Haven station with the maids, the rest of us walked or ran the few blocks to home.

The town had two cabs and a horsecar that ran on rails. Bowen's cottage was a the end of the horsecar line, and though she thought it "a grand thing" to ride through town in such style, it cost her week's allowance of five cents for fare. So more often she recalls walking the half-mile through the marshes to the sailing docks, pestered by flies and mosquitoes along the way.

The Region's Railroad Giants

James Buckelew (1801–1869)

James Buckelew is not well known outside northern New Jersey, but he is the man after whom Jamesburg was named, a town where his house still stands on an avenue now called Buckelew. He is remembered as a regional leader in the fields of agriculture, commerce, and particularly transportation.

One of eleven children, Buckelew became a Jersey farmer who also ran a mill. He championed agricultural innovations, including the use of Jersey marl as fertilizer. He operated factories that produced bricks and draining tiles, and he established a bank in Jamesburg. He was the organizer and first president of the Jamesburg Agricultural Fair.

Working with a partner, Buckelew established stagecoach service between Freehold and Jamesburg, and he eagerly welcomed the prospect of railroads. He favored the creation of the Camden and Amboy Railroad and became a contractor for the construction of its original lines. He later became a promoter for the Freehold & Jamesburg Agricultural Railroad.

In 1840, Buckelew obtained a contract to provide mule teams for towboats for the Delaware and Raritan Canal Company, holding it for a quarter century and becoming one of America's largest mule dealers. He housed hundreds of mules in brick barns that he built on his property.

When he married in 1829, Buckelew purchased a house, part of which had originally been constructed in 1685. As his family and various business interests grew, Buckelew expanded the dwelling to mansion size. The borough of Jamesburg purchased it in 1979, and today it is open to the public under the care of the Jamesburg Historical Association, which houses many artifacts of local history there.

Jay Gould (1836–1892)

Jay Gould was the son of a farmer and shopkeeper in upstate New York. Gould worked in his father's store before he was able to start a business as a self-taught surveyor.

In New Jersey railroad history, Gould is associated with the Lackawanna, New Jersey Central, and Reading. He also made major improvements to the Union Pacific Railroad, which he acquired in 1874. After Gould sold his Union Pacific stock, he gained control of many other American railroads in the West, Midwest, and Southwest in his effort to forge a transcontinental system.

Gould has had the misfortune of being remembered as the quintessential robber baron. He joined forces with James Fisk and Daniel Drew in a conflict popularly called the Erie War to prevent Cornelius Vanderbilt from taking over the New York & Erie Railroad. He also initiated an expansion program at the Erie that forced the Pennsy and its other rival, the New York Central Railroad, to expand and compete. His effort to corner the nation's gold supply blackened his reputation, causing many contemporaries and later scholars to depict him as a predatory villain. Modern business historians are lately beginning to rehabilitate his reputation.

Gould's various enterprises resulted in bringing railroads to a great deal of previously undeveloped American territory. During his lifetime, he acquired a fortune estimated at $75 million. Gould suffered from neuralgia and chronic tuberculosis;

Jay Gould
LIBRARY OF CONGRESS

contemporaries described him as thin and sickly. He died at his home on New York's Fifth Avenue, leaving a will intended to keep his fortune in the family.

George Jay Gould (1864–1923)

Jay Gould's eldest son, George Jay Gould, was well remembered in Lakewood, New Jersey, for the lavish entertainments he held at the estate he called Georgian Court. Many of its buildings remain standing and are used by students at today's Georgian Court University, where they serve as reminders of just how much money the Gould family made in the railroad business and related industries.

George Jay Gould attended private school, became a partner in the brokerage house of one of his father's friends, and received a seat on the New York Stock Exchange as a gift for his twenty-first birthday. His father's will gave him control over the family's millions and its thousands of miles of railroads, as well as his father's interests in two other businesses: Western Union Telegraph Company and the Manhattan Elevated Railway.

Gould did not inherit his father's business instincts or capacity for hard work, instead developing his own talent of spending the family money. He liked parties and the theater as well as the expensive sport of polo, which he helped popularize in the United States. He did build and extend

George Jay Gould
LIBRARY OF CONGRESS

many railroads in an attempt to realize his father's dream of controlling America's first coast-to-coast rail system. But he lost control of most of them following a financial panic in 1907 and turned from active participation in business to management of his investments.

In 1916, members of his own family sued him, claiming he had mismanaged their father's estate, a family dispute that the newspapers eagerly followed for years. Gould made the papers one last time when he died abroad soon after visiting King Tut's recently discovered tomb. Although he died of pneumonia, people seemed to want to believe he was a victim of King Tut's curse.

Sampling the Region's Railroad History

Riding the Rails at the North Jersey Shore:
Present and Future

The North Jersey Coast Line combines the routes of the old New York & Long Branch Railroad, built under the auspices of the New Jersey Central, a Pennsy branch line between Perth Amboy and Rahway, and portions of NJ TRANSIT's Northeast Corridor and Morristown lines. On weekdays most of the year, commuters use the New Jersey Coast Line to get from their seashore homes to places of business in Newark, Hoboken, and New York. During racing season, the train also stops at the Monmouth Park Racetrack. In the summer, this line takes New Yorkers and residents of New Jersey's northern urban areas to the shore. Passengers often have to change in Long Branch from the electric train that brought them there to a train with a diesel locomotive to take them the rest of the distance to Bay Head. At Asbury Park, Belmar, Point Pleasant Beach, and Bay Head, passengers can easily walk to a beach. They can also reach the beach and boardwalk at Spring Lake and Sea Girt, but only after a fairly long hike through town.

The Monmouth–Ocean Development Council has recently joined forces with the Central Jersey Rail Coalition and the New Jersey Association of Railroad Passengers to promote a second passenger line in this region that would run roughly parallel to the North Jersey Coast Line, but located farther inland. Known as the Monmouth-Ocean-Middlesex Rail Project, or MOM, its trains would run between Lakehurst and South Brunswick on the Northeast Corridor Line, with a possible branch connecting with the North Jersey Coast Line at Red Bank, and a future extension south to Toms River and perhaps even Atlantic City.

Citizen activists started campaigning for the rail service around 1997, and their brochures, which can be found in public places in northern Jersey, carry the title *Let's Bring MOM to Central New Jersey*. In 2000, they won the endorsement of New Jersey's legislature and governor by citing studies showing that this region will be home to nearly a quarter of New Jersey's population by the end of this decade, and arguing that rail service would relieve the steadily growing traffic congestion on Route 9, the

Garden State Parkway, and other highways. The rail service promoters are still trying to win over residents of some communities who object to commuter trains running past their backyards, even though freight trains currently operate on these active tracks.

A Small Museum in Ocean Gate

South of the town named Toms River and busy Route 37, which takes tourists to the beaches east of Barnegat Bay, Ocean Gate lies well off the beaten track on the southern shore of Toms River. On a weekday in June 2004, no one was strolling its narrow boardwalk, and the only people on its beach were the lifeguard and the young woman whose job it was to check and sell beach tags.

The town is located on a small cape projecting into Barnegat Bay that was once called Good Luck Point. In 1881, the Pennsylvania Railroad Company built a single track from Whiting to Toms River, through a farm in this area, and out across the bay to the barrier island where seaside resorts later developed between Seaside Park and Bay Head. To get some idea what most of the Jersey Shore looked like in the days before railroads, cross over to the barrier and go south to Island Beach State Park, an area that no railroad ever served. By the early 1900s, many members of the beachgoing public had decided that Good Luck Point was also a nice place with a water view just right for building one's sum-

The Ocean Gate Historical Society occupies the town's old railroad station.

mer cottage, and by 1918, the growing community took a new name: Ocean Gate.

In 1909, the Pennsy constructed a railroad station on Lakewood Avenue. In 1990, the recently organized Ocean Gate Historical Society purchased the station and moved it to its present location at Cape May and Asbury Avenues, restoring it and dedicating it in 1992, and later adding a small museum at this site. The station's waiting room and ticket office now house a number of objects recalling both the railroad history and local history of Ocean Gate. Memorabilia in the collection includes a Pennsy two-man fire-fighting hand pumper.

The museum's hours are very limited, and it was closed when we arrived, but after we spent a few minutes taking pictures, we were joined by an active member of the historical society who was just passing by to check the sprinklers dousing its lawn. Yes, he told us, the structure we were photographing was a real Pennsy railroad station used by tourists coming from both Philadelphia and New York. He explained that the organization's latest project was the restoration of a Pennsy caboose, but the group was interested in acquiring all sorts of objects that illustrated the history of the town. "Gonna be in town Wednesday evening?" he asked us. "Stop by for our meeting. We need new members."

The Pine Creek Railroad in the Park

Not far from the beaches at Spring Lake and Belmar, Allaire State Park occupies about 3,000 acres of Monmouth County. Named for its former owner, James Peter Allaire, the site had been an iron forge since the early 1790s. When Allaire acquired it, he named it the Howell Works, using its facilities to produce iron castings and pig iron for the foundry in New York where he manufactured steamship engines and boilers. The site grew into a self-contained community with mills, shops, a church, and a school. Iron-workers and their families resided there until the mid-nineteenth century.

Many structures remained intact in what local folks came to call the Deserted Village, and they were used for various purposes in the early twentieth century, including a Boy Scout camp and a filming location for movie studios. In 1941, the site's owners deeded it to the state of New Jersey. In 1957, citizens interested in restoring and interpreting the structures formed Deserted Village at Allaire, a volunteer organization today known as Allaire Village, which cooperates with the state's Park Service on programs and events at this location.

Whether or not the Howell Works ever had some primitive form of railroad for moving around heavy things, Allaire State Park became the home of a live steam narrow-gauge preservation railroad called the Pine

Creek, which had been operating in Marlboro since 1952. The railroad's operators reincorporated as the New Jersey Museum of Transportation, and they moved the Pine Creek Railroad piece by piece to Allaire State Park in 1963 and 1964.

The New Jersey Museum of Transportation now has an impressive collection of rolling stock, and the organization offers train rides every weekend from Palm Sunday through October, weather permitting. Its special trains include a Christmas Express and a Haunted Nights Express, which runs at night for three "spooktacular" weekends in October. In September, the organization hosts its annual Railroaders' Weekend Celebration and Machine Show, during which members try to put every piece of equipment they can get to move on their tracks.

In September 2004, a retired surveyor explained to us how the vintage equipment he had on display might have been used to construct an engineering feature like the Horseshoe Curve. Some guys in the shops told us what really went on when they got together for restoration work sessions, and a fellow named Charley showed off his collection of maps illustrating the former railroad systems of Jersey City.

We chose seats in an open car for our ride on the railroad's circular track, but we peeked at the original seats and bathroom fixtures in the restored Canadian National passenger car just ahead of our car on the train. Our conductor commented on that day's lack of "track inspectors," his name

Equipment on display during Pine Creek Railroad's Railroaders' Weekend Celebration.

The train arrives for its first passenger run during the Railroaders' Weekend Celebration.

for the deer and woodchucks that were so accustomed to the trains that they nonchalantly watched them go by. We passed the yard limit sign, went around the track a second time, and then disembarked at the station.

All staff members of New Jersey Museum of Transportation are volunteers who donate thousands of hours of time each year. The group's income comes from dues, donations, gift shop sales, and train fares.

Locomotives Underwater

In the autumn of 2004, the towns of Long Branch and Asbury Park briefly captured the nation's attention when two rare mid-nineteenth-century locomotives were discovered nearby, but railfans will have a hard time studying them unless they rent a boat and diving gear, as these locomotives are resting on the ocean floor about 5 miles off the coast.

The locomotives were first discovered in 1985 by the captain of a charter boat who spread the word to a local historical divers' organization. Generally interested in shipwrecks, the divers became fascinated by the sunken engines and began asking questions. In the ensuing years, railroad historians have identified them as six-wheeled locomotives manufactured in the 1850s, an important and unique discovery because they are in mint condition, covered with barnacles perhaps, but bearing no later alterations. The divers broke the news to the rail enthusiasts associated with the New Jersey Museum of Transportation, better known as the Pine Creek Railroad.

News of the find was kept from the general public until the lost loco-motives could be granted legal protection from souvenir hunters with diving gear. In September 2004, a U.S. marshal dove to the site and attached a notice to one of the engines to warn off poachers. That same month, a documentary aired on the History Channel informed the world about the underwater locomotives. The show addressed the interesting question of where the locomotives came from and how they got to the bottom of the Atlantic.

Railroad historians dismissed the notion that they might have been on a boat sunk by Germans during World War II, speculating that they had been built in New England around 1850. They may have been en route to some Pennsylvania railroad via the port of Philadelphia when the ship carrying them ran into a storm. The engines probably had been secured to the ship's deck, and they may have slipped off in rough seas or been purposely ditched to lighten the ship's load.

The public will get to see more of the locomotives once they have been raised and cleaned of the barnacles and other underwater life forms that now call them home.

Lorett Treese Travels

Having checked out of the library a 1904 edition of Baedeker's guide-book for touring the United States, my husband and I set out to see what had become of what the little red volume described as the "Summer and Winter Resorts of New Jersey." Our Baedeker informed us that a century ago, we might have arrived here from New York on the New York & Long Branch Railroad or from Philadelphia on the Pennsylvania Railroad. We contemplated using the North Jersey Coast Line to get around the area, but with a spring northeaster blowing up the coast, we decided that the train did not run frequently enough to get us everywhere we wanted to go, so we ended up driving from town to town.

Our first stop was Ocean Grove, founded by Methodist ministers who formed the Ocean Grove Camp Meeting Association in 1869, which evolved into a middle-class family resort by the 1880s. Our Baedeker described it as an "extraordinary settlement, possible only in America, in which many thousands of persons, young and old, voluntarily elect to spend their summer vacations under a religious autocracy, which is severe both in its positive and negative regulations." The vintage guidebook told us that visitors could not purchase alcohol or tobacco, nor could they swim or drive on Sunday, when the town's gates were barred against undesirables. No railroad line ever proceeded directly into this town, and an NJ TRAN-SIT train just crossed our path as we drove over the city limits to Broadway.

Today Ocean Grove is a national historic district with late-nineteenth-century cottages and small hotels constructed suffocatingly close together, their gingerbread architectural trim painted in decidedly more conservative colors than the historic structures of Cape May. We easily located the Great Auditorium, built in 1894 and still used by the faithful on Sunday mornings, as well as by orchestras, vocalists, and other entertainers the rest of the week during tourist season. We also found several blocks of canvas tents, which had offered inexpensive accommodations in days gone by. They are now prized by their owners and often have been handed down in families from generation to generation. They were empty that day in early May, and since the men cleaning up the pavilion outside the auditorium did not seem to mind, we took our time and explored them.

We drove north across the bridge over the lake separating Ocean Grove from Asbury Park, founded in 1871 by James A. Bradley. Although named for Methodist bishop Francis Asbury, Asbury Park was conceived as a slightly more worldly alternative to Ocean Grove; it too was alcohol-free, however, and trains were not permitted to stop there on Sunday. According to our Baedeker, Asbury Park was "a prosperous town with at least 50,000 annual visitors, largely frequented by those who object to the religious management of Ocean Grove but appreciate the 'no license' policy of its sister-town."

What we knew about the place we had learned from Bruce Springsteen and various newspaper stories bemoaning its economic decline in the 1970s and 1980s. Developers had tried to reclaim it in the mid-1980s and 1990s, but many of them ended up bankrupt. We had recently read in the

Asbury Park is easily reached from New York by train, but do you really want to go there?

Wall Street Journal, however, that developers were again planning hip new residential units and attractions on the beachfront designed to lure New Yorkers without cars to a seashore destination easily reached by train.

We found paint peeling on the decrepit Metropolitan Hotel as we neared the beach, where the old amusement complex buildings were deserted and neglected. The boardwalk was utterly empty, and though the Stone Pony nightclub was still in business, it did not look like a place that a lady ought to visit. We had heard that the Berkeley-Carteret, the city's classic hotel, had been renovated, but even that had a few boarded-up broken windows. And still standing in the midst of all this desolation was the steel skeleton of a never completed high-rise condominium, now rusted and sagging, but sporting a sign that implied it was still a viable work in progress optimistically renamed Esperanza.

Putting Asbury Park on our list of places to revisit in, say, a decade or three, we headed quickly out of town.

The scenery improved the moment we hit neighboring Allenhurst. From there through Deal to West Long Branch, Ocean Avenue was a boulevard of mansions and a catalog of architectural styles from the turn of the last century. Beaux Arts, Tudor, and Iberian domiciles were interspersed with triple-wide ranch houses built later in the twentieth century, each carefully landscaped. A chain-link fence protected the Church of the Presidents (so called because seven U.S. presidents had attended services there), which had recently been awarded a restoration grant from the New Jersey Historic Trust.

Our century-old guidebook had a long entry for Long Branch, calling it "one of the most popular watering-places in the United States (50,000 summer guests) and also one of the most fashionable, in the sense in which the word is used by those who fondly imagine that lavish display of wealth is evidence of high social position. . . . The modern watering place occupies a bluff, which here faces the sea, at a height of 20–35 ft. above the beautiful sandy beach." I was also carrying a map dated 1878, which showed that there had been large hotels fronting on Ocean Avenue facing the sea, including the Mansion House, Ocean Hotel, Clarendon, and East End Hotel near where Jay Gould had owned considerable beachfront property.

My husband and I had visited Long Branch about a decade earlier because relations of his recalled being there circa World War II. Back then, we had found Ocean Place Resort and Spa, which looked like a nice place, but nothing else appealing about this town.

As we proceeded from West Long Branch into Long Branch in 2005, we found a whole lot of condo developments, either newly opened or

The Twin Lights of Navesink were a familiar landmark to those arriving by steamer at Atlantic Highlands, where travelers boarded trains.

still under construction. A gated community called Renaissance on the Ocean seemed to have taken its name from the trend. Having thought that Ocean Place would be the only place in town where we might want to have lunch, we were delighted to find numerous restaurants and bistros on and near Ocean Avenue. We finally chose the Portuguese cuisine of a new eatery right outside the Ocean Place parking lot on a street that my old map told me used to be called Depot Avenue.

We continued north through Monmouth Beach, Sea Bright, and Highlands Beach on a narrow strip of land between the Atlantic Ocean and the Navesink River. We stopped at Twin Lights Historic Site, where we visited the brownstone lighthouses built in 1862, visible from 40 miles at sea and a landmark for New Yorkers arriving at the shore via the steamboats of yesteryear. It was well worth a drive up a steep hill for a magnificent view of Sandy Hook and the Verrazzano Narrows Bridge and Manhattan skyline, which was just barely visible beneath the clouds of the approaching storm.

Passengers in yesterday's steamboats would have changed to railroad cars at Atlantic Highlands, a town that still has signs directing visitors to a Manhattan Ferry. We followed them through a pleasant town to a marina where vessels dock for a carrier called *Seastreak* ("Call 1-800-BOATRIDE!"). There were quite a few cars in the parking lot but no boats at the dock.

We continued on to the village of Leonardo, where the state of New Jersey opened a marina to the public in 1949. We located the Trail Activity

You can still reach Manhattan by ferry from Atlantic Highlands.

Center and trailhead for the rail trail on the old New Jersey Central line called the Bayshore Branch. We might have walked the trail, but it had turned cold and windy, so we abandoned the coast for Route 35. The highway runs roughly parallel to the tracks of today's North Jersey Coast Line, where we witnessed an NJ TRANSIT train crossing the bridge across the Navesink at Red Bank.

We followed NJ TRANSIT rails through the pleasant towns of Belmar, Spring Lake, Sea Girt, and Manasquan. Spring Lake and Sea Girt had the finest mansions, Manasquan the best selection of restaurants. Spring Lake also had the largest and most interesting downtown, frequented by tourists as well as people who actually live there. We stayed in a Spring Lake hotel very near the railroad station, and the first sound I heard the next morning was the grade-crossing toot of a NJ TRANSIT diesel locomotive horn.

There was one more northern Jersey resort we wanted to see: the former spa called Lakewood, once visited by Americans rich and famous from October through May from its founding around 1880. The town's most opulent estate belonged to the convivial George Jay Gould, who named it Georgian Court, either after himself or the Georgian Revival style of his mansion built by architect Bruce Price overlooking Carasaljo Lake. Gould helped popularize polo in the United States, and his estate included a structure to house and train his polo team. It was also furnished with a bowling alley, swimming pool, and other amenities. John D. Rockefeller Sr. was Lakewood's other famous resident, but unlike Gould, he was not known for entertaining.

After Gould died in 1923, New Jersey's Sisters of Mercy purchased Georgian Court and moved their College of Mount Saint Mary to the site, renaming the school Georgian Court University at the family's request.

Today Lakewood has another school, called Beth Medrash Govoha, which is famous for rabbinical and Talmud studies, and a great many orthodox Jews live in the town. It seemed strange driving through town on a Saturday morning looking for a Catholic university while men in hats and prayer shawls and boys with curls and yarmulkes were heading on foot for Sabbath services. Since Georgian Court University's campus is a national historic landmark and an arboretum open to the public, we were permitted to park and wander the grounds at leisure.

We found the building, now called the casino, where the polo team had trained; the university uses it as a gymnasium. Gould's mansion is not open for touring but is still most impressive from the exterior. Steps lead down from one side to a water gate—Gould's private canal off the lake. Here and in the extensive Italianate gardens, Gould's sculptures and

Georgian Court, the estate of George Jay Gould in Lakewood, now houses a Catholic university. Statues of saints have joined the pagan decor of its garden.

garden decor fraught with antique pagan motifs now share the landscape with the Sisters' statues of the Madonna and Jesus.

The cash that built Georgian Court did not come entirely from railroads, but the place is an artifact illustrating the kind of opportunity that once existed in the transportation and related industries.

The Region's Rail Trails

Monmouth County's Henry Hudson Trail extends 9 miles from Aberdeen to its Trail Activity Center near Avenue D in Leonardo, just outside the town of Atlantic Highlands. Users can conveniently park at the center, pick up a trail map, and use the restrooms.

The trail occupies part of a former Central Railroad of New Jersey (CNJ) right-of-way, once known as that railroad's Bayshore Branch, which was used for passenger service until 1966. Conrail took over the line but abandoned it in 1984. That same year, Monmouth County officials issued bonds to acquire the right-of-way for possible future development as a light rail line. It was instead turned over the Monmouth County Park Service, which developed it as a recreational trail.

Trailhead of the Henry Hudson Trail

Part of the Freehold and Jamesburg Railroad Trail.

The trail, which opened in 1995, includes quite a few renovated railroad bridges that carried the line over streams and wetlands. Users pass a former railroad station in Port Monmouth. The trail's wide, paved surface makes it easy to navigate. An attendant at the Trail Activity Center told us, "You can rollerblade the entire thing." Horses are also permitted; motorized vehicles are not.

Someday this trail system may be extended to the marina at Atlantic Highlands, where a ferry now runs to New York City. Work is currently under way to open 12 more miles of trail south from Matawan's train station to Freehold Borough, where it will terminate at a CNJ train station. This southern extension will be constructed on the right-of-way of the former Monmouth County Agricultural Railroad, opened in the 1860s to take farm products to a rail pier in Keyport. It will be called the Monmouth Heritage Trail.

The Freehold and Jamesburg Railroad Trail is 4 miles long, extending from Allenwood to Farmingdale along a portion of the old Freehold & Jamesburg Agricultural Railroad. The trail website, called Traillink, cautions users that it has "some interruptions" and is not marked as well as it could be. A map of Allaire State Park showed us where it ran through the park, but after we thought we had located it by crossing the tracks of the Pine Creek Railroad and climbing a fence, there was nothing to confirm that we were on an established rail trail. At Allenwood, this trail joins the Edgar Felix Memorial Bikeway, which runs another 4 miles to North Main Street in Manasquan and occupies another portion of the Freehold & Jamesburg Agricultural Railroad.

In Ocean County, the planning board is purchasing segments of the CNJ's former Barnegat Branch to construct a bike trail and linear park extending 14 miles from South Toms River to Barnegat, roughly parallel to Route 9.

Greater Atlantic City Region

Great Railways of the Region

The Pennsy Down the Shore

From 1871, when the Pennsy acquired the United Companies and the West Jersey system, until market forces demanded the Pennsy's consolidation with the Reading, the Pennsylvania Railroad Company actively expanded toward the Atlantic coast. Its acquisition of the Camden and Atlantic Railroad would be the cornerstone of this program, designed to offer its services to people who might want to vacation down the Jersey Shore.

In 1879, the Pennsy purchased a small railroad between Pemberton and a town called Whiting's (now Whiting), where passengers could take the Tuckerton Railroad to the port of Tuckerton. The Pennsy constructed a line east from Whiting through the town of Toms River to a small cape on Barnegat Bay called Good Luck Point (now Ocean Gate). The railroad built a trestle bridge across the bay, which was relatively narrow here, to a formerly isolated Baptist retreat called Sea Side Park on Long Beach Island. By the end of summer in 1881, the line extended north on the island to Bay Head.

It would necessarily be a while until Long Beach Island could take off as a tourist destination, so the Pennsy simultaneously mounted an effort to compete for passengers traveling to New Jersey's far more popular Atlantic City. Prevailing on the West Jersey Railroad, which it controlled, the Pennsy constructed a branch from Newfield to Atlantic City via Mays Landing and Pleasantville, which was chartered as the West Jersey & Atlantic Railroad. Opened in 1880, this new railroad extended its reach south to Somers Point when it acquired a narrow-gauge line built in 1880, which it converted to standard gauge in 1882.

The Pennsy expanded operations in the northern shore counties by leasing the Freehold & Jamesburg Agricultural Railroad Company, which had started out in 1851 as a local railroad serving farmers who used its connection with the Camden and Amboy (C&A). The C&A had invested in this small railroad, which had prospered financially, making Freehold a transshipment point for freight. The railroad carried a lot of marl, a type of earth that could be extracted for use on farms as fertilizer. Following the Civil War, the railroad expanded toward the coast through Jersey's marl region, merging with the Sqankum and Freehold Marl Railroad and the Farmingdale & Squan Village Railroad Company in 1879. It increased its trackage to more than 27 miles, extending southeast to Farmingdale as well as Sea Girt on the coast, the town where Robert Field Stockton happened to own a summer home.

Following a fierce rate war, the Pennsy finally acquired the competitive Camden and Atlantic line to Atlantic City and started coordinating its operations with the Pennsy's West Jersey Railroad, making considerable improvements to both lines. It double tracked the Camden and Atlantic between Berlin and Atlantic City and began standardizing the equipment used by both subsidiaries. In Atlantic City itself, the Pennsy expanded the Camden and Atlantic terminal so that it could also serve West Jersey Railroad trains to that destination. By the early 1890s, the West Jersey main line to Cape May had extensions making it possible to take trains to Sea Isle City, Ocean City, Wildwood, Avalon, and Stone Harbor.

In 1893, the Pennsy completed a spur from the Tuckerton Railroad's Manahawken station to Long Beach Island, which it leased back to the Tuckerton. Three years later, the Pennsy created the West Jersey and Seashore Railroad Company through one big merger of the various operations it controlled in South Jersey.

The Pennsy project that most significantly improved its service to South Jersey was the bridge it opened across the Delaware River in 1896. The Delair Bridge made it possible to move freight and passengers from Pennsylvania and the west to the shore and the southern part of New Jersey without transferring people or goods to a ferry or routing them via Trenton. The Pennsy selected a site well north of where ferries plied the river between Camden and Philadelphia, and the railroad obtained charters from the legislatures of both Pennsylvania and New Jersey enabling them to begin construction work in 1895. When completed, the bridge was more than 1,900 feet long and would carry trains 50 feet above the river's high-water mark. In 1897, the Pennsy completed its extension from the bridge to Haddonfield and its Atlantic City main line, and began advertising Atlantic City as a destination to potential tourists in western Pennsylvania, Ohio, West Virginia, and points even farther west.

During the early 1900s, while the Pennsylvania Railroad Company was constructing tunnels beneath the Hudson as well as its Pennsylvania Station in Manhattan, managers made the decision to electrify one of its Camden-to-Atlantic City lines. The railroad chose its longer route through Newfield and Mays Landing, originally constructed by its West Jersey Railroad. Its first electric trains began running to the shore in 1906.

Through the early years of the twentieth century, competition between the Pennsylvania Railroad Company and the Reading for traffic to New Jersey's shore points remained fierce. In places, the two railroads' lines were nearly parallel. Both railroads kept their physical assets in peak condition, providing top-rate accommodations and constantly seeking to shave minutes off the length of their runs.

Once these two major railroads faced additional competition from automobiles operating on improved highways, the parallel lines seemed increasingly redundant, and it became obvious that merging them into a single entity would make a great deal of sense.

Rail Stories of the Region

The Camden and Atlantic

In 1820, Dr. Jonathan Pitney established his medical practice in Absecon, a fishing village and port on the Jersey mainland with a harbor that never seemed to freeze in winter. His rounds sometimes took him to an island also named Absecon, but locally known as Further Island. Its broad beaches, tall dunes, and sea breezes convinced him that a great many people would come for recreation or to improve their health if only they had a cheap and convenient way to get there.

Members of the Leeds family had lived on Further Island ever since 1793, when Jeremiah Leeds built a log hut there. By midcentury, the island had a saltworks and a few other modest frame homes that had been constructed by Leeds family descendants. Aunt Millie Leeds took in boarders, generally sportsmen who came to fish or hunt ducks.

Pitney's idea for a railroad to Further Island found little support among the businessmen of Atlantic County who shipped the oysters, clams, and wood they harvested to New York by seagoing vessels. He joined with other railroad promoters and sought support among the glass and iron manufacturers elsewhere in South Jersey's Pine Barrens. Pitney and his fellow visionaries finally approached the New Jersey legislature in 1851, but their idea for a railroad to a bathing village that did not yet exist was met with some preliminary objections, followed by indifference. The Camden and Amboy monopolists allowed the Camden and Atlantic Railroad to be chartered in 1852 largely because they did not regard the project as competition, but a "railroad to nowhere" that would certainly fail.

The new railroad's original directors made their first official visit to their remote proposed terminus in June 1852. Some questioned whether tracks could be constructed over the salt marshes between the port of Absecon and Further Island, but Richard Boyse Osborne, a civil engineer making preliminary surveys, assured them that it could be done. The

Trains heading for Atlantic City passed through Hammonton when the 1868 edition of John W. Barber's and Henry Howe's *Historical Collections of New Jersey* was published.

opportunity for land speculation persuaded them to move forward; the island's real estate could be had very cheaply to be resold as building lots once the railroad was built.

Construction began that year from Cooper Point in Camden, through Haddonfield and the stagecoach stop then known to travelers as Long-A-Coming, to the town of Atco (location of a glassworks), then along an almost straight line to Absecon, where the railroad constructed a wharf on Absecon Inlet. Service began in July 1854 with a ferry transporting passengers to the island until a bridge could be built over the bay. On Further Island, passengers could board another train and ride the remaining distance to a large, brand new structure called the United States Hotel. On opening day, six hundred invited guests enjoyed a banquet in this building, which was only partially completed at the time.

The new railroad faced financial difficulties in the 1850s, but business improved the following decade. The key to its success was the day trip that it made possible for Philadelphians of modest means who got little time off and could not afford the price of a visit to Long Branch or Cape May. By the 1870s, the railroad was cleverly offering excursion rates to groups and organizations, allowing them to keep a percentage of the money made by enticing passengers to purchase tickets on a particular train for a group outing in Atlantic City.

The railroad purchased new locomotives and passenger cars in the early 1870s. Anticipating increased traffic during the nation's centennial in 1876, the Camden and Atlantic built a new terminal near Atlantic

City's Atlantic and South Carolina Avenues. Near Cooper Point, the railroad purchased land and developed a picnic area.

By 1883, when the Pennsylvania Railroad purchased a majority of its stock, the Camden and Atlantic had managed to survive an uncertain beginning, create a new city on an isolated and virtually uninhabited island, and even see some reasonably profitable years.

The Philadelphia & Atlantic City

In 1876, the Camden and Atlantic Railroad lost its own monopoly on transportation to the then thriving Atlantic City when the Philadelphia & Atlantic City Railway Company (P&AC) was incorporated. Founded by renegade Camden and Atlantic directors, this line was intended to bring even more tourists to Atlantic City with better service and cheaper fares, improving the resort's business climate and raising its property values. The founders hoped that their decision to construct a narrow-gauge railway would lower the expense of construction per mile and keep operating costs down. The railroad would be able to use lighter locomotives and cars that could run faster and cover the distance more quickly.

The P&AC began construction in 1877, laying tracks between Atlantic City and Pleasantville. Within about ninety days, all the work was done, the contractors having worked day and night, breaking records for speed of construction. On July 7, 1877, the inaugural train from Camden arrived in Atlantic City, where invited guests feasted at a downtown hotel. Passenger service began one week later.

By 1878, the P&AC was running five round-trips on weekdays and two on Sundays. Passengers could choose excursion or first-class coaches. They arrived at a terminal on Atlantic Avenue between Missouri and Arkansas Avenues, initially a remote area, but one that quickly became developed once the trains were running. Two years later, the P&AC built a branch off its main line from Pleasantville to Somers Point, where tourists could take a ferry across the bay to a community called Ocean City out on a barrier island.

The P&AC charged less for tickets than the Camden and Atlantic and greatly increased the demand for Atlantic City day trips. It was unable to price its product in a way that made its revenues exceed its operating costs, however, and the railroad entered bankruptcy in July 1878.

The directors of the Camden and Atlantic were very interested in purchasing their rival, intending to use the parallel narrow-gauge line for freight, but a court injunction prevented this takeover. When the P&AC was sold at a foreclosure sale in 1883, the railroad found a willing buyer in the Reading Railroad, which was at that time intent on expanding its empire. The Reading converted the railroad to standard gauge and double tracked it, making it ready to take even more tourists down the shore.

Atlantic City, the Railroad Town

While the Camden and Atlantic Railroad was under construction, Richard Boyse Osborne and other railroad directors began planning a resort at the end of its line. By December 1853, they envisioned a city with parallel avenues named after the world's oceans and intersecting streets named after America's states, which then numbered twenty-seven. Osborne designed a city intended to accommodate large crowds, with a grid system that would be familiar to people who lived in Philadelphia, making it easy for them to get around. Further Island would never do as a name for this place, so Osborne came up with Atlantic City, which was enthusiastically received by the railroad's board.

The Camden and Atlantic directors incorporated the Camden and Atlantic Land Company in 1853 to purchase land and sell building lots. They also planned the United States Hotel, intended to be the world's largest. They promoted construction of a lighthouse, which went into service in 1857 and became a tourist attraction, offering a great view of the Jersey coastline. By 1870, Atlantic City had nearly three hundred houses and over a thousand permanent residents, plus accommodations for ten thousand summertime visitors in its hotels and boardinghouses.

The beach and Boardwalk of Atlantic City, from the Pennsylvania Railroad Company's 1885 *Summer Excursion Routes.*

That year, Alexander Boardman, a conductor for the Camden and Atlantic Railroad, and Jacob Keim, a hotel owner, persuaded the city to build a long, wooden walkway on beach pilings from the lighthouse to Missouri Avenue to prevent tourists from tracking sand into the hotels. It was constructed in sections so that it could be removed in the winter to prevent its destruction by storms. Known as the Boardwalk, the popular structure was extended and widened over the years. Entrepreneurs established businesses on the Boardwalk, some giving rides to tourists in rolling chairs while others manufactured postcards and saltwater taffy they could take home as souvenirs. By the turn of the century, taking a slow walk on the Boardwalk in Easter Sunday finery had become an Atlantic City tradition.

Atlantic City's first ocean pier was constructed in 1881, but its most famous one, called the Steel Pier, was built in 1898. Designed for recreation, it had a casino, music hall, dancing pavilion, and auditorium. On some occasions, as many as eighteen thousand people visited Steel Pier.

To keep the visitors coming through the month of September, in 1921 business leaders came up with the Miss America Pageant, a bathing-beauty contest that was supposed to identify the most beautiful girl in

Trains once brought many conventioneers to Atlantic City's old convention center, now called Boardwalk Hall.

By the time the Pennsy published its 1903 edition of *Summer Excursion Routes,* Atlantic City had grown in popularity.

the nation from among those who won contests in their states. Although not as popular as it used to be, the Miss America Pageant continues to be held each year.

Following World War II, tourists ceased to come to Atlantic City in such great numbers, and the city deteriorated. Atlantic City appealed to the New Jersey state legislature to legalize casino gambling in an effort to bring the visitors back. Atlantic City's first casino opened in 1978, and today the casinos bring in millions of people each year.

In 1989, Atlantic City got a new rail terminal in a location where it would soon be joined by a new convention center. Both Amtrak and NJ TRANSIT ran trains to Atlantic City from 1989 until 1995, when Amtrak pulled out.

Railroads had a tremendous impact on Atlantic City's development. Indeed, the Camden and Atlantic was responsible for the city's very existence. Today most visitors do not come by train, however, and many do not even realize that such a thing is possible. Those interested in learning about Atlantic City's unique and fascinating history and the city's relationship with its railroads should visit the Atlantic City Historical Museum, open daily and located on Garden Pier.

Walt Whitman Travels

Born on Long Island, Walt Whitman became a journalist and editor in New York City and elsewhere, but he is best remembered for his 1855 volume of free verse called *Leaves of Grass,* depicting American life at the time the book was published. He lived in New Jersey from 1873, and in 1879, he chronicled a trip to Atlantic City for an essay for a newspaper called the *Philadelphia Times:*

> As I went to bed a few Saturday nights ago, it entered my head all of a sudden, decidedly yet quietly, that if the coming morn was fine, I would take a trip across Jersey by the Camden and Atlantic Railroad through to the sea. . . .
>
> Walking slowly, or rather hobbling (my paralysis, through partial, seems permanent), the hundred rods to the little platform and shanty bearing the big name of "Pennsylvania Junction," were not without enjoyment to me, in this pleasant mixture of cold and sunbeams. While I waited outside the yet unopened hut, two good-looking middle-aged men, also journey-bound, held animated talk on gunning, ducks, the shore, the woods, the best places for sport, etc. Each had a long story to tell about "his gun," its properties, price and history generally. Their anecdotes of wonderful shots, bird events, and such—all with many idioms, and great volubility. . . .
>
> From the car-windows a good view of the county, in its winter garb. These farms are mostly devoted to market truck, and are generally well cultivated. Passing the little stations of Glenwood and Collingswood—then stopping at old, beautiful, rich and quite populous Haddonfield, with its fine tree-lined main street. . . .
>
> Some four or five miles south of Haddonfield we come to the handsome railroad station of Kirkwood. Here is a beautiful broad pond or lake. They are getting the ice from it, and a good sight it is to see the great, thick, pure, silvery cakes cut and hauled. In summer, the pond with its young groves and adjacent handsome pavilion, forms a favorite destination for Philadelphia and Camden picnics. . . .
>
> Five miles from Kirkwood we strike the thrifty town of Berlin (old name Long-a-Coming, which they had much better kept). We reach Atco, three miles further on—quite a brisk settlement in the brush, with a newspaper, some stores, and a little branch railroad to Williamstown. At the eighteen mile post the grade of the railroad reaches its highest point, being one hundred and eighty feet above the level of the sea. Here is what is called by the engineer, "the divide," the water on the west flowing to the Delaware, and on the east to the ocean.
>
> The soil has now become sandy and thin, and continues so for the ensuing forty miles; flat, thin, bare gray-white, yet not without agreeable features—pines, cedars, scrub oaks plenty—patches of clear fields, but much larger patches of pines and sand. . . .
>
> After this a broad region of interminable salt-hay meadows, intersected with lagoons and cut into everywhere by watery runs—the strong sodgy perfume, delightful to my nostrils, all reminding me again of "the mash" and the continuous South Bay of old Long Island. . . .

Passing right through five or six miles (I could have journeyed with delight for a hundred) of these odorous sea prairies we come to the end— the Camden and Atlantic depot, within good gun-shot of the beach. I no sooner land from the cars than I meet impromptu with young Mr. English [of the *Atlantic City Review* newspaper] who treats me with all brotherly and gentlemanly kindness, posts me up about things, puts me on the best roads and starts me right.

A flat, still sandy, still meadowy region (some of the old hummocks with their hard sedge, in tufts, still remaining) an island, but good hard roads and plenty of them, really pleasant streets, very little show of trees, shrubbery, etc., but in lieu of them a superb range of ocean beach—miles and miles of it, for driving, walking, bathing—a real Sea Beach City indeed, with salt waves and sandy shores ad libitum.

The Region's Railroad Giants

Jonathan Pitney (1797–1869)

Jonathan Pitney was born in 1797 in Mendham, Morris County, New Jersey, and studied medicine at Columbia College. After having practiced medicine on Staten Island and in Morris County, in 1820 he took up residence in Absecon, a port town then in Gloucester County, and married Caroline Fowler, a local girl. Pitney supported the creation of Atlantic County out of part of Gloucester County and was chosen the first director of the new county's Board of Chosen Freeholders in 1837. Pitney represented Atlantic County at a constitutional convention to rewrite the state constitution in 1844.

He first became involved in local improvements in 1835, when he began requesting that America's Congress appropriate funds for a lighthouse on Absecon Island, also called Further Island, where a body of water had become known as Graveyard Inlet thanks to numerous shipwrecks there. He collected sworn statements from many ships' captains whose vessels had gone down at this treacherous spot. Congress finally came up with $35,000 for Absecon Lighthouse, but not until 1854. After additional funds were appropriated in 1856, the lighthouse was put into operation in 1857.

Having come to appreciate the health benefits of sea air, Pitney envisioned a bathing village on that same island that would rival Long Branch and Cape May. He began writing letters to the editors of Philadelphia newspapers but enticed few visitors because of the difficulties of reaching the place.

Now a bed-and-breakfast, Dr. Jonathan Pitney's house still stands in Absecon. A sign points the way to the city he founded.

Pitney began lobbying the state legislature for a railroad in 1851, but he was unsuccessful until he attracted the support of Jersey entrepreneurs in the glass and iron industries who recognized the benefits of a railroad to their businesses. Pitney became a director of the Camden and Atlantic Railroad once it was formed and served on committees to purchase land, select the site for Atlantic City's depot, and supervise construction of the railroad.

He later participated in efforts to develop the town of Absecon, where he had invested in many tracts of land. Pitney died of tuberculosis in 1869.

Richard Boyse Osborne (1815–1899)

Born in Ireland in 1815, Richard Boyse Osborne split his engineering career on different projects in Ireland and the United States. Osborne first came to the United States in the 1830s, and he learned about building railroads from Moncure Robinson, one of the world's foremost civil engineers.

By the early 1840s, Osborne had become chief engineer for the Reading Railroad. While back in Ireland visiting family, he was hired to build the Waterford and Limerick Railroad.

In the late 1840s and 1850s, Osborne once again resided in America, where he worked on railroads in Pennsylvania's anthracite region concurrently with his work on the Camden and Atlantic. Besides designing Atlantic City, Osborne engineered the railroad's route and the structure that would support the weight of a train across the salt marshes to Absecon Island.

Following a bout with typhoid fever, Osborne retired to England in 1856. He lived to see Atlantic City succeed and the Camden and Atlantic become part of the Pennsylvania Railroad Company.

Sampling the Region's Railroad History

The Miniature Trains of Atlantic County

Spend a whole week down the shore, and chances are that by day three or four, you and your loved ones will be sunburned and bored with the beach. You may find yourselves looking for something else to do within easy driving distance. Atlantic County has two destinations that make good beach alternatives, and both offer train rides in open coaches drawn by modern replicas of the 1863 C. P. Huntington locomotive.

Storybook Land, in Egg Harbor Township, has been operated by the same family that built it in 1955. A huge statue of Mother Goose presides over a landscape of structures that illustrate beloved children's stories and nursery rhymes, such as the Little Red Schoolhouse and Alice in Wonderland. Geared for preschoolers, Storybook Land specializes in nonscary rides, including a classic carousel and old-fashioned automobiles. The J&J Railroad makes a circuit of the park, providing a good way to preview the other attractions. When the kiddies get cranky, families can retreat to the Caboose Café for refreshments.

The town of Smithville has a much longer history, having been founded in the eighteenth century along a route known as the King's Highway to the colonials who constructed it over an existing Indian trail. This road is now called New Jersey Route 9, or the Old Shore Road. In 1787, James Baremore constructed the Smithville Inn to accommodate people traveling that route by stagecoach. In 1949, Fred W. Noyes and his wife purchased and restored the inn, reopening it as a restaurant in

The Smithville Railroad Company is one of two attractions not far outside Atlantic City that offer train rides.

1952. Over the years, the Noyeses created a new nostalgic Smithville by identifying old buildings earmarked for destruction and relocating them near their restaurant, where they rented them to shopkeepers.

Today there are two retail complexes near the Smithville Inn, joined by a bridge across a lake. The inn is still the heart of Smithville Village, also known as the Old Village. Village Greene operates on the other side of the lake. This destination is for adults, who can browse shops stuffed with antiques, knickknacks, garden ornaments, baskets, and handcrafted items such as scented homemade soap; sample wine at the two tasting rooms operated by New Jersey's Tomasello Winery; and stay overnight at a newly opened B&B. Colorful roosters wander the grounds freely, entertaining visitors with their loud crowing and annoying the shopkeepers by perching on merchandise displayed outdoors.

The Smithville Railroad Company operates from the back room of a diminutive railroad station in Village Greene. The day we visited, the miniature train was in its tiny maintenance yard behind the parking lot. Its locomotive was being serviced for a craft festival the following day, when a great many people were expected to descend on this site and probably want to ride it. Its engineer, who was using his downtime to operate Village Greene's carousel, told us that the railroad had been purchased from a company that manufactures amusement rides and constructed at Village Greene, where it had been an attraction for about fifteen years. When we left, I noticed the roosters chasing each other down the tracks and wondered how many had ended up as roadkill over the life of the railroad.

Dr. Jonathan Pitney's House

In 1824, Dr. Jonathan Pitney purchased a house in Absecon, another town on the Old Shore Road that had long been a stagecoach stop. The house had been built in 1799, and toward the middle of the nineteenth century, as Absecon grew, Pitney renovated and gentrified the structure in the Italianate style, which was popular at the time. He constructed a three-story addition with a hipped roof and cupola. His office was on the first floor at the rear. Pitney left the house to his two sons, and it remained in the hands of various family members until 1946.

Still standing at 57 Shore Road, the house is now operated as a bed-and-breakfast, where guests can stay in one of its rooms, furnished with colonial or Victorian antiques, or in a suite in the adjacent guest quarters. A collection of before and after pictures illustrates the restoration of this house in the 1990s.

Lorett Treese Travels

A sign on one of the NJ TRANSIT vending machines in Thirtieth Street Station warned us that the machines preferred "old, non-tinted twenty dollar bills." We inserted two of them, and since the round-trip fare to Atlantic City was less than $24 for my husband and myself, a whole lot of Sacajawea and Susan B. Anthony dollars plummeted down into the change compartment, making me anticipate the slot machines that we knew we would find in the city fondly nicknamed AC.

Most of the people waiting on the platform for the Atlantic City Line were women of a certain age in a holiday mood. Several couples were carrying luggage, as we were, for a midweek getaway. The train pulled in right on time, and we were soon admiring Boathouse Row as we traveled parallel to the Schuylkill Expressway. We crossed the Schuylkill on the same viaduct used by SEPTA's R7 and followed its route past the North Philadelphia Station.

We slowed as we approached the Delair Bridge. We didn't get much of a view of the bridge itself as we began rumbling over it, but for some reason our train stopped just as we were exactly midway across the Delaware, giving us the peculiar sensation of being indefinitely suspended in midair.

Light pours into Atlantic City's new train station, located near its convention center.

At Cherry Hill, the train stopped behind a shopping center, and when we pulled in at Lindenwold, where it is possible to change to or from PATCO Speedline trains, a great many people joined us. We sped up after that, and the historic railroad station at Berlin, where we did not stop, did not seem all that long-a-coming. We zipped smartly through pine forests and over flat farmland glazed with an icing of snow on this February morning, picking up more passengers at the stops along the old route of the Camden and Atlantic: Atco, Hammonton, Egg Harbor City, and Absecon. Then we were crossing the salt marshes on a route where we could share the billboards with those driving cars on the Atlantic City Expressway.

We had read that plans were being discussed to link NJ TRANSIT's Atlantic City Line with its northern Jersey commuter system and its new RiverLINE. A brochure we picked up during our stay mentioned a planned link from Atco to the Cape May Seashore Lines, which would make it possible for people staying in Atlantic City to reach Cape May by train and vice versa. Any of these plans would have put more riders on our Atlantic City–bound train, which was hardly half full by the time we arrived, but then, it was a weekday in February.

We marched through the city's new ultramodern train station, filled with light but few people except for those we followed off our own train. In days gone by, visitors could hire a carriage to take them to their hotel or boardinghouse, or step onto a one-horse coach whose driver would get them to any point in town. NJ TRANSIT includes free shuttle service to all the casino hotels, provided on the same vehicles by the same drivers who run the city's jitneys, or private bus system.

We checked in at the hip, new, very cool Borgata, a casino hotel popular enough to incur a lengthy wait in a snaking airport-style line before we got our room keys. While waiting, I overheard another excited guest exclaim into her cell phone, "I'm here! I'm in my happy place!"

The Borgata reminded me a great deal of a train station. Its restaurants, shops, and lobby are all built off its casino floor, which makes for a great deal of foot traffic through the casino. At any hour of the day, half the people there are hurrying to get someplace else while the other half are patiently waiting, not for a train, but for the right combination of symbols to appear in the window of a slot machine.

I thought I knew how to operate a slot machine but discovered that, like many NJ TRANSIT ticket-vending machines, the Borgata's slots wanted nothing to do with my proffered dollar. Finally a gentleman whose job it was to keep the wrong people out of a VIP lounge gave me and my equally puzzled husband some instruction. You need a $5 bill to activate the Borgata slots. To our utter disappointment, those same machines did not reward the lucky winners with cascades of change. Win and you get a receipt.

It took but a few minutes for us to lose $5, and that was the extent of the gambling we did in two days in Atlantic City. Let me be the first to admit that I just do not get gambling. We walked all around the Borgata's casino, observing other people gamble, and saw no one who looked like he or she was having a really good time. I watched a guy place $100 bill on a blackjack table and lose it on the very next cards that were dealt. Okay, our lunch the following day cost more than $60, but it was a lot more fun spending money on pasta and pizza in a cozy Italian restaurant with a wood-burning oven after hiking the Boardwalk in the brisk winter air.

We did enjoy the Borgata, however. Our beautifully appointed room had a glass wall with a view of AC's skyline of beach hotels in one direction and Jersey salt marshes in the other. Because of the orientation of the hotel, we could watch the winter sun rise over the Atlantic at one corner of our window and set in the other. Each evening, we turned our chairs

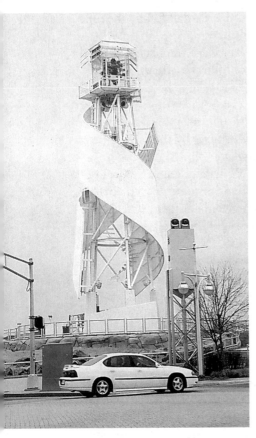

See it while you can. This work of art resembling a lighthouse in a park on roughly the site of Atlantic City's old Atlantic City Railroad depot and 1934 Union Station may soon make way for an expansion of an outlet mall called The Walk.

toward that window and stared out at city lights while sipping red wine.

I had brought along a map that showed where the hotels and railroad stations of yesteryear were located, and we went in search of historic remains. On the site of the old United States Hotel, we found a parking garage. Where Pennsy trains once stopped at the head of what is now Bacharach Avenue (formerly the railroad's roadbed), we saw a bank and parking lot. The sites of the old Atlantic City Railroad station and 1934 Union Station were occupied by a park dominated by a structure intended to suggest a lighthouse. Atlantic Avenue, once furnished with a tramway, was lined with dollar stores and shops offering loud music and flashy jewelry, not to mention peep shows with "live girls." But Michigan Avenue between Atlantic Avenue and the new Convention Center had been reclaimed with an outdoor outlet mall called the Walk, which had already proven to be lucrative enough for the city to consider expanding it into the neighboring park. See that lighthouse work of art while you still can.

In the winter of 2005, a great deal of construction work was being conducted on and near the Boardwalk, where we also discovered a few tributes to the city's past, including a small billboard with some railroad history and a picture of the United States Hotel. We found more railroad information at the Atlantic City Historical Museum on Garden Pier, where the exhibits and an excellent orientation film told the story of Atlantic City and its railroad lines.

One of AC's historical selling points was its location within a curve of the Atlantic coast that sheltered it from storms and moderated its climate. In a history of the county published in 1900, I had read: "There is a mildness and balminess in the air that cannot be expressed in words, it must be felt to be understood. So pronounced is this, that invalids coming here in the winter from snow-bound cities call Atlantic City the 'Florida of the North'; they unbutton their heavy wraps, walk up and down the board-walk, or along the beach, and thoroughly enjoy the climate." The February day when we walked the Boardwalk, it was far too chilly for us to unbutton our coats, but the brisk air kept the beach deserted and reminded me of many winter walks taken during my youth in Stone Harbor, where my parents had a vacation home.

As for AC's casino hotels, if you like historic architecture, stay at Resorts or the Claridge. The Tropicana has been remodeled to suggest Old Havana, and the Showboat was in the process of reconstructing New Orleans. Besides the Borgata, we liked the Atlantic City Hilton Casino Resort best.

For a transportation experience that is a lot of unintended fun, ride the local privately operated public transportation system run by the Atlantic City Jitney Association. The jitneys are minibuses that follow four routes roughly connecting the city's casinos and other points of interest. The little vehicles seat only thirteen people, and when they are full, the drivers let on only the same number of people as those getting off at that stop. A fistfight nearly broke out when someone bucked a line,

Atlantic City's famous Boardwalk.

separating the members of a party, until those about to be left behind figured out that they could simply board the next jitney and meet up at their destination. Three ladies kept reminding one increasingly irritated driver to let them know when they had arrived at the stop nearest the Hilton. After their fourth request and his reply, "I'll let you know," he added under his breath, "Turn up the hearing aid, honey."

Looking for amusement rides in Atlantic City? If Steel Pier is crowded, just try your luck on a jitney.

The Region's Rail Trails

The Linwood Bikepath extends 5 miles through Atlantic County from Pleasantville to Somers Point. Its wide, paved surface attracts many users from the mainland residential communities through which it passes. Early in the morning, it is busy with those walking or bicycling for exercise, who often greet the crossing guards posted at its numerous street intersections like old friends.

The pleasant Linwood Bikepath allows recreation where trains once ran between Pleasantville and Somers Point.

This rail trail occupies the right-of-way of a line built in 1880, later called the Somers Point Branch for the Pennsylvania-Reading Seashore Lines, which ran from Atlantic City through the mainland communities and back out to Ocean City. Freight trains once shared its tracks with an interurban trolley that ran until 1948. Rail traffic ceased in 1966. In the town of Linwood, trail users pass a replica train station with a rail-crossing sign.

In 2002, the Atlantic County Park System created the Atlantic County Bikeway, another wide, paved recreational trail covering the 8 miles between Mays Landing and the Egg Harbor Shore Mall. Also a former right-of-way on the Pennsylvania-Reading Seashore Lines, this trail was funded by a federal grant and the Atlantic County Open Space Trust Fund. Its users are separated from vehicular traffic except where the trail intersects one avenue where they can activate a traffic signal for safe crossing.

Estell Manor Park, also located in Atlantic County, has recreational trails in a forested area with a nature center, but they are not located on former rail corridors.

SECTION SIX

Southern Shore Region

Great Railways of the Region

The Reading in Jersey

Throughout its history, the railroad commonly known as the Reading did most of its business in Pennsylvania. It got its start as the Little Schuylkill Navigation, Railroad, & Coal Company in 1826, serving the mining industry primarily in the Schuylkill River Valley and surrounding Pennsylvania counties. It became an important anthracite railroad as well as a major passenger carrier and rival to the Pennsy for Philadelphia-area commuter traffic.

Once the Reading acquired the Philadelphia & Atlantic City Railway Company in 1883, the Reading renamed it the Philadelphia and Atlantic City Railroad Company and initiated a major rebuilding program that included converting its narrow-gauge tracks to standard gauge. The Reading's shops built new locomotives for this railroad's new passenger trains, and by 1885, the railroad could offer customers a faster trip to Atlantic City in much nicer surroundings. The gauge change also improved this line's freight revenue. Within a few more years, the Reading expanded its Camden terminal and double tracked the route. All the improvements began to draw business from the Pennsy's Camden and Atlantic line, forcing that railroad to compete. Both railroads worked hard to maintain the tracks, where they operated some of the world's fastest trains.

In the 1880s, the Reading extended another of its acquisitions in southern New Jersey, the Williamstown & Delaware River Railroad, chartered in 1871, in order to link Williamstown with the Camden and Atlantic Railroad and the New Jersey Southern Railroad at Atco. By 1888, this railroad also extended to Mullica Hill via Glassboro.

The next year, the Reading integrated operations in South Jersey, creating the Atlantic City Railroad Company by consolidating the Philadelphia and Atlantic City Railroad; Williamstown & Delaware River Railroad; and two smaller properties, the Camden, Gloucester and Mount Ephraim Railway and Kaign's Point Terminal Railroad.

In the following decade and the early years of the twentieth century, the Reading built tracks to Sea Isle City with one branch into Ocean City and another to Cape May via Tuckahoe. By 1901, the Reading brought into the Atlantic City Railroad Company the smaller southern Jersey lines that it had leased or purchased, including the Camden County, Seacoast, and Ocean City railroads, becoming a serious challenger for the Pennsy's traffic to New Jersey's southern shore resorts. Real estate developers on barrier islands called Seven Mile and Five Mile islands brought the towns of Avalon, Stone Harbor, and Wildwood into the Reading system in the 1910s by promoting construction of two additional short lines connecting with the Atlantic City Railroad.

By the 1920s, the Reading's Atlantic City Railroad still carried a lot of people to the shore but was having a hard time turning this traffic into profit. The Benjamin Franklin Bridge and the development of New Jersey's highway system made automobile excursions easier, also fostering the development of bus companies that offered rides to the shore. In 1929, the Reading tried to compete by running its own buses between Philadelphia and Atlantic City. Because the Pennsy was facing the same problems, it made sense to form a joint company called the Pennsylvania-Reading Seashore Lines in 1934 in an attempt to eliminate redundancies.

Meanwhile, the Reading faced an even larger problem starting around 1930, as gas and petroleum, as well as other forms of energy, largely replaced coal, its major freight commodity. Losses continued to grow through the 1960s, and the Reading filed for bankruptcy in 1971. Its Philadelphia-area commuter lines became part of SEPTA, and its remaining viable freight lines were later absorbed by Conrail.

The history of the Reading is currently preserved by the Reading Company Technical and Historical Society and the Anthracite Railroads Historical Society.

Rail Stories of the Region

The West Jersey of Southern Jersey

When it was chartered in 1853, the West Jersey Railroad Company was not the first attempt to connect Camden with Cape May. Such a route was a logical business proposition because Cape May had been a popular resort since the early years of the 1800s, but Philadelphians had to reach it by steamboat or stagecoach, neither of which operated during the winter months. A railroad running between Camden and Cape May could also count on freight business from the glass factories in New Jersey's southern counties, which might be able to grow and expand if they had a better way to ship their products. Two previous attempts had been made to build railroads in this region, but neither had seen any success.

Because the Camden and Amboy monopolists were busy obstructing what would become the New Jersey Southern Railroad's proposed line, they were inclined to view the prospective West Jersey as an alternative

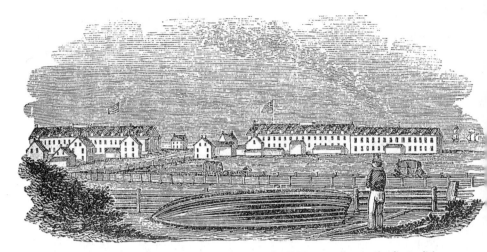

Cape May was already a favorite vacation spot in 1845, according to the first edition of *Historical Collections of the State of New Jersey.*

that posed less threat to their own enterprises. Their support for the West Jersey was intended to appease the residents of southern New Jersey and their elected representatives. The Joint Companies invested in the railroad, and Robert Field Stockton became its first president.

Construction began in 1855, and two years later, equipment borrowed from the Camden and Amboy was running between Camden and Woodbury. Inspired by significant stock subscriptions from the residents of

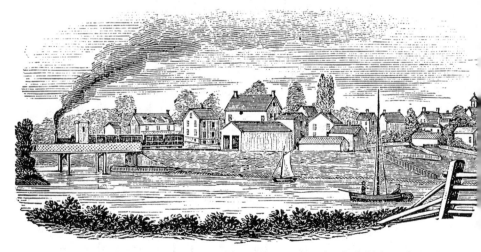

The West Jersey Railroad was supposed to reach Cape May, but its initial terminus was Woodbury. Construction had not actually begun when the 1845 edition of *Historical Collections of the State of New Jersey* was published.

The beach at Cape May, from the Pennsy's 1903 *Summer Excursion Routes.*

Bridgeton, the next segment of railroad completed reached that town by way of Glassboro. In 1859, other South Jersey residents formed the Millville and Glassboro Railroad Company, whose rights to extend to Cape May were acquired by the Cape May and Millville Railroad, completed in 1863.

In 1868, the New Jersey legislature permitted the Millville and Glassboro Railroad Company to be merged with the West Jersey, which leased the Cape May and Millville the same year. The West Jersey also leased four other South Jersey short lines, thus gaining control of most of the railroad mileage in that part of the state.

The resulting West Jersey rail system made Cape May even more popular and also allowed South Jersey farmers to ship produce to Philadelphia more quickly. Canning factories sprang up near new railroad spurs, and the newfound ability to ship milk by rail made dairy farming profitable for the first time in the region.

When the Pennsy acquired the United Companies in 1871, the railroad gained control of the West Jersey rail system, as the United Companies had always had

Wildwood had woods back in 1903, when the Pennsylvania Railroad Company published this photo in *Summer Excursion Routes.*

an interest in this network and by then owned the majority of its stock and bonds. All the railroads in the West Jersey system were formally consolidated in 1896 as the West Jersey and Seashore Railroad Company, which was officially leased to the Pennsy in 1930.

Pennsylvania-Reading Seashore Lines

In 1932, when the Board of Public Utility requested that South Jersey's two major competing railroads consolidate, such a concept had ceased to be revolutionary or even all that new. Pennsy and Reading managers had discussed such a merger several times during the late 1920s, and in 1931, New Jersey's legislature had directed the state's public utility commissioners to determine whether a merger was feasible.

At the time, the Reading's Atlantic City Railroad was suffering annual deficits, but the Pennsy's West Jersey and Seashore was still making a profit thanks to the Delair Bridge, though its Atlantic City traffic was declining too. Because the Pennsy and the Reading competed not only in South Jersey, but also in Pennsylvania's coal regions and the corridor between Philadelphia and New York, there was no doubt that the ultimate deal would be vigorously contended, but that the Pennsy would probably dominate whatever sort of entity might emerge.

On November 2, 1932, the presidents of the two railroads announced their unification agreement in Atlantic City. As of January 1934, New Jersey would have a new railroad called Pennsylvania-Reading Seashore Lines (PRSL). The Pennsy would own two-thirds and the Reading one-third of this railroad, which would not include the Pennsy's relatively new Delair Bridge, though PRSL trains would use it. The stockholders of the original railroads approved the deal, with the only opposition coming from people who owned shore property in Stone Harbor and Avalon, who protested the proposed abandonment of rail service to their towns.

The merger made it possible for both the Pennsy and the Reading to eliminate duplicate trackage. The Camden and Atlantic route became the main line to Atlantic City. The Reading took up the tracks between Winslow Junction and Atlantic City. The Pennsy eliminated more than 40 miles of tracks in Cape May County.

The new railroad would construct a new Union Station in Atlantic City on Reading property a block away from the existing station of the Atlantic City Railroad. The building cost $4 million and was completed in February 1935. The masonry station was classical in design, and surviving photographs and architectural drawings show that it had a shape and facade resembling Pennsy's Thirtieth Street Station in Philadelphia, which was constructed around the same time.

The Reading and the Pennsy also consolidated their Atlantic City bus services, forming a PRSL subsidiary called the Pennsylvania-Reading Motor Lines in 1933, although their ultimate goal was to unload the marginally profitable service to another carrier.

The exigencies of World War II canceled vacation plans for many Americans, but business remained good for PRSL during the war because the U.S. Army took advantage of Atlantic City's ample hotel rooms and turned the town into a basic-training center for new recruits. Troops drilled in the city's Convention Hall and practiced amphibious landings on the beaches. The troopers' family members also traveled by way of PRSL to visit relatives in uniform before their deployment overseas.

Not long after the war ended, Atlantic City's Race Track opened in 1946. The railroad constructed a spur enabling gamblers to get to the track, naming the trains that took them there Pony Expresses.

Despite PRSL improvements, such as adding new self-propelled rail diesel cars and air-conditioning the passenger coaches, business declined in the 1950s as more and more vacationers chose to fly to distant locations or drive to developing shore resorts other than Atlantic City. In 1965, work being done on the Atlantic City Expressway made it necessary to remove the PRSL tracks in downtown Atlantic City, forcing the railroad to move its terminal to the edge of town. The Union Station was turned into a bus terminal.

Despite annual losses approaching $5 million, PRSL continued to receive cash advances until 1970 from the Reading and the new Penn Central Railroad, which had been created by the merger of the Pennsy with the New York Central. The PRSL became part of Conrail on its creation in 1976. In 1982, passenger service to Atlantic City was terminated because of track problems on the main line, and NJ TRANSIT substituted buses for the few riders it had left. It would be seven years before Amtrak and NJ TRANSIT brought back passenger service to Atlantic City in 1989.

The Oyster Wars of Cumberland County

Native Americans were first to enjoy the tasty oysters to be found in the Maurice River Cove. Colonial Americans developed the Maurice River oyster industry, shipping the shellfish by wagon through the Pine Barrens to Philadelphia. By the mid-nineteenth century, oystermen were using improved dredging equipment and shipping their product to the city by schooner.

Once the West Jersey Railroad was open for business from Camden to Bridgeton in South Jersey, shipping oysters by rail became a much desired

Much commercial fishing and processing still goes on in Bivalve and Shellpile, along the Maurice River, but the massive freight station that once occupied this river shore is gone, as is the town of Maurice River on the opposite shore.

possibility. In 1866, local merchants incorporated the Bridgeton & Port Norris Railroad Company. Constructed in 1872, the railroad permitted oystermen to ship oysters to destinations along the Pennsylvania Railroad Company's main line to cities as far distant as Pittsburgh and New York.

The Bridgeton & Port Norris Railroad went bankrupt in 1878, but it was reborn the following year as the Cumberland & Maurice River Railroad. As the original tracks had been rather cheaply constructed, the new railroad's managers borrowed money and made needed improvements. Shipments increased in the early 1880s, and the railroad also instituted passenger service, enabling oystermen to commute to work.

By 1887, the CNJ had purchased most of the Cumberland & Maurice River Railroad's stock and leased the line to its Southern Division. South Jersey oysters began reaching their ultimate consumers via connections of the CNJ and Reading railroads, rather than those of the Pennsy.

To reclaim the oyster freight business, the West Jersey, then controlled by the Pennsy, retaliated by establishing the Maurice River Rail Road Company on the river's opposite (eastern) shore. Before 1887 was over, this railroad had built nearly 10 miles of tracks from a town called Manumuskin to a point opposite the wharf that its CNJ competitors called Bivalve. The new terminus was named Maurice River.

For many years, the two railroads competed to ship Maurice River Cove oysters. The West Jersey added ferry service to Bivalve via tugboat.

The processing and freight complexes on both sides of the river grew. Business peaked in the 1920s, when motor carriers also began to compete for South Jersey oyster freight. The Depression suppressed the industry, but it managed to survive until the 1950s, when an oyster blight attacked the Delaware Bay, causing harvests to fall dramatically.

Today rural Route 553 runs roughly parallel to the old route of the Bridgeton & Port Norris Railroad through towns where trains used to stop: Fairton, Cedarville, Dividing Creek, and Port Norris. Other roads branch out through the salt marshes to Delaware Bay beach towns such as Gandys Beach and Fortesque, once the "Weakfish Capital of the World" and still the destination of many sportfishermen.

The grid of streets in Port Norris has many fine late-nineteenth-century dwellings dating from its oyster industry heyday. Commercial fishing vessels are lined up at the piers between Bivalve and a neighboring village called Shellpile. A narrow road and parallel bike trail connect these points, perhaps on the railbed of the former freight station. I had heard that a genuine oyster boxcar was being restored for display in Bivalve but found no sign of it when we visited the Maurice River Cove area in the spring of 2005.

Nothing is left of competing operations on the opposite shore, where the town of Maurice River seems to have vanished. In fact, there is no way to cross the river south of Mauricetown. The tracks of the Maurice River Rail Road Company are still visible here and there on the eastern shore, but trees of respectable size growing in between the rails indicate that they've been unused for a very long time.

Richard Atwater Travels

The Atwater family of Millville were among those who purchased property in Sea Isle City, a resort just being developed in the early 1880s. Richard Atwater kept a diary in which he described purchasing the family's lot and building their vacation home. Parts of his entries for 1881 and 1882 describe the initial primitive nature of their surroundings and the improvements following the completion of the West Jersey's spur from Sea Isle Junction (near Seaville) to the island:

> 1881: The life this first year was unique and can never be repeated. We were nearly alone on the island. A few prospectors during the middle of the day were the only disturbers of our solitude. The beach was rich with shells and strewn with old wrecks, some high and dry and others showing the timbers at the fall of the tide. The flowers and berries were luxuriant and in great variety. We used to take long strolls in bathing costume. Boys and girls alike were barefoot and were clad in the simplest garments. A pair of goats with

their kid afforded much amusement and some annoyance as they ate cloth-
ing, stole food from the fire and climbed the stairs in quest of food or fun.

1882: We moved down June 11 with Alice Atwater and two servants.
We came to Seaville Station and rode to the house in carriages, an improvement over the previous year but we looked enviously at the railroad not
yet quite completed to the island. . . .

On July 11 the trains ran and the transit to the island became a far easier matter. Since this event, although the island has lost its peculiar charm
of isolation, it has gained in many substantial ways.

As our commissariat, starting from Millville at five o'clock p.m. with a
can of milk and a basket of meat and groceries, I landed at Seaville and was
met by the stage specially provided by agreement with Mr. Landis, the
founder. At Seaville I bought berries and bread. At Henry Corson's I added
vegetables. At Ezekial Bossi I added ice. I filled our water can and took in
melons, etc. The stage was usually well filled by the time we reached the
thoroughfare and the transfer of the freightage from the stage to the ferry
boat was thence by cart to our castle. It was no easy task.

After August 1 the bridge was completed and the butcher and baker
wagons came over twice a week. Public wells supplied water for washing
and cooking. We had no communication with the shore at night until the
bridge was completed. Fortunately we had no sickness nor accident during
the whole season requiring a doctor or other help from the mainland. On
September 13 we moved back to Millville.

The Region's Railroad Giants

Charles Kline Landis (1833–1900)

Charles Kline Landis was born in 1833 to an upper-class Philadelphia
family. He studied law and practiced in Philadelphia but is now remembered mainly as a South Jersey real estate developer and the founder of
several of the region's towns.

In 1857, soon after the Camden and Atlantic Railroad was operating,
Landis purchased 5,000 acres where the railroad had established a stop it
called Hammonton. Landis advertised the merits of the area and induced
a number of would-be farmers living in New England to buy property.
Within a few years, those farmers were shipping surplus to Philadelphia
and New York City.

When Landis heard that another railroad was being constructed
between Glassboro and Millville, he purchased about 20,000 acres along
its route, where he planned a second city to be called Vineland. Landis
envisioned an ideal community, including a town with industries, shops,

Charles Kline Landis founded Vineland, which looked like this when the 1868 edition of *Historical Collections of New Jersey* was published. The train through town would have been part of the West Jersey system.

and schools surrounded by farms, orchards, and vineyards. In 1861, he drove a stake into the ground to mark the center of town, renaming the main road through the area Landis Avenue. While hired workers were still cutting down trees, Landis managed to get America's postmaster general to agree to establish a post office in a location where no one yet lived, and Landis was appointed Vineland's first postmaster.

Landis advertised Vineland real estate in newspapers published in Boston, New York, and Philadelphia. He is said to have personally greeted everyone who stepped off the train. Around the time of the Civil War, a few Italians had settled in Hammonton, and Landis invited more to Vineland, where he hoped they would use their skills to cultivate grapes. Many Italian and Sicilian immigrants bought land in an area that Landis named New Italy, where the streets were given Italian names. By the late 1880s, the borough of Vineland had nearly three thousand inhabitants.

A former New Yorker named Uri Carruth, who had become editor of a Vineland newspaper, characterized Landis as a greedy landlord and dictator. Landis grew depressed and paranoid. In 1875, when Carruth wrote about his personal life and accused him of madness, Landis confronted him and shot him in the head. Landis's friends rallied, and he was acquitted of murder by reason of "temporary insanity" and set free.

Landis planned a third town called Sea Isle City on an island formerly known as Ludlam's Beach. The West Jersey Railroad agreed to build a spur from a junction just north of Seaville to his community, which he planned to furnish with canals, fountains, and artwork, possibly inspired by his 1874 travels in Europe, where he had been seeking a cure for his depression. Landis published real estate advertisements in 1881, and the following year, those who were building Sea Isle City cottages could reach them by rail.

Landis's fourth community was considerably less successful. The town called Landisville still exists in South Jersey, but it never did become the seat of a new county that Landis had hoped would also be named for him.

Sampling the Region's Railroad History

Miniature Train at Wheaton Village

Glass manufacturers were among the initial advocates of rail service in southern New Jersey. Those interested in learning about traditional glass-making processes can visit Wheaton Village, named for Dr. Theodore Wheaton, a pharmacist who started a glass factory in nearby Millville in 1888. His grandson Frank acquired the collection of American glass now on display in a museum in this village, which is designed to resemble a rural glassmaking community around the turn of the twentieth century. Visitors can also watch receptacles being made at the village's glass factory, where contemporary artists find the facilities and equipment to develop their craft.

The village's other attractions surround its village green. Its shops include a Christmas shop, paperweight shop, and general store. A train station originally constructed in 1897 by the Ocean City Railroad (later part of the Reading system) in rural Palermo was moved to Wheaton Village. Once used to load freight traveling to Camden or Ocean City, this station is now where visitors can board the village's miniature train, another C. P. Huntington replica. Since 1975, the train has traveled its loop through the village's woods, reminding visitors of the importance of railroads and delighting the many children visiting Wheaton Village on school tours.

Cape May Seashore Lines

The first tracks to reach Cape May were constructed by the Cape May and Millville Railroad in 1863. In the 1890s, the Reading built tracks to Cape May, and by the turn of the century, its trains often raced those controlled by the Pennsy on its West Jersey and Seashore Railroad Com-

The C. P. Huntington Train at Wheaton Village awaits passengers in the shed that houses it next to the Palermo station.

A Cape May Seashore Lines train on the tracks at Historic Cold Spring Village.

pany, on parallel lines between Cape May Court House and Cape May. After formation of the Pennsylvania-Reading Seashore Lines, largely the Reading's tracks remained in Cape May County.

After Conrail halted passenger service to Cape May in 1981 and freight service in 1983, a man named Tony Macrie of Hammonton formed Cape

May Seashore Lines (CMSL), a privately owned passenger railroad with a long-term lease agreement with NJ TRANSIT. Although the railroad was founded in 1984, it was not until 1999 that trains were running between Cape May Courthouse and Cape May. Today its three daily passenger trains, named the Resorter, Mermaid, and Sun Tan, operate during the summer. A Halloween Transylvania Express runs in October, and a Santa Express operates around Christmas. The railroad also offers charter service to schools, clubs, and organizations.

The trains cross a bridge across the Cape May Canal, which, unlike Jersey's other major canals, was not constructed in the nineteenth century. This canal was built by the U.S. Army Corps of Engineers during World War II, so that ships could avoid German submarines lurking off Cape May Point at the entrance to the Delaware River bay. CMSL trains also stop at Historic Cold Spring Village, allowing passengers to visit this tourist attraction as well as Cape May in a single day. Soon CMSL may put into service a Blue Comet observation lounge car built in 1927, currently undergoing restoration in the Jersey town of Rio Grande.

CMSL plans to extend service to Tuckahoe, and then farther north to a junction with the Atlantic City Rail Line. Macrie has recently signed contracts enabling CMSL to bring freight service back to Cape May County.

In the meantime, CMSL serves Cape May County's biggest industry: tourism. It can be difficult to find a place to park among the brightly painted Victorian cottages of historic Cape May. CMSL allows day trippers to park elsewhere and trade the hassles of traffic for a scenic train ride.

Historic Cold Spring Village

The costumed interpreters of Historic Cold Spring Village show visitors what life was like in a nineteenth-century farm village in southern New Jersey. They demonstrate trades, crafts, and activities in structures moved to this site from other locations in Cape May and Cumberland counties by the Salvatore family in the years since they acquired the property in 1973. During the 1800s, Cold Spring was a popular destination for those visiting Cape May who wanted to taste the therapeutic water of its spring, said to be the southernmost source of fresh water in New Jersey.

Railfans may appreciate the fact that they do not have to purchase tickets and actually enter Historic Cold Spring Village in order to see its railroad artifacts, which are all located outside the village proper in the parking lot near the tracks of Cape May Seashore Lines. In 1975, a train station built in 1894 in neighboring Rio Grande was moved to the village. The frame station had been built by the West Jersey Railroad and later used by Pennsylvania-Reading Seashore Lines. The station's sign now reads "Cold Spring," and CMSL trains use it for their station at Historic Cold Spring Village. Nearby is a West Jersey Railroad signal tower, constructed in 1894 at Woodbine Railroad Junction. Another building at this location may look like a railroad freight station, but it is actually a reproduction that houses the site's restrooms.

Historic Cold Spring Village hosts several annual special events, including a Celtic festival, Revolutionary War encampment, Confederate weekend, Union encampment, and the Railroad Days Festival, when visitors can ride miniature trains and observe model and garden-scale railroads.

South Jersey Railroad Museum

If CMSL can extend service to Tuckahoe, South Jersey visitors might be able to ride its trains to this town's South Jersey Railroad Museum, located in a building that once housed a school and later a municipal building. The museum has been operated by the Shoreline Railroad Historical Society for about six years.

Its old classrooms are now filled with operating model railroads in different gauges, illustrating railroad equipment and scenery from different

The South Jersey Railroad Museum operates in a former school building in Tuckahoe. Its classrooms now contain model layouts.

eras. "It's a place where a bunch of guys get together and play," one member told us. One room had a layout that climbed its wall, with trains operating on different levels. This layout had many moving figures, including children on swings in a park and gandy dancers fixing the tracks of a railroad. We were invited to examine a layout, still under construction in the basement, that would re-create the ride between the yards in Camden and Cape May. In answer to our question about when the layout would be finished, our guide shrugged, smiled, and replied, "Nothing's ever really finished around here."

Lorett Treese Travels

I spent many weekends in Cape May County in my life, but very rarely have I gone down the shore in the summer. One June weekend in 2005, however, my husband, Mat, and I officially became "Shoobies," the word that Jersey residents have been using since the 1920s to describe people who come to the seashore for a short time in the summer—possibly for only a single day. The summer solstice had passed, school was out, and we were driving over the Commodore Barry Bridge, gateway to the lower Jersey Shore, where we planned to spend a weekend.

We left pretty early on Friday morning and encountered little traffic heading south on Route 55. The highway quickly took us below Millville, where we made our choice among several backroads through the Pine Barrens to the Garden State Parkway and the Old Shore Road, the two major highways that run parallel to the coastline. My dad used to know every possible shortcut in this area, and I thought we must have happened upon one of his favorites, because we passed no more than two cars between Port Elizabeth and Tuckahoe.

Soon we were riding south on Route 9. The Old Shore Road of my childhood memories had frame houses, antique shops that my mother insisted on visiting, and here and there an old church and fenced cemetery. A lot of those same structures were still around, but now they shared the highway with auto dealers and strip malls.

I've always liked the town of Cape May Court House, which we inevitably passed through to get to the vacation house my dad built in Stone Harbor. We stopped there for lunch and so that I could revisit its tree-lined streets and colonial-style buildings. Outside the public library, patrons were sitting on park benches reading novels in the shade.

We continued south on Route 9, and I recognized the intersection with Route 47 where one could turn east and head into wild, wild Wildwood. I did not recall the Wal-Mart or other big-box stores at this location, but I could understand how convenient they must be for people who own rental property. We used to buy things for the house at a much smaller operation called Seashore Home Supply.

Ever since we had driven through Whitesboro, we had been traveling parallel to the tracks of Cape May Seashore Lines, passing occasional grade crossings. As we approached Historic Cold Spring Village, there before us, lying idle, was one of this railroad's trains. Drawn by a bright red locomotive with Lehigh Valley lettering, its two passenger cars were so shiny they almost sparkled in the Jersey sun. It was just about the spiffiest train I had ever seen.

A conductor noticed us walking around the train snapping pictures, and he obligingly got out to offer us a train schedule and see if we had any questions. When we said we wanted to ride CMSL into Cape May the following day, he had some unpleasant news: CMSL trains were making only abbreviated trips between Cape May Court House and Historic Cold Spring Village that weekend, because repairs were being made on the railroad bridge over the Cape May Canal.

He let us board the train to look around, though. We examined the passenger car identified as Pennsylvania-Reading Seashore Lines equipment, which was every bit as spotless inside as out. Its bright blue upholstery looked new, and it was decorated with vintage shore tourism posters. This train also had a dining car furnished with tables, chairs, and a snack bar, where two other crew members were awaiting departure time. They answered our questions about the railroad and its equipment, advising us to return when they could offer a ride all the way from Cape May to Tuckahoe, a station marked "coming soon" on the railroad's printed schedule.

We decided to try for a better look at what else we could find of the railroad. We found the Blue Comet observation car that CMSL is restoring on sidings off Route 47 just east of the big intersection with Route 9 in Rio Grande. Much other CMSL rolling stock was stored there too. We then hunted for roads parallel to the Cape May Canal, hoping for a good view of the bridge, but we had a hard time getting closer than a parking area near the Route 109 bridge over the canal. We could see that the railroad drawbridge was open but were too far away to observe any repairs in progress.

To head back north, we used the Garden State Parkway, still a pleasant, divided, tree-lined thoroughfare. I had a map that showed where I might find two existing railbeds jutting off what is now CMSL's main line. There was too much foliage for me to spot the one just north of Exit 4, which proceeds east of Wildwood Junction, but the Garden State Parkway does have an overpass precisely where this railbed should be. Farther north, as we approached Palermo, there was a break in the trees lining the parkway,

Cape May's station for trains and buses.

giving me a great view of the salt marshes stretching out to the barrier islands. Just where the map said it should have been, I noticed a flat railbed, also lined with shrubbery, reaching out toward Ocean City.

The following morning, we were back on the Garden State Parkway on our way to Cape May. We had no trouble parking in a metered lot in the heart of town, but then, we had arrived around 9 A.M. The only difficulty we encountered was finding sufficient quarters to feed the meter, as each quarter purchased only twenty minutes of parking time and the clerks at a nearby convenience store had been instructed not to make change.

As we were driving toward town, we had observed several signs informing visitors that parking was free in the lot of the local elementary school, where there was trolley service downtown. Upon investigation, we discovered that parking was indeed free, but the trolley was not, nor did we notice it arriving very frequently at the school's parking lot, which was a healthy distance from the main attractions of Cape May. It wasn't a real trolley, either, just an open-sided bus run by a tour operator.

Our advice for Shoobies on the way to Cape May: Take along a roll of quarters and get there early—or park in Cape May Court House or Historic Cold Spring Village and ride CMSL. The train stops very close to the pedestrian mall in the heart of Cape May, and inside the transportation station is an information desk where cheerful ladies will greet you and load you down with pamphlets, maps, and insider advice.

Cape May has a wide, clean beach separated from the town by an asphalt walk called the Promenade. The beach requires tags, which can be purchased from attendants at its entrances, but the Promenade is free and lined with benches.

The pedestrian mall, also called the Washington Street Mall, consists of three blocks of stores facing a street closed to vehicular traffic. You can buy saltwater taffy, fudge, beach togs, or even pastries and cappucino.

Cape May makes a great day-trip destination because it has historic houses and inns open for tours, as well as walking tours, bus (excuse me, trolley) tours, and boat tours. Cape May even offers live theater performances. You can also wander the streets perpendicular to the Promenade and admire its Victorian Ladies: brightly painted nineteenth-century cottages now serving as B&Bs or rental properties.

With only a few hours to spend, we decided to visit the town's wonderful monument to shore tourism: Congress Hall, a hotel already in operation while railroads were still a gleam in John Stevens's eye, and which continues to draw tourists today. Built in 1816 by Thomas Hughes, this hotel was a very large structure for its day, so large that contemporaries called it the Big House until Hughes was elected to Congress. It is painted pale yellow with white and black trim, and its front and back porches are furnished with varnished rocking chairs that invite passersby to sit and contemplate its elegance. In a marble-floored hallway running the length of the building, we discovered photographs and artifacts hanging on the walls between the hotel's shops. Congress Hall even had a museum shop. We also discovered some tributes to one of Cape May's most famous visitors, John Philip Sousa, who performed there in 1882.

One of the best things about Cape May is its great selection of restaurants, and this Jersey Shore resort is not a dry town with religious roots like some of the others. On and near the pedestrian mall, you can find Northern Italian, Southwestern, Caribbean, and just about any other trendy cuisine, as well as long-established steak and seafood houses.

We decided on another time-honored Cape May tradition: the Lobster House at Fisherman's Wharf at Schellenger's Landing. Fishing has always been an important industry in Cape May County, and about a century ago, the Atlantic City Railroad built a branch to a wharf at a location then called Cold Spring Harbor. The railroad also built an icehouse for the commercial fishermen and operated excursion trains from Camden to accommodate sportfishermen.

The Lobster House is actually part of a complex, including the seafood restaurant, an outdoor raw bar and deck, and a fish market. It has been in operation for about fifty years. It was always a favorite of my dad's because it had great fresh seafood, a water view, and a location outside Cape May proper that was easy to reach with ample parking. While I was growing up, for a long time I thought Schellenger's Landing was Cape May.

We found that nothing much had changed at the Lobster House, which still served up a great lobster. We got a table where we could watch fishing boats depart, just as they have done for a century.

We headed back toward Route 55, taking a shortcut through the Pine Barrens on Route 347. It was Saturday afternoon, and we discovered that a whole lot of other people had also reasoned that this backroad would make a good shortcut, but fortunately all of them were heading south, in the opposite direction. As we sped north, their cars were barely moving. One desperate couple had pulled off onto the shoulder, where they were diapering a wailing infant on the grass.

We were glad we had missed all these other tourists. The town had been crowded enough without them.

Cape May had been delightful, though, and we were eager to return. But in the winter, when we can have a really good time.

The Region's Rail Trails

In Cape May County, the Woodbine Railroad Trail now occupies 3 miles of Pennsy railbed that was abandoned as redundant when the Pennsylvania-Reading Seashore Lines were formed. The trail is wide, paved, furnished with benches, and parallel to Dehirsch Avenue or Route 550, which runs through the heart of Woodbine.

The Seashore Line Trail appears to be a work in progress. It is located on railbed once part of the West Jersey system between Millville and Cape May, and it is said that plans are under way to open this corridor from Millville south to Cape May Court House. The website called Traillink reports that the trail currently extends 10 miles from Belleplain State Forest near Weatherby Road to Woodbine, but it cautions prospective users that parts of the trail are "unimproved." We drove the length of Weatherby Road from Port Elizabeth to the Atlantic County line, but we never found the Seashore Line Trail or any indication that it could be accessed nearby.

The Cold Spring Bike Path of Lower Township opened late in 2002. It occupies about 3 miles of former West Jersey and Seashore railbed and

NJ TRANSIT converted Ocean City's old train station to a bus station. The Ocean City Trail starts nearby.

incorporates a new truss bridge over a stream near the entrance to Historic Cold Spring Village. The trail is parallel to the tracks of today's Cape May Seashore Lines; this is where Reading and Pennsy trains once raced each other to Cape May. Today trail users can wave to CMSL passengers in the summer when this railroad's trains are running.

Although it is not very long, the Middle Township Bike Path, opened in 2003, connects some favorite destinations near Cape May Courthouse, including Cape May County's 4-H Fairgrounds and the Cape May County Park Zoo. It crosses tracks now used by Cape May Seashore Lines.

Running for many blocks through the middle of Ocean City, the Ocean City Trail occupies the former Ocean City Branch of the Pennsylvania-Reading Seashore Lines. The trail begins near the Ocean City Transportation Center, formerly the Pennsylvania-Reading Seashore Lines Ocean City station, where buses now deliver tourists to this town. Although it is too narrow to be a real street, its asphalt surface seems to encourage drivers to use it as a shortcut, forcing those on foot or bicycle to make way.

The town of Wildwood Crest also has a 1-mile bike path near the beach.

CONTACT INFORMATION
FOR REGIONAL SITES

All Regions

Anthracite Railroads Historical
  Society
P.O. Box 519
Lansdale, PA 19446-0519
http://arhs.railfan.net

National Railway Historical
  Society
National Office and Library
100 N. Seventeenth St.,
  Suite 1203
Philadelphia, PA 19103-2783
215-557-6606
www.nrhs.com
[Local chapters listed on website]

NJ TRANSIT Corporation
One Penn Plaza East
Newark, NJ 07105-2246
800-772-2222
www.njtransit.com

Rails-to-Trails Conservancy
www.traillink.com

United Railroad Historical
  Society of New Jersey
732-928-7758
www.urhs.org

Delaware River Region

Camden and Amboy Historical
  Society
P.O. Box 3277
South Amboy, NJ 08879

Delaware and Raritan Canal
  State Park
625 Canal Rd.
Somerset, NJ 08873
609-397-2000
www.dandrcanal.com

Long-A-Coming Historical
  Society
59 S. White Horse Pike
Berlin, NJ 08009
www.long-a-coming.com

Morven Museum and Garden
55 Stockton St.
Princeton, NJ 08540
609-924-8144
www.historicmorven.org

North Penn Railroad Station
3 Fort Dix Rd.
Pemberton, NJ 08068
609-894-0546
www.pemberton_two.com/north_
  pemberton_station

PATCO Speedline
Box 4262
Lindenwold, NJ 08021-0218
877-567-3772
www.drpa/patco/index

Pennsylvania Railroad Technical
   and Historical Society
www.prrths.com

Trenton Rail Station
72 S. Clinton Ave.
Trenton, NJ 08609

Skylands Region

Belvidere & Delaware Railway,
   Black River & Western Railroad
c/o Black River Railroad System
P.O. Box 200
Ringoes, NJ 08551
908-782-9600
www.brwrr.com

Black River Railroad Historic Trust
P.O. Box 232
Ringoes, NJ 08551

Central Railroad of New Jersey
   Historical Society
P.O. Box 4226
Dunellen, NJ 08812-4226

Clinton Station Diner
Route 173 & Bank St.
Clinton, NJ 08809
908-713-0012
www.clintonstationdiner.com

Friends of the New Jersey
   Transportation Heritage Center
P.O. Box 2968
Hamilton Square, NJ 08690-2968
www.njthc.org

Lehigh Valley Railroad Historical
   Society
P.O. Box RR
Manchester, NY 14504-0200
585-289-9149
www.lvrrhs.org

Liberty State Park
Morris Pesin Drive
Jersey City, NJ 07305
201-915-3440
www.libertystatepark.com

New Jersey Midland Railroad
   Historical Society
P.O. Box 6125
Parsippany, NJ 07054

New York, Susquehanna &
   Western Technical & Historical
   Society, Inc.
P.O. Box 121
Rochelle Park, NJ 07662
877-TRAIN-RIDE
www.nyswths.org

Northlandz
495 Highway 202 South
Flemington, NJ 08822
908-782-4022
www.northlandz.com

Phillipsburg Railroad
  Historians, Inc.
P.O. Box 5104
Phillipsburg, NJ 08865

Stevens Institute of Technology
Castle Point on Hudson
Hoboken, NJ 07030
201-216-5000
www.stevens.edu

Waterloo Village
525 Waterloo Rd.
Stanhope, NJ 07874
973-347-0900
www.waterloovillage.org

Whippany Railway Museum
P.O. Box 16
Whippany, NJ 07981-0016
913-887-8177
www.whippanyrailwaymuseum.org

Gateway Region

Erie Lackawanna Historical
  Society
http://erielackhs.org

Hoboken Rail Station
1 Hudson Place
Hoboken, NJ 07030

Jersey City Landmarks
  Conservancy
P.O. Box 68
Jersey City, NJ 07303-0068
201-792-3386
www.jclandmarks.org

Maywood Station Historical
  Committee
108 Stelling Ave.
Maywood, NJ 07607

National New York Central
  Railroad Museum
P.O. Box 1708
721 S. Main St.
Elkhart, IN 46515
574-294-3001
www.nycrrmuseum.org

Newark Penn Station
Raymond Plaza
West Newark, NJ 07102

New Jersey Historical Society
52 Park Place
Newark, NJ 07102
973-596-8500
www.jerseyhistory.org

New York Central System
  Historical Society
Department W
P.O. Box 81184
Cleveland, OH 44181-0184
www.nycshs.org

NY Waterway
Pershing Rd.
Weehawkin, NJ 07086
800-53FERRY
www.nywaterway.com

Paterson Museum
Thomas Rogers Building
2 Market St.
Paterson, NJ 07501
973-321-1260

PATH
225 Park Ave. South, 18th Floor
New York, NY 10003
212-435-7777
www.panynj.gov/path/

Union Model Railroad Club
295 Jefferson Ave.
P.O. Box 1146
Union, NJ 07083
908-964-9724
www.tmrci.com

Shore Region

Allaire State Park
P.O. Box 220
Farmingdale, NJ 07727
732-938-2371

Georgian Court University
900 Lakewood Ave.
Lakewood, NJ 08701
800-458-8422
www.georgian.edu

Jamesburg Historical Association
203 Buckelew Ave.
Jamesburg, NJ 08831
732-521-2040
www.jamesburgnj.org

New Jersey Museum of
  Transportation
  (Pine Creek Railroad)
P.O. Box 622
Farmingdale, NJ 07727
732-938-5524
www.njmt.org

Ocean Gate Historical Society
P.O. Box 895
Cape May Ave. & Asbury Ave.
Ocean Gate, NJ 08740
732-269-3468

Stafford Township Historical
  Society
Manahawkin, NJ 08050
609-597-7416
www.telecottage.com/staffordhist/
  heritage.html

Tuckerton Seaport
120 W. Main St.
P.O. Box 52
Tuckerton, NJ 08087
609-296-8868
www.tuckertonseaport.org

Greater Atlantic City Region

Atlantic City Historical Museum
Dept. NJ
P.O. Box 7273
Atlantic City, NJ 08404
609-347-5837
wwwacmuseum.org

Atlantic City Rail Terminal
One Atlantic City Expressway
Atlantic City, NJ 08404

Dr. Jonathan Pitney House
57 Shore Rd.
Absecon, NJ 08201
609-569-1799
www.pitneyhouse.com

Smithville Village and Village
Green
1 N. New York Rd. (Route 9)
Smithville, NJ 08205

Storybook Land, Inc.
6415 Black Horse Pike
Egg Harbor Township, NJ 08234
609-641-7847
www.storybookland.com

Southern Shore Region

Cape May Seashore Lines
P.O. Box 152
Tuckahoe, NJ 08250-0152
609-884-2675
www.seashorelines.com

Historic Cold Spring Village
720 Route 9
Cape May, NJ 08204
609-898-2300
www.hcsv.org

Reading Company Technical
and Historical Society
P.O. Box 15143
Reading, PA 19612-5143
610-372-5513
www.readingrailroad.org

South Jersey Railroad Museum
1721 Mt. Pleasant Rd.
P.O. Box 327
Tuckahoe, NJ 08250
609-628-2850

Wheaton Village
1501 Glasstown Rd.
Millville, NJ 08332
800-998-4552
wwww.wheatonvillage.org

BIBLIOGRAPHY

Alexander, Edwin P. *On the Main Line: The Pennsylvania Railroad in the Nineteenth Century.* New York: C. N. Potter, 1971.

Anderson, Elaine. *The Central Railroad of New Jersey's First 100 Years, 1849–1949: A Historical Survey.* Easton, PA: Center for Canal History and Technology, 1984.

Archer, Robert F. *The History of the Lehigh Valley Railroad.* Forest Park, IL: Heimburger House Publishing Company, 1977.

Baedeker, Karl. *The United States: With an Excursion into Mexico: Handbook for Travelers.* New York: C. Scribner, 1904.

Baer, Christopher T., William J. Coxey, and Paul W. Schopp. *The Trail of the Blue Comet: A History of the Jersey Central's New Jersey Southern Division.* Palmyra, NJ: West Jersey Chapter of the National Railway Historical Society, 1994.

Barber, John W., and Henry Howe. *Historical Collections of the State of New Jersey.* New York: S. Tuttle, 1845.

———. *Historical Collections of New Jersey: Past and Present.* New Haven, CT: privately printed, 1868. [Updated edition of previous book.]

Baxter, Raymond J., and Arthur G. Adams. *Railroad Ferries of the Hudson.* New York: Fordham University Press, 1999.

Bednar, Mike. *Lehigh Valley Railroad: The New York Division.* Laurys Station, PA: Garrigues House Publishers, 1993.

Biemiller, Lawrence. "Where the Only Station Stop Is Princeton." *Chronicle of Higher Education,* May 16, 2003.

Bogen, Jules I. *The Anthracite Railroads: A Study in American Railroad Enterprise.* New York: Ronald Press Company, 1927.

Bowen, Catherine Drinker. *Family Portrait.* Boston: Little, Brown and Company, 1970.

Boyd, Jim, and Tracy Antz. *The Lehigh and Hudson River.* Scotch Plains, NJ: Morning Sun Books, 2001.

Brakeley, Anna. "The First Railroad in New Jersey." *Proceedings of the New Jersey Historical Society* 10 (1928): 273–82.

Brinckmann, John. *The Tuckerton Railroad: A Chronicle of Transport to the New Jersey Seashore.* 2nd ed. Edison, NJ: privately printed, 1992.

Buchholz, Margaret Thomas, ed. *Shore Chronicles: Diaries and Travelers' Tales from the Jersey Shore, 1764–1955.* Harvey Cedars, NJ: Down the Shore Publishing, 1999.

Buckingham, James Silk. *America: Historical, Statistic, and Descriptive.* 2 vols. New York: Harper & Brothers, 1841.

Burgess, George H., and Miles C. Kennedy. *Centennial History of the Pennsylvania Railroad Company, 1846–1946.* Philadelphia: Pennsylvania Railroad Company, 1949.

Carey, Henry Charles. *Beauties of the Monopoly System of New Jersey.* Philadelphia: C. Sherman, Printer, 1848.

——. *Letters to the People of New Jersey: On the Frauds, Extortions, and Oppressions of the Railroad Monopoly.* Philadelphia: Carey & Hart, 1848.

Catlin, George Lynde. *The New Line between New York and Philadelphia to the Centennial.* New York: n.p. [probably Reading Railroad], 1876.

Cawley, James S., and Margaret Cawley. *Along the Delaware and Raritan Canal.* Rutherford, NJ: Fairleigh Dickinson University Press, 1970.

Clayton, W. W. *History of Bergen and Passaic Counties, New Jersey.* Philadelphia: Everts & Peck, 1882.

Collins, V. Lansing. *Princeton: Past and Present.* 1931. Reprint, Princeton, NJ: Princeton University Press, 1945.

Cook, Joel. *Brief Summer Rambles near Philadelphia.* Philadelphia, PA: J.B. Lippincott & Co., 1882.

Cook, W. George, and William J. Coxey. *Atlantic City Railroad: The Royal Route to the Sea.* Oaklyn, NJ: West Jersey Chapter, National Railway Historical Society, 1980.

Coxey, William J., ed. *West Jersey Rails: A Series of Stories about Southern New Jersey Railroad History.* Conshohocken, PA: West Jersey Chapter, National Railway Historical Society, 1983.

——. *West Jersey Rails II: A Series of Stories about Southern New Jersey Railroad History.* Haddonfield, NJ: West Jersey Chapter, National Railway Historical Society, 1985.

——. *West Jersey Rails III: A Series of Stories about Southern New Jersey Railroad History.* Palmyra, NJ: West Jersey Chapter, National Railway Historical Society, 2002.

Coxey, William J., Frank C. Kozempel, and James E. Kranefeld. *The Trains to America's Playground.* Allentown, PA: West Jersey Chapter, National Railway Historical Society, Custom Print Express, 1988.

Cudahy, Brian J. *Rails under the Mighty Hudson.* New York: Fordham University Press, 2002.

Cunningham, John T. *Railroads in New Jersey: The Formative Years.* Andover, NJ: Afton Publishing Company, 1997.

Cushing, Thomas, and Charles E. Sheppard. *History of the Counties of Gloucester, Salem, and Cumberland, New Jersey.* Philadelphia: Everts & Peck, 1883.

Damato, Karen. "Developments Aim to Restore Jersey Shorefront Charm to Springsteen's City of Ruins." *Wall Street Journal,* June 23, 2004.

Della Penna, Craig P. *24 Great Rail-Trails of New Jersey.* Amherst, MA: New England Cartographics, 1999.

Department of Conservation and Development. *Report on Final Disposition of Delaware and Raritan Canal.* Trenton, NJ: New Jersey Department of Conservation and Development, 1942.

Dorwart, Jeffery M., and Philip English Mackey. *Camden County, New Jersey, 1616–1976: A Narrative History.* Camden: Camden County Cultural & Heritage Commission, 1976.

Fazio, Alfred E. *Hudson Bergen Light Rail.* Piscataway, NJ: Railpace Co., 2002.

Gibson, David. *Delaware and Raritan Canal State Park: Historic Structures Survey.* Trenton: New Jersey Department of Environmental Protection, 1982.

Gladulich, Richard M. *By Rail to the Boardwalk.* Glendale, CA: Trans-Anglo Books, 1986.

Hall, John F. *The Daily Union History of Atlantic City and County, New Jersey.* Atlantic City, NJ: Daily Union Printing Company, 1900.

Halsey, Edmund D. *History of Morris County, New Jersey.* New York: W. W. Munsell, 1882.

Holton, James L. *The Reading Railroad: History of a Coal Age Empire.* 2 vols. Laurys Station, PA: Garrigues House, 1989–92.

Honeyman, A. Van Doren. *History of Union County, New Jersey, 1664–1923.* New York: Lewis Historical Publishing Co., 1923.

"John Bull at 150 Can Still Make It down the Rails." *Smithsonian* 12, no. 9 (December 1981): 151–54.

Klein, Aaron. *New York Central.* New York: Bonanza Books, 1985.

Knox, Nancy. "Princeton Basin." *Princeton History* 4 (1983): 17–28.

Kramer, Frederick A. *Pennsylvania-Reading Seashore Lines.* Ambler, PA: Crusader Press, 1980.

Lane, Wheaton J. *From Indian Trail to Iron Horse: Travel and Transportation in New Jersey, 1620–1860.* Princeton, NJ: Princeton University Press, 1939.

Lee, Warren F. *Down along the Old Bel-Del: The History of the Belvidere Delaware Railroad Company, A Pennsylvania Railroad Company.* Albuquerque: Bel-Del Enterprises, 1987.

Lowenthal, Larry, and William T. Greenberg Jr. *The Lackawanna Railroad in Northwest New Jersey.* Morristown, NJ: Tri-State Railway Historical Society, 1987.

Lucas, Walter Arndt. *From the Hills to the Hudson: A History of the Paterson and Hudson River Rail Road.* N.p.: Railroadians of America, 1944.

Madeira, Crawford Clark. *The Delaware and Raritan Canal: A History.* East Orange, NJ: Easterwood Press, 1941.

McIlroy, David. "The Dinky: Decades of History and Lore." *Princetonian,* April 29, 2004.

Messer, David W., and Charles S. Roberts. *Triumph V: Philadelphia to New York, 1830–2002.* Baltimore: Barnard, Roberts and Co., 2002.

Miller, Jacquelyn C. "Breach over Troubled Waters: Special Interest Groups and Public Policy Formation: The Morris Canal Abandonment Controversy." *New Jersey History* 109, no. 1–2 (Spring–Summer 1991): 1–26.

Mohowski, Robert E. *The New York, Susquehanna & Western Railroad.* Baltimore: Johns Hopkins University Press, 2003.

Mott, Edward Harold. *Between the Ocean and the Lakes: The Story of Erie.* New York: John S. Collins, Publisher, 1900.

National Cyclopaedia of American Biography. 63 vols. New York: J. T. White, 1898–1926.

New Jersey Mirror, "First Public Railroad Meeting," January 16, 1828.

New York Herald, Editorial, May 21, 1871.

Paulinskill Valley Trail Committee. *The Paulinskill Valley Trail: Before and After.* Andover, NJ: Paulinskill Valley Trail Committee, 2003.

Pennsylvania Railroad Company. *Ceremonies upon the Completion of the Monument Erected by the Pennsylvania Railroad Company at Bordentown, New Jersey, to Mark the First Piece of Track Laid between New York and Philadelphia, 1831, November 12, 1891.* Washington, DC: W. F. Roberts for the Pennsylvania Railroad Company, 1892.

———. *Summer Excursion Routes, 1885.* Philadelphia: Passenger Department of the Pennsylvania Railroad Company, 1885.

———. *Summer Excursion Routes, 1903.* Philadelphia: Passenger Department of the Pennsylvania Railroad Company, 1903.

Pike, Helen C. *Greetings from New Jersey: A Postcard Tour of the Garden State.* New Brunswick, NJ: Rutgers University Press, 2001.

Power, Tyrone. *Impressions of America during the years 1833, 1834, and 1835.* 2 vols. London: R. Bentley, 1836.

Prowell, George Reeser. *The History of Camden County, New Jersey.* Philadelphia: L. J. Richards & Co., 1886.

Ricord, Frederick W. *History of Union County, New Jersey.* Newark: East Jersey History Co., 1897.

Rosenbaum, Joel, and Tom Gallo. *NJ TRANSIT Rail Operations.* Piscataway, NJ: Railpace Company, 1996.

Russell, William Howard, Sir. *My Diary, North and South.* Edited by Fletcher Pratt. New York: Harper, 1954.

Scull, Theodore. *Hoboken's Lackawanna Terminal.* New York: Quadrant Press, 1987.

Shaw, William H. *History of Essex and Hudson Counties.* Philadelphia: Everts & Peck, 1884.

Snell, James P. *History of Hunterdon and Somerset Counties, New Jersey.* Philadelphia: Everts & Peck, 1881.

———. *History of Sussex and Warren Counties, New Jersey.* Philadelphia: Everts & Peck, 1881.

Stansfield, Charles A., Jr. *Vacationing on the Jersey Shore: Guide to Beach Resorts Past and Present.* Mechanicsburg, PA: Stackpole Books, 2004.

Stevens, John. *Documents Tending to Prove the Superior Advantages of Rail-Ways and Steam-Carriages over Canal Navigation.* New York: T and J Swords, 1812.

Things as They Are; or, Notes of a Traveler. New York: Harper & Brothers, 1834.

Treese, Lorett. *Railroads of Pennsylvania: Fragments of the Past in the Keystone Landscape.* Mechanicsburg, PA: Stackpole Books, 2003.

Turnbull, Archibald Douglas. *John Stevens: An American Record.* New York: American Society of Mechanical Engineers, 1928.

Twain, Mark. *Mark Twain's Travels with Mr. Brown.* Collected and edited by Franklin Walker and G. Ezra Dane. New York: Knopf, 1940.

Vigrass, J. William. *The Lindenwold Hi-Speed Line.* Palmyra: West Jersey Chapter, National Railway Historical Society, 1990.

Walker, Edwin Robert, and Trenton Historical Society. *A History of Trenton, 1629–1929.* Princeton, NJ: Princeton University Press, 1929.

Watkins, J. Elfreth. *The Camden and Amboy Railroad: Origin and Early History.* Washington, DC: Bedney, 1891.

Winfield, Charles Hardenburg. *History of the County of Hudson, New Jersey.* New York: Kennard & Hay Printing Co., 1874.

Winpenny, Thomas R. "The Engineer and Promoter: Richard B. Osborne, The Camden and Atlantic Railroad and the Creation of Atlantic City." *Essays in Economic and Business History* 22 (2004): 301–12.

INDEX